AMATEUR HORSEMAN'S

THEORY & PRACTICAL TEXTBOOK

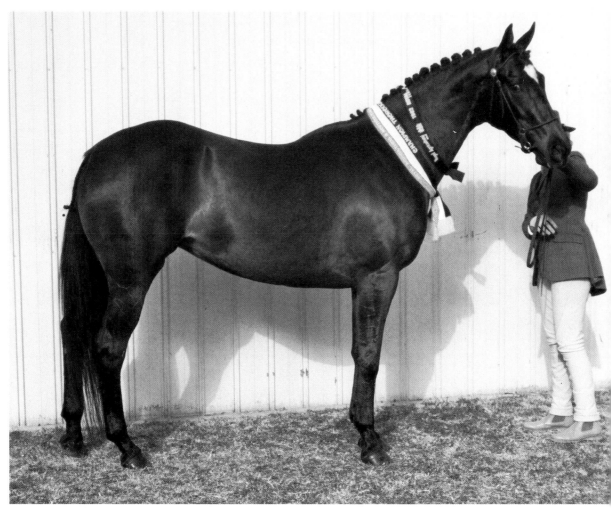

'Phylton's Pride (Proud Boy-Chalette) has conformation and presence enough to win led-in championships at the Adelaide Royal Show and has many other honours to her name. Her neat head fits the body and there is ample length of rein due to the well laid-back shoulder and correctly shaped neck. She has good width of forearm and short cannons, but is a little long in the pasterns. Her gently sloping wither, short back and neatly set-on tail ensure a good top-line. A good thigh and gaskin (2nd thigh), big, strong hocks and a reasonably straight hind leg give good balance to her body. She has an ample girth but shows a fraction too much daylight in the flank area. She is owned by A & P Borg, Phylton Park Stud, South Australia. Photograph by Jenny Carroll.

AMATEUR HORSEMAN'S
THEORY & PRACTICAL TEXTBOOK

BY MARGARET I. CLARKE, E.S.C.

First Edition – First Printing

1989

230 Park Avenue
New York, N.Y. 10169

Many thanks to Erica Taylor and 'Crown Law' for modelling the movements for this book.

Editor: Jo Rudd
Design: Susan Kinealy
Drawings: Pam Crellin

Published 1989 by Howell Book House Inc.
230 Park Avenue, New York, N.Y. 10169

Library of Congress Cataloging-in-Publication Data

Clarke, Margaret I.
Amateur horseman's theory & practical text book.

Sequel to: Care of the Australian horse and pony.
Includes index.
1. Horses. 2. Horsemanship. I. Clarke, Margaret I.
Care of the Australian horse and pony. II. Title.
III. Title: Amateur horseman's theory and practical text book.
SF285.C5545   1988   798.2'3   88-9113
ISBN 0-87605-876-4

Originated by Lansdowne Press, Sydney, Australia

Printed in Singapore

CONTENTS

Introduction 7

1 Development of the Equine 9

2 Structure and Movement 14

3 Bodily Systems 24

4 Conformation 37

5 Horse Behaviour and Psychology 51

6 Gaits 60

7 The Horse's Position under the Rider 68

8 The Rider's Position on the Horse 79

9 Riding Aids 96

10 Education, Fitness and Exercise 126

11 Jumping 143

12 Safety with Horses 149

13 Lungeing 157

Glossary 161

Index 173

Horseplay, which can be notoriously rough, is the horse's way of establishing the pecking order. Here, 'Bombalo' (right) is above 'Bold Eagle' in the pecking order. Photograph by Cindy Lade.

INTRODUCTION

This book is a sequel to *Care of the Australian Horse and Pony* which has been so successful since its appearance in 1966. It is intended to complement and extend the information in that book, which is still pertinent today and will be for many years to come.

Over the years the compliment most often paid to *Care of the Australian Horse and Pony* is that it is very easy to read and understand compared with some of the more technical books which are difficult to take in unless studied deeply. And most amateur horse owners have little time to spend studying.

During my years as a riding instructor, I have often been asked about the usefulness of books. Having one of the most comprehensive private libraries on the subject of the horse, it is quite clear that I consider books to be very important in the quest for knowledge. Invariably my advice is that the universal practice of 'reading' the pictures and glancing through the text leaves readers with only a superficial knowledge; they must read the text as well as look at the pictures if they really wish to increase their knowledge, so I have tried to make this book as interesting and as easy to read as possible.

The word 'amateur' in the title does not mean novice – it means that those concerned are involved in a sport which is not their full-time occupation. Therefore, an amateur can be a highly qualified and experienced person. Even so, because of the amateur status, they have not had the experience of dealing with the large numbers of horses and different situations which the professional horseman encounters, so the provision of this extra knowledge is necessary.

I have been influenced in my work as an instructor by several professional people, both Australian and from overseas. Many years ago I attended several schools at which the late great Franz Mairinger officiated, and had many conversations with him on the subject of horse education. His empathy with the horse has reinforced my own belief that a rider can get more out of the horse if he/she asks for it, rather than demands it.

My time at Mrs Sivewright's Talland School of Equitation in England and with the lady herself in Australia has convinced me that the rider's greatest asset is an ability to think. In my studies I have found inadequate instructors giving 'guided tours' rather than lessons, and others who are exceptionally talented. However, riders themselves are the ultimate instructors – they are the ones who must understand and apply themselves if they wish to become expert, or even just good, riders.

Until recently the word 'dressage' held a mystique which discouraged a large number of riders from attempting to understand its meaning and implications. This has been fostered – intentionally or otherwise – by books and articles written by dressage experts who do not explain the fundamentals of the art, and in some cases attempt to bamboozle the reader with obscure technicalities.

Dressage is, in fact, a method of communication with the horse which teaches him what he is required to do while at the same time developing his ability to carry out these instructions. It develops and strengthens his muscular, respiratory and circulatory systems, while protecting his psychological balance from frustration and pain. It is an educational program which systematically develops the horse's muscles, while teaching him how to use them efficiently.

There are many people I must thank for assisting me in this work. Fran Harvey of Katherine in the Northern Territory typed and retyped and typed again without demur, until I was reasonably satisfied with my text.

Pam Crellin, also of Katherine, is responsible for the drawings in this book and has worked under the most difficult circumstances. Being a pupil at an English riding school takes up most of one's time, and Pam must have burned the midnight oil on many occasions to get through her own studies and complete the drawings I requested.

The photographs are the work of many photographers; some were already in existence and others had to be specially taken. Each has its own acknowledgement so I will simply say to the photographers: "Thank you so much for your assistance. This book could not have been produced without you."

The name of the person who has had the greatest influence on me is lost to posterity. He was an old man when I was still at school. I saw him no more than once or twice a year, but I heard from him every week when he would send a message back with my grandmother, telling me how to care for the horse she drove to town.

He was a hostler at the hotel where the horse was put up during my grandmother's stay in town and he had been with horses all his life. At different times he had been head groom in both polo and racing stables and stud master at a Thoroughbred stud. Automatic actions I have taken all my life can be traced back to his influence and he must be given his due for the success of my previous books. Alas, I cannot remember his name, and those who might have remembered it for me are now all dead.

This book attempts to pass on in simple language what it has taken me — a professional — a lifetime and the handling of nearly a thousand horses to learn.

CHAPTER 1

DEVELOPMENT OF THE EQUINE

The horse has been a major factor in the development of the world. Perhaps the best example of his importance in the past is the term still used today to describe the pulling ability of the combustion engine – horse power.

Although a great deal of research has been carried out into his origins, most of it has been combined with research into life generally, and palaeontologists are still discovering previously unknown facts about the horse.

It is generally accepted that the horse developed from an animal the size of a fox, with four toes in front and three behind. It is important to understand the evolution of the horse because the way the modern horse acts and reacts is a direct result of his prehistoric experiences.

The modern horse, *Equus caballus,* belongs to the family Equidae. His first known ancestor, of some fifty million years ago, belonged to the fossil genus *Eohippus.* We believe *Eohippus* began his existence in the marshy forests of North America and it was this marshy ground which necessitated the separate toes to prevent him from sinking into the marsh as he would undoubtedly do today under the same conditions. In those early days there were probably few predators – he certainly could not move fast on those toes.

Each of the toes ended in a small hoof, covered by a hard surface, much the same as our fingers and toes have nails. He lived on leaves from the trees and included bark from the trunks in his diet. (People who have tried to keep trees from being damaged in a horse paddock will now know why it is so hard to do.)

Over the many years of the horse's development several situations have combined to change his appearance. The marshy forests began to dry out and he had to travel greater distances for food. Predators became more prevalent and he had to move faster to avoid them. Grazing on pastures provided a much more efficient diet and he began to grow bigger and taller.

As *Eohippus* developed, he found it easier to move faster on his centre toe and the two lateral toes were used less and less. Like all animal structures, what is not used regularly soon begins to atrophy and the horse began to lose these lateral toes.

During this time *Eohippus* changed his name several times, first to *Orohippus*, then

Eohippus

Mesohippus

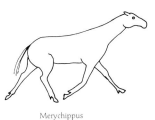

Merychippus

Equus caballus

EOHIPPUS TO CABALLUS

Mesohippus and *Merychippus*, before finally being identified as *Equus caballus*.

During all these millions of years his only defence of any great value was his ability to travel fast away from danger. His other defences, biting, kicking, rearing and bucking, are not particularly efficient, but are employed when speed fails. The horse's courage is rarely assessed by how he attacks but rather by how fast and how far he can run. Chapter 2 describes how the horse's body has developed to enable him to use his speed to the best advantage.

During these early times the horse migrated to Asia over a land bridge, which then existed, and spread throughout Europe. On several occasions he was virtually wiped out but emerged again in the same North American marshes. When the land bridge disappeared into the sea the horses already in Europe and Asia continued to thrive, while those in the Americas died out. The horse did not reappear in America until the Spaniards took him back there in comparatively modern times.

As the horse evolved in Europe and Asia he tended to remain in certain regions and his body structures developed in a way that would accommodate him for these areas. In the north-east of Europe an animal developed which was rather like a small Shetland pony. He stood about 12.2 hands and was usually of brown or bay colouring with a thick waterproof coat to keep out the weather. Widely distributed throughout Central Europe there was a heavier-boned animal, better at trotting than galloping. He also had a thick frost-proof coat and was usually of a dun colour with a dorsal stripe.

In Central Asia a taller animal was developing. He was about 15 hands with a long narrow head, straight or Roman nose, long straight neck, sloping croup, long lopped ears, slab-sided with fairly shallow hoofs, and sparse mane and tail. He was of clay colour and had an ambling gait (from which many of the present-day faults have developed).

In Western Asia another small animal measuring around 12.2 hands was found. This one had a very fine head, straight or concave profile, flat-topped croup, a silky, abundant mane and tail set very high. He was of varied colours.

These four types moved around and intermingled. The features which were useful to them developed, while those that were of little or no value faded into the background – but without disappearing completely.

Better conditions such as more nutritious food, sufficient shelter and the rule of 'survival of the fittest' have combined to enable the horse to continue to develop in height and weight.

Even today authors are perpetuating the erroneous theory that all horses evolved from *Equus przewalskii*. Anyone with any knowledge of the Arab and his near relation, the Thoroughbred, will agree that such a thing is impossible. No animal could change in such a 'short' space of time from the phlegmatic, coarse-looking *Equus przewalskii* to the elegant clean-limbed Arab or Thoroughbred.

Eohippus

Mesohippus

Merychippus

Equus caballus

EVOLUTION OF THE FOOT

There is no documentation of the evolution of the Arab horse; there was no evidence of the breed, then suddenly he was the valued mount of the Bedouin and other Middle Eastern riders and today is the oldest pure breed of horse in the world.

The purpose of man's first confrontation with the horse was to kill him for food – large deposits of bones which can only have been horse skeletons attest to this fact. Even then man thrilled to what he saw and painted the animal's likeness in his caves, faithfully portraying the colours – particularly the particoloured (piebald and skewbald), golden chestnut (now referred to as the Palomino) and the beautiful diluted colours of the bay (buckskin or dun).

Soon man learned to use the horse to do his heavy pulling and carrying. It was only much later that he dared to ride him. Horse flesh was still consumed but only the young and the useless were eaten. Milk from the mares was used in the same way as we use cow's milk.

A good horse remained his master's servant for many years, and so it is today. If we teach the horse to behave the way we wish him to, and to work willingly, he will never lack a good home; but let him become the bad-tempered monster into which he can develop and no one but the meat factory will want him.

The heavy horse so recently used for working the land was developed from a big horse produced in earlier times – first by the Prussians and later by the Crusaders – to carry them into battle. The Prussians invented heavy armour for the protection of the warrior in battle. This often weighed up to 180 kg (400 pounds) and a big strong horse was needed to carry the weight of both the armour and the rider.

A team of six horses bring in the harvest on a South Australian farm earlier this century, before tractors were in vogue. Note the top condition in which these horses were kept – neatly trimmed feet, good-fitting and well-kept harness. With this attention to detail the horses were able to remain in work for long periods. Photograph from Lade family album, Kangaroo Island.

Riding began in Persia and Mongolia around 2000 BC, although saddles were not used until very much later. These ridden horses were used mostly by warring factions and they were also harnessed to war chariots, and used much as tanks are today.

Probably because horses and riding became so much a part of life before there were many historians around, there is very little written about the invention of the saddle and other harness. Having been invented, there has been little major change over the years. Saddles are less cumbersome than they were originally, but most of the essential features have been retained.

Horses were important to the economy of every country until well into the twentieth century. They were as essential to the farmer as the tractor is today, and the only alternative form of transport to that of horse-drawn vehicles or ridden animals appeared with the invention of the railway. However, even the railway was not a great threat to the horse as the train had to remain on its tracks and could go only where the tracks were laid.

Horses were used to draw public coaches, private carriages and individual vehicles, such as the trap, governess cart and hay wagon. They were ridden when speed was essential and used as pack animals over rough terrain; they still remain indispensable in some rough mountain areas.

Large teams, sometimes as many as twenty or more animals, helped to till and reap the fields. They also did the work of today's heavy transport vehicles and, even taking into account the extra time needed, they were more economical and often more efficient than our modern transport companies – they did not go on strike. Such big teams are only seen today when collected from several owners for special occasions.

The ever-patient horse, donkey or mule was asked to walk round in a very small circle from dawn to dusk working the windmills and grinding the corn; also, for many centuries, all three went to war with their masters and died beside them without knowing or caring about the issues involved.

In fact, the horse has been used for every conceivable purpose for which we now use the combustion engine, gas, electricity, steam or, more recently, solar and atomic energy. The horse's compatriots as beasts of burden were the donkey, mule and the slow-moving ox, but none of these was used for fast or fashionable travel.

Our present-day knowledge of the horse and his ills owes much to the past. We still diagnose lameness and other ailments by the same methods used by our ancestors. Modern techniques such as the X-ray can confirm our diagnosis and modern medicine can repair damage that was not repairable in earlier times, but the knowledge passed down to us from the experts of the past (who were far more numerous than they are today) is just as important to the horse's maintenance as our understanding of his history is in our handling of the modern animal.

Just as in earlier times, the horse still runs away when he feels threatened by fear or pain; he still kicks, bites, bucks and rears in self-defence. Those who accuse him of being an outlaw when he behaves in this fashion have little sympathy with the horse or, more likely, little knowledge of the reason for these actions. In their ignorance, their own reactions often lead to more frequent repetition, until the horse's behaviour becomes an established pattern which is very difficult to eradicate.

At one time it was believed that the horse would become obsolete with the coming of the combustion engine and other sources of energy, but this has not happened. If anything, the horse is more popular today than ever before. He is viewed with much more sentiment today and has found his way into the possession and the hearts of many people who would never have been able to own a horse in earlier times. This, in itself, is a mixed blessing as many people with limited knowledge have caused great suffering to the horse through their ignorance.

In the past, the young people of the family learned the basic facts of horse husbandry from their parents and grandparents, as well as from the family groom. Today there is little knowledge of horses within most families. Often one or two members within a family which has no recent connection with horses want to keep one, and discovering how to do this becomes a challenge.

The knowledge possessed by the old-fashioned groom has been lost, because it was never written down when it seemed that the horse was becoming obsolete. The grooms' sons and daughters found other work more compatible to them and the old grooms died, taking their knowledge with them. This also occurred within the ranks of associated industries such as farmers, horse dealers and, to some extent, fodder merchants. Most of the knowledge acquired over the thousands of years that horses were used was lost in one generation and we must now try to regain it for the sake of the horse.

Przewalski mare and foal – this breed, or type, of horse was discovered on the Steppes of Siberia by the man whose name they bear. They are found mainly in zoos today, where authorities aim to keep the breed pure. Przewalski horses were once thought to be the original ancestor of all horses, but are now known to match the description of one of the four types found throughout Europe when man first discovered horses. Photograph by David Langdon.

CHAPTER 2

STRUCTURE AND MOVEMENT

One of the first essentials in the study of the equine species is to know and understand the anatomy of the horse, both external and internal. Almost every book on the subject of horsemanship has a diagram of the horse with the 'points' marked on it, but how many people either amateur or professional can mark them all in from memory?

To be able to understand and handle the horse efficiently it is important that these charts be studied and the points learned off by heart. They are as important to the student of horsemastership as tables are to the student of mathematics.

To enable the horse owner to diagnose problems effectively it is also necessary to understand the functions of the several systems of the horse's body. If we ask the horse for a performance of which he is incapable, not only will he be unable to carry out our instructions but our unreasonable requests will make him sour and perhaps affect his disposition for the rest of his life. It will also do untold harm to his body functions.

The systems we are most concerned with are the bone structure and the muscular, respiratory, circulatory, digestive and nervous systems. The reader is not studying to be a

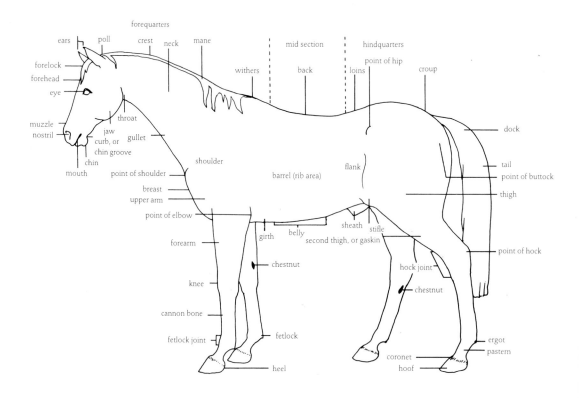

POINTS OF THE HORSE

veterinary surgeon, but those who have a basic knowledge of the systems will be less inclined to panic when something happens and help is needed. It will be possible to give the veterinarian precise details of the visible symptoms when it is necessary to call him, or to be reasonably certain whether the matter is urgent or not.

Bones

The bone structure, or osseous system, performs at least six important body functions, the major one being the support of the body itself; it provides a framework around which the body is built. For instance, all the other leg tissues would collapse under the weight of the horse without the bones in the leg.

An interesting point was made recently when it was reported that prolonged weight-lessness, such as that experienced by astronauts, would result in the bones of the body becoming superfluous. Eventually the body would become similar to that of a snake and would no longer be able to support itself upright. This would take a considerable time to accomplish, of course, but it does remind us that what we do not use will eventually be taken away.

Bones also supply anchorage for muscles, most of which could not function without this aid. Bone marrow produces red blood cells which carry oxygen from the lungs to the heart. Oxygen is then distributed to the body through the circulatory system. Manufacture of these blood cells occurs particularly in the vertebrae and the bones of the skull, although in young animals the long bones also do their share. Marrow in the bone also produces antibodies for the fight against infection. These are called white blood cells or leucocytes.

To a limited extent, bones are reservoirs of calcium and phosphorus and other materials essential to the digestive system. If calcium and phosphorus are not supplied in correct proportions, the body will leach these essentials from the bones, leaving them brittle and liable to break easily.

There are approximately 54 vertebrae bones and 36 ribs. (The figures are approximate because some horses have more vertebrae and ribs than others.) Thirty-four bones are found in the skull and 80 bones in the limbs, plus one breast-bone, making a total of about 205 bones of varying shapes and sizes.

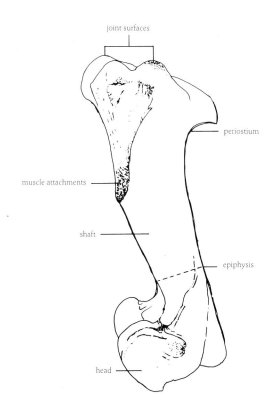

joint surfaces

periostium

muscle attachments

shaft

epiphysis

head

HUMERUS, SHOWING THE FUNCTIONS OF A BONE

JOINTS

Some of these bones are connected by joints: a joint is a place where movement occurs between two or more sets of bones. The horse has five different types of joints which allow him to propel himself forward and to keep himself upright when in a standing position. They also allow him to lie down if he wishes or to sleep standing up, locking into position to prevent him falling down.

In a typical joint, the joint surface of the bone is covered by the synovial membrane. This membrane is continuous around the side of the joint, thus producing a completely enclosed space called the joint cavity. As these membranes rub against one another when the joints move, they are lubricated by synovial fluid which is found in the space. Ligaments on either side of the bones hold them in place and a bursal sac between the ligaments and the tendons of a particular muscle acts as a buffer. The articular cartilage on each end of the bone reduces friction and wear.

Damage to any one of these structures and, in particular, release of the synovial fluid results in more or less serious injury: capped hocks or elbows – unsightly but not serious – or poll evil and fistula – very serious and difficult to cure. Sometimes more than one

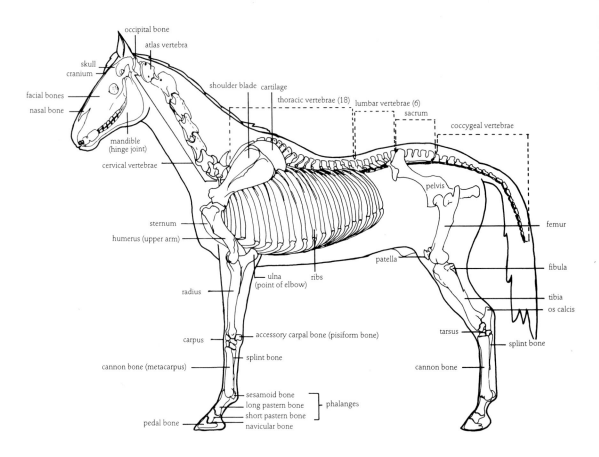

SKELETON OF THE HORSE

A Palomino class at Glenelg, South Australia. Study the riders' positions, looking for turned-out toes, raised heels and hollow backs, and mentally make the slight adjustments that would improve the positions of most of the riders. Look for horses above the bit and behind the bit. Study the muscle development and halt position of each horse where possible. Only one horse is completely at ease! Photograph by Keith Stevens.

Erica Taylor on 'Crown Law' demonstrates a working canter while waiting her turn to enter the dressage arena at the Royal Adelaide showgrounds. 'Crown Law' is slightly behind the bit, but the rest of his body is working correctly. Note the long, forward-driving hind leg stride and the swinging tail. Photograph by Peter Gower.

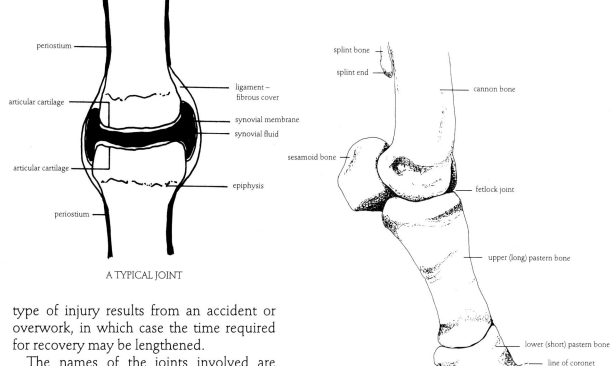

A TYPICAL JOINT

Labels (left diagram): periostium, articular cartilage, articular cartilage, periostium, ligament – fibrous cover, synovial membrane, synovial fluid, epiphysis

LOWER LEG BONES (hinge joints)

Labels (right diagram): splint bone, splint end, cannon bone, sesamoid bone, fetlock joint, upper (long) pastern bone, lower (short) pastern bone, line of coronet, navicular bone, pedal bone

type of injury results from an accident or overwork, in which case the time required for recovery may be lengthened.

The names of the joints involved are suture, gliding, ball and socket, hinge and ginglymoid.

A suture joint does not allow movement and is found in the sacrum where the pelvic bones join and slot into the vertebrae (backbone) and in the cranium (skull). These joints occur only in young animals; once bone growth has been completed the bones unite and the joints disappear.

Gliding joints, where bones slide over one another, are found in the knees, hocks and vertebrae.

Ball and socket joints, allowing movement in several directions, are found at the hip and shoulder joints.

Hinge joints are found in the mandible (jaw), fetlock, stifle and elbow joints.

The strangely named **ginglymoid joint** allows movement in one direction only and is found in elbows, hocks and stifle. Note that the elbow, hock and stifle areas have two kinds of joints.

There are two major injuries which can occur in joints: luxation, when they shift or are misaligned, and dislocation, when the bones do not articulate.

It is interesting to note that the horse stands, literally, on the tips of his toes. The bottoms of his hoofs are equivalent to the ends of our fingers and toes, with the horn of the hoof corresponding to our toe and finger nails. This fact, together with the number of joints involved in the legs, is the source of many problems associated with unsoundness in both the young and the older horse.

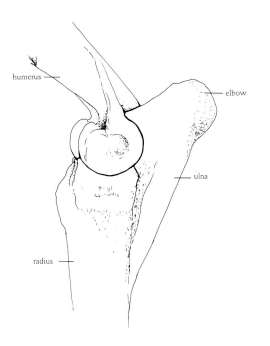

UPPER LEG BONES – FORE (hinge and ginglymoid joints)

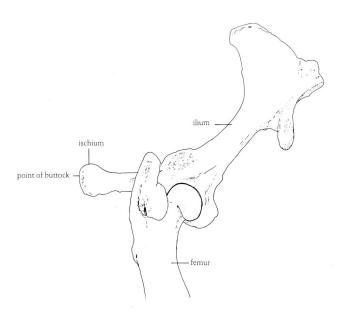

RIGHT PELVIS (ball and socket joint)

EPIPHYSIS

No study of bone formation would be complete without an explanation of the epiphysis. When a foal is born, like all young animals including humans, its bones are soft and quite pliable. Just a little way back from each end of the long bones there is a cartilage-type plate. All longitudinal growth occurs at these plates and they maintain their gristle-like form until the animals reach their potential, or some environmental problem has intervened. At this stage the cartilage forms into bone and the plate disappears. The closing of the plate occurs at different ages in different breeds of horses and under different conditions.

The epiphysial plate of the Thoroughbred, which is an early maturing breed, will often be found to have closed at an early age, while that of the Arab, which is a late maturing breed, may not close before three or four years of age. The closing of the epiphysial plate is a gradual process; although it is foolish to ride or even work a young horse with a fully open plate it is possible to do some work as the plates close.

The only way to assess the state of the plate accurately is to have the animal X-rayed before work begins.

Next time there is a chicken carcass in the house, inspect the end of the breast-bone and you will be able to see for yourself the cartilage-cum-bone formation at the end of the breast-bone. The cartilage in a very young chicken will be soft and pliable and of a whiteish colour, and will break away from the breast-bone with the lightest touch. The older the chicken, the stronger the cartilage will be and old boilers will have no cartilage at all – the bone will be completely formed.

Several different situations affect the development of the epiphyses. They can be brought to maturity much earlier than nature intended by a high percentage of protein in the diet and/or injections of anabolic steroids, which give a kind of hot-house plant forcing. Whether or not the injection of anabolic steroids at this stage is detrimental is not yet clear. The full effects are not yet known even to the experts.

Under these circumstances the animal does not grow any bigger than its potential size; it just reaches this potential at an earlier age. When this happens, the epiphysial plate will close and the animal may be worked without ostensibly doing harm. This is why many Thoroughbreds can be raced as early two-year-olds without apparent harm.

On the other hand, the potential size of the animal can be stunted by premature closure due to some physical inadequacy such as poor husbandry, chronic illness or excess worm burden. Animals born under drought conditions often do not grow to their full potential, because the limited amount of food available is only just sufficient to keep them alive. They stop growing, the plates close before their potential is reached, and the animals mature much smaller than nature intended.

Somewhere in between is the ideal. Good paddocking for the mare before and after foaling is important. A supplementary balanced ration, again before and after foaling, and continued throughout the foal's formative years, will also help to ensure the animal reaches its full potential and the plate closes as nature intended.

Extensive use of a young horse before the plate closes may at best retard growth and at worst cause irreparable damage to the bone growth. This applies not only to the legs, but to the backbone as well. A study of the skeleton will reveal that there are dorsal spines of

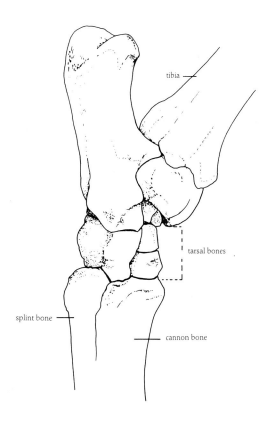

RIGHT HOCK (ginglymoid and gliding joints)

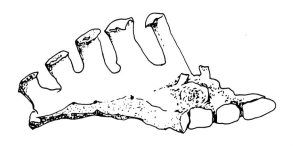

SACRUM (suture joint)

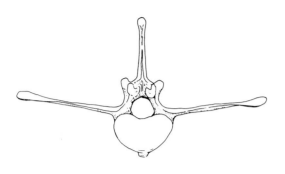

SECOND LUMBAR VERTEBRA (gliding joint)

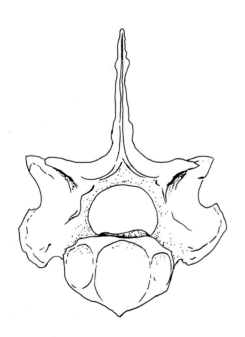

THORACIC VERTEBRA (gliding joint)

varying length and shape which project upwards from the vertebrae. Weight on these spines before the animal is mature may result in two or more fusing together, thus reducing still further the limited movement in the horse's backbone.

LEG BONES

Several small bones in the legs are important as they are also sources of potential unsoundness if damaged by overwork or injury. The first group consists of the seven bones in the knee, which are roughly equivalent to the human wrist. These bones should be completely formed and the knee 'closed' before any ridden work is commenced. An 'open' knee is obvious to the naked eye as there is a marked indentation across the front of the knee. It is necessary to confirm closure by X-ray before a young horse is put into work for racing or other fast work.

Lower down the leg at the back of the fetlock joint there are two sesamoid bones over which tendons work, rather like pulley ropes or belts over wheels. These bones are easily broken if a horse is asked to move fast before the bones are fully formed or if the animal is not completely fit. They can also be spread by lungeing or riding the horse in small circles before the bones are mature.

Deep in the foot is another sesamoid bone referred to as the navicular bone. This also works like a pulley wheel and is a major source of trouble from extreme concussion of the leg joints and other kinds of misuse or disease. Hereditary malfunction, poor conformation or injury can cause a number of problems in any or all of these bones, resulting in unsoundness and restricted use of the horse.

Bones grow not only in length but also in width or thickness. A membrane known as the periosteum adheres closely to the shaft of the bone and this contains bone-forming cells called osteoblasts. These bone-forming cells add more bone to the outside of the shaft (diaphysis) of the bone while bone-eroding cells, called osteoclasts, remove corresponding bone from the marrow cavity; thus the cavity increases in size as the shaft of the bone grows in diameter.

Shin soreness is the result of a shattering of the periosteum while the animal is young and still growing. Once growth is complete and/or fitness established it is unlikely that shin soreness will occur.

Like human bones, horse bones could, under the same circumstances, be easily set and would mend just as easily. However, the problem with the horse is that he cannot be immobilised as a human can. The horse must always be able to keep his feet and cannot be 'kept in bed' or sent off on crutches. Attempts have been made to repair the broken bones of valuable horses and in rare cases they have been successful, but they are prohibitively expensive and have a very low success rate.

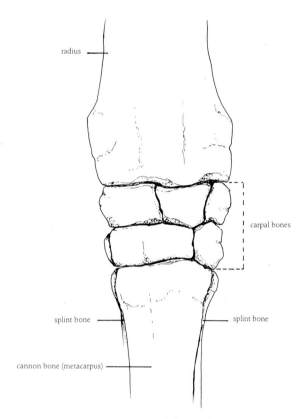

radius

carpal bones

splint bone   splint bone

cannon bone (metacarpus)

KNEE – CARPUS (gliding joint)

epiphysis

epiphysis

A TYPICAL BONE

CHAPTER 3

BODILY SYSTEMS

MUSCLES

The muscular system, which for our purpose includes the tendons and ligaments, provides the body with the means of movement. A muscle is usually attached at one end directly to a firm non-moving bone by means of a tendon. When the muscle contracts it causes the two bones to be brought together, and when it relaxes the bones regain their original position.

The other end of the muscle (the insertion) is usually attached to the surface of a moving bone by means of a tendon.

There are three kinds of muscle tissue found in the horse's body: smooth or involuntary, striated or voluntary, and cardiac. The smooth muscle is involuntary or automatic in its contraction and is active in the digestive system, the urogenital system and the respiratory and circulatory systems.

The voluntary muscles are involved in the movement of the horse and a knowledge of these, together with an understanding of the role of tendons and ligaments, especially the flexor and extensor systems in the legs, is very important when training the horse.

These voluntary muscles are moved by nerve impulses from the brain or by reflex action resulting from thought processes. Muscles work in one direction only.

The cardiac muscle is, of course, the heart which has an intricate labyrinth of branches linking each cell to its neighbour. The heart is automatic and when this muscle ceases to work the horse is dead.

Tendons, which are enclosed in a sheath, can be damaged by overuse when the horse is unfit or over-tired, or by sudden changes of direction undertaken before the horse is co-

ordinated under the rider. The tendon itself can be stretched or torn, or the surrounding sheath can be damaged, or both.

Damage to the tendon sheath is more easily and quickly repaired than damage to the tendon itself, and stretched tendons will usually mend more quickly than torn tendons. Veterinary assistance is necessary to ascertain the extent of the damage and to recommend treatment. It would be unwise to cut short the period of rest that will undoubtedly be recommended.

The horse is born with a given number of muscle cells, which cannot be increased in number. Exercise and educational work cannot increase the number of cells, only the size.

Ligaments hold bones and muscles in position and can be damaged by strain, tearing by unfit or tiring muscles, or by travelling over rough terrain faster than the system can accommodate.

The intercostal muscle underlies the skin area from wither to loin and down over the ribs. The panniculus muscle, also in this area, assists the intercostal in its sensitivity. This is the muscle that 'shivers' the skin to remove flies that have landed. Because of the nerves which are close to the surface in this area, the horse is more sensitive to touch; this is an advantage to the rider as this is where the rider's legs lie.

The muscles with which the horse propels himself forward run from the poll, along the neck, under the rider's seat, through the loin area and fan out over the hindquarters. The front leg muscles join in at the wither.

Imagine the horse standing upright on his

hind legs and compare him with the human body. At first sight it would seem that the difference begins in the hind leg where the horse's hocks bend backwards and the human knees bend forward. But think again! The horse is standing on the tips of his toes and his hind feet correspond to the human centre toes. His fetlock joint is the beginning of a human toe, his hock is equivalent to the human heel and his stifle to the human knee. Pelvis, hips, loins and rib cage approximate to the human body and the only real difference is that a horse does not have a collar-bone.

The horse may have a longer neck but the muscling and set-on of head are the same. The forelimbs stand on the equivalent of a human centre finger, the knee of the horse corresponding to our wrist and his elbow correctly named.

As an experiment, try to lengthen your stride without bending your neck forward, and you will immediately understand why a horse must lengthen his neck to be able to lengthen his stride.

To be able to use his back muscles to carry a rider, the horse must first develop them sufficiently to do so – and to be able to do this efficiently the rider must sit balanced and still. Try carrying a load that is unbalanced or moving around and you will understand the problems presented to the horse when the rider cannot sit still and remain balanced.

Other muscles which affect the efficiency of the horse in carrying weight are the strong internal abdominal muscles, which are equivalent to the human stomach muscles. To be able to move his hind legs well forward, the horse must contract these muscles, lifting the stomach upwards towards the backbone.

There is one fact which few horse riders

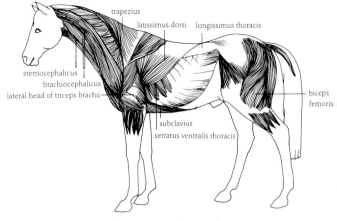

SUPERFICIAL MUSCLES

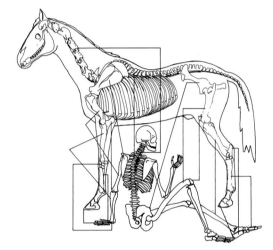

RELATIONSHIP BETWEEN THE HUMAN AND EQUINE SKELETONS

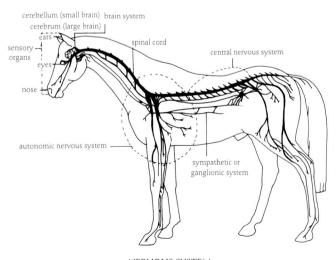

NERVOUS SYSTEM

know, or if they do know, do not take into account when training or working the horse. Nature has developed the horse to go forward in a straight line and any activity which requires forward movement is not difficult for him. But when free, the horse is seldom required to turn, change direction or continue on a curve for any length of time and is therefore not naturally equipped to carry out these movements efficiently.

However, it is not possible to play polo, jump a showjumping course, compete in a show, or carry out many other activities on a straight line only, so the horse must learn to adapt his body to perform circles and sharp changes of direction without injuring himself. He needs help in accomplishing this efficiently, hence the need for education and suppling work, activities which are the basis of dressage.

To be able to turn efficiently, the horse must be developed in the back muscles so that he can use his strong hindquarter muscles to position his leg, on the side to which he is turning, well under his body and then to contract his back muscles on the same side and extend them on the other side to assist the small amount of bend he has in his backbone and rib cage. Not only must he learn how to do this initially but he must also be given time to redevelop these muscles after every rest period.

Nervous System

The nervous system includes the central nervous system (CNS), the peripheral nervous system (PNS) and the specialised sensory organs, the eyes, ears and nose.

The CNS consists of the brain, brain stem and spinal cord. The PNS may be regarded as a network of communications throughout the body which records both inner and external sensations.

The whole can be likened to a telephone system where the brain represents the exchange and the nerves leaving the spinal column are the individual lines to houses, which in this case are the muscles.

Just as the telephone system relays messages, the nerves convey information from various parts of the body to the brain or, automatically on shorter paths (like local exchanges), back to the muscles to cause them to contract or relax according to the state of the motion.

Nerves regulate the supply of nutrients to the muscles via the blood stream and control and regulate the synchronisation of muscles working in co-ordination. The elastic walls of the small arteries which provide oxygen and nutrients are operated by nerve impulses. Without control by the nerves the flexion of a limb could result in a bone fracture or other disastrous accidents.

The autonomic nervous system is designed to regulate the supply of blood to each organ in accordance with requirements. This system is involved in heart rate and is important in work for fitness.

The nervous system registers sensations and stores them in the memory for future use. The memory in the horse is unusually active – this fact and the horse's low tolerance to pain give him an unusual learning ability and enable him to be trained. The foal starts learning on the day it is born and continues to do so throughout its life, forgetting nothing. Although the horse can overcome traumatic experiences, he never forgets them.

Nervous disorders in the horse are difficult to treat, so it is important for the handler to understand the psychology of the horse and be aware that it can suffer nervous breakdowns as easily as man (see Chapter 5).

DIGESTION

The digestive system of all animals, including the horse, starts at the mouth and, although the mouth is also used for other purposes, it should always be remembered that its primary function is to provide an entrance to the horse's stomach. Any injury caused by the bit, however accidental, will mar the efficiency of this primary function.

Food is processed in a tube of varying width and thickness, which extends from the mouth to the anus and is called the alimentary canal. The process of dealing with the food eaten is called digestion. As the food moves along the canal it is broken down into simpler substances so that they can be absorbed into the bloodstream through the wall of the intestine. Grass, hay and oats, for example, are turned into the relatively simple forms of carbohydrates, proteins, fats, minerals and vitamins.

The nutritive material in this food is made available to the rest of the body for muscle building, cell maintenance and storage for future use in the form of fat. The fibre in the food aids digestion and is a very necessary part of the horse's diet. Water, of course, is essential.

Starting at the mouth, the lips select the food then, if necessary, the incisor teeth (front teeth) bite off what is chosen. Then the molars (back teeth) grind the food into a pulp for swallowing. With the help of the hard palate, the tongue forces the food into a ball and then pushes it into the oesophagus (at which stage the soft palate closes off the nasal passage).

The oesophagus conveys the food into the stomach, which is relatively small compared with other animals and the size of the horse. During this time the salivary glands are adding moisture to the balls of food – there

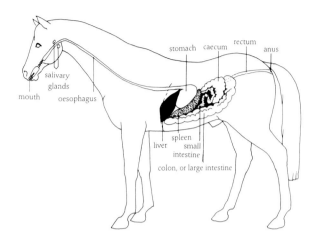

DIGESTIVE SYSTEM

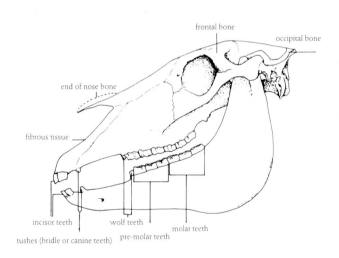

SKELETON OF THE HEAD

are three pairs of salivary glands in the sides of the face. Another source of moisture is the water the horse must drink.

The first part of the stomach is a storage space, but the latter part secretes a strong acid substance which begins to break down the food in preparation for passing it along the small intestine. Immediately the food leaves the stomach and enters the small intestine this acid is neutralised so that it cannot damage the tissue of the intestines.

Digestion continues through the caecum (pronounced 'see-cum') which is roughly equivalent to the human appendix, then through the large intestine and colon. All this time substances are being passed into the bloodstream for the nutrition of the body cells and organs. Finally, the unwanted material is stored in the rectum to be discharged as faeces from time to time.

Organs which are also involved in the digestive processes are the pancreas, the kidneys and the liver, which act as filter and storage areas. Horses have no gall bladder to store bile, but produce it as required.

The whole of the intestinal mass is looped back and forth to fill the area allotted to it, but it is not connected to the outer frame of the horse. The intestines themselves are lightly joined by connective tissue which is rather like a very thin plastic.

Starting from the mouth, let us look at the organs as they affect the horse owner.

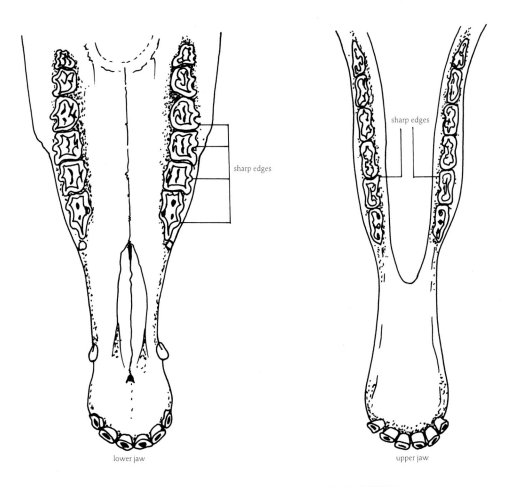

sharp edges

lower jaw

sharp edges

upper jaw

MOUTH, SHOWING TEETH EDGES THAT BECOME SHARP

Teeth

The teeth are of first importance. The incisor teeth seldom need attention once they are fully mature except in cases of injury or 'caps', but the molar teeth should be checked regularly as they can cause considerable discomfort to the horse if allowed to become sharp or if teeth are missing. Incisor teeth are very useful to us as well as to the horse, as they are used to tell the age of the horse.

Young horses up to the age of four years lose their baby teeth and replace them with adult teeth from time to time. Problems occur when the baby teeth (or caps as they are called) refuse to let go and may have to be removed. They are not difficult to remove once they are ready, and a flick of the thumbnail will usually dislodge them. Although they may bleed a little, this should not be too severe. These caps should be left until they are ready to lift, but if it is necessary for some reason to remove them, this should be done by an experienced person.

On the other hand, molars often cause trouble by becoming too sharp, especially in very young or very old horses. The horse's teeth are not like human teeth – they have no central nerve cavity and they continue to grow from the gum as they are worn away by the grinding action.

Because modern fodder is not hard to grind, particularly in the case of stable-fed horses, the grinding action is not completed across the whole tooth, and edges are left at each side which become sharper with time. The bottom teeth have sharp edges on the outside and the top teeth become sharper on the inside. These sharp edges cut into the tongue and the cheek, causing discomfort and considerable pain which is often accentuated by the action of the bit.

Regular attention should be arranged either with a veterinary surgeon or a horse dentist, at least every six months until four years of age, then once every twelve months. When the horse is older, it will be necessary to go back to six-monthly inspections. The process of filing the teeth is known as 'floating' the teeth.

Should a horse lose a molar tooth, it is essential that the tooth left above or below the cavity is floated regularly. This tooth will continue to grow even though it is not being worn away and will grow into the cavity from above or below, cutting the gum where the tooth above or below it used to be. Misbehaviour which has mystified the owner can often be traced to this cause.

The space between the incisors and the molars, commonly known as the bars of the mouth, allows us to place an instrument of communication – the bit – in the mouth. This space is sufficient for a single bit, or even two bits, to be placed in the mouth. These bits cause little inconvenience if fitted correctly and **used** correctly.

However, there are situations which can cause the horse considerable inconvenience and sometimes great pain.

Between the two sets of teeth, and a little lower than the correct position for the bit, there is sometimes a tooth which erupts at the age of about four years. This tooth is called a canine or bridle tooth. The canine tooth is usually associated with the male animal but occasionally a mare will produce canine teeth.

Trouble can be experienced when these teeth first erupt. As in any tooth eruption, the gums become hot and red and sore and when the bit is introduced to the mouth it causes considerable pain. However, as soon as these teeth have cleared the gums, the soreness disappears and the bit no longer troubles the horse.

It is wise to stop working with a bit in the mouth while these teeth are erupting, as problems which arise at this time can easily become bad habits and continue after the teeth are no longer sore. The canine teeth may appear only on the bottom jaw or on both top and bottom.

A small tooth without roots which erupts in front of the molars is called a wolf tooth. This tooth can appear in front of the upper molars on one side, on both sides, in front of the lower molars only, or in a few cases in front of both upper and lower molars. They cause little trouble until the bit is introduced to the horse's mouth or when they appear after the horse has been bitted. Increased head tossing and obvious discomfort should result in an inspection of the mouth to determine if such teeth are present.

If wolf teeth are in existence they will appear as small teeth growing out of the gum in front of the molar teeth; they have no roots. These wolf teeth should always be removed. It is a simple job for a veterinary surgeon or a horse dentist, the most difficult part being to keep the horse's mouth open. This work can be carried out during a routine check, unless the problem is urgent.

Whenever a horse is misbehaving, having been well behaved in the past, an inspection of the mouth is indicated. Trouble, such as new teeth erupting, can be easily combated by resting the horse until the teeth are through and the gums are no longer sore.

If the trouble is caused by wolf teeth, these can be removed. It is not necessary to remove canine teeth unless they are infected or causing trouble for some reason.

Other mouth problems

If the teeth are not the cause of the problem, the other likely answer is grass or cereal seeds. Coarse grasses have large seeds which sometimes pack up between the lips and the gums or back behind the molar teeth. A much more difficult problem occurs when the tiny sharp spikes of the seed casing become embedded in the lips, tongue or cheeks of the horse. This is as painful to the horse as splinters or thistle spikes are in our fingers. They can be picked out with a sterilised pair of tweezers if the horse is easy to handle – if not, it might be a job for the veterinary surgeon.

A good way to ensure that grass seeds do not cause trouble is to hose out the mouth every day during the seeding season. Do not have the hose on full pressure – just a gentle trickle of water under a little pressure will clear the mouth and most horses learn to appreciate this treatment.

Not only do these problems affect the behaviour of the horse, they can also affect his digestion. At best, they cause the horse to deal inefficiently with his food and, at worst, they can make it impossible for him to eat at all.

Other problems can occur with the mouth, such as lampas (inflammation of the palate), but such problems must be diagnosed by a veterinary surgeon. Any treatment necessary to the actual entrance to the alimentary canal itself and on down the length of the digestive system is a matter for the veterinary surgeon.

It is necessary to point out, however, that forcible dosing such as drenching should be done with care, as the soft palate must close over the nasal passages and the epiglottis must close over the larynx to prevent liquids from entering and causing considerable damage. If the horse is to do this successfully, his head must not be forced up too high.

Stomach

As the horse has a very small stomach it is quickly filled up at mealtimes and any work – particularly fast work – should not begin until at least one hour after feeding. As the horse breathes diaphragmatically, fast work such as that required of a racehorse should be done when the stomach is relatively empty. This is one of the reasons why racehorse training usually takes place in the early morning when the trainer can be reasonably sure that the horse's digestive system is least active, and there is room for the expansion of the lungs towards the stomach cavity. This is also a consideration for polo ponies, endurance horses and all horses or ponies which take part in fast sports.

Caecum

Further down the canal, the caecum receives the food after it has travelled along the small intestine. The entrance to the caecum is bigger than the exit so that it can take in any large undigested particles. These particles cannot leave the caecum if they do not break

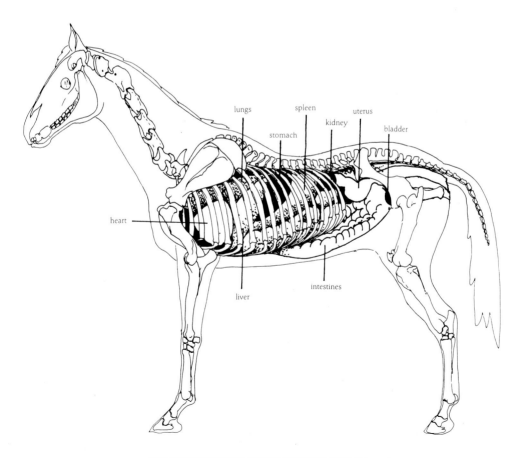

ORGANS PROTECTED BY THE SKELETAL FRAME (mare)

down and it is possible that a blockage will occur and cause colic. Unless the blockage can be cleared, the horse is in serious trouble.

If such a blockage occurs, the large intestine and colon continue to be cleared by the natural process, and are then left empty due to the blockage. They can easily twist as the horse rolls and throws himself around in pain.

The bacteria in the caecum develop the ability to deal with a particular diet and any change in the diet should be made gradually so that the bacteria can change. New season's chaff and hay and other cereal products constitute a change of diet and should be mixed with the old season's products.

A blockage or gas build-up can also occur anywhere along the alimentary canal and there is always a danger of twisting – virtually a death sentence for the average horse. Some very expensive horses have been saved by a timely operation, but even the operation itself can be dangerous as horses have a very low tolerance to pain.

Worms

Much has been written about the danger of a large worm burden and the need for an efficient program to combat this problem. Worms reduce the value of their host's fodder, thus keeping the horse in poor condition. They also burrow into the tissues and bloodstream, causing aneurisms and weakening the walls of the blood vessels and damaging the organs.

This damage becomes dangerous when blood vessels and organs are stressed, as in racing, when the horse is straining every tissue in his body to take the lead or to stay there. A weakened blood vessel can give way at this time and the horse literally drowns in his own blood.

A less dramatic result is an unnatural lethargy caused by anaemia and/or lack of nutrition, the worms having gained the most benefit from the horse's food. Another dangerous situation occurs when a horse is suffering from colic, caused either by blockages or gas build-up. A weakness in the intestine wall can rupture, spilling the contents into the stomach cavity, the result of which is peritonitis – almost always a death sentence to a horse.

The food which is moving along the alimentary canal is quite liquid until it reaches the colon when this liquid is removed by the body, leaving the waste quite dry by comparison. Faeces should be large and soft enough to break or spread a little on landing. Small hard nuts or sloppy cow-like dung suggest something is wrong with the digestive system. A slight change of diet may correct the problem, especially if the horse shows no signs of a more serious situation, such as high temperature, increased respiration or fast pulse.

Always remember that the ridden horse is an athlete, no matter what his duties are, and he should be treated as such. Diet and exercise should be aimed at keeping the horse in a fit and healthy condition.

Respiration

A knowledge of the respiratory and circulatory systems is very important to anyone involved in training horses. The more fit a horse has to be, the more important is this knowledge. The function of the respiratory system is to supply oxygen to the body, remove carbon dioxide and other wastes and assist in temperature control.

The respiratory system begins with the nasal cavity by which air enters the body, continues down the pharynx and larynx to the trachea and thence to the bronchial tubes and air cells. The last two together form the lungs.

Lungs are composed of a spongy substance made up of vast numbers of small lobules that are connected and kept separate by cellular tissue. Each lobule is composed of many minute air cells and is supplied with a small tube which conveys air to these cells. The alveoli are covered with capillary blood vessels so that while air in one cell acts on one side of the capillary, the air in the adjoining cell acts on the other side, transferring oxygen in the first instance and receiving waste in the second instance.

The lung cavity is lined with two smooth glistening membranes which cover the lungs and form two separate compartments. Their purpose is to prevent friction between the lungs and the walls of the chest. Called the 'pleurae', they secrete serous fluid to lubricate their inner surface. Infection in this area is called pleurisy.

Nasal passages, pharynx, larynx and bronchial tubes are lined with a mucous membrane which can become damaged by dust and other foreign substances. The subsequent disease is called bronchitis.

Because the horse breathes diaphragmatically, he cannot use the intercostal muscles of his chest in an all-out effort at the gallop. Instead, he must take a huge breath and expel it gradually, while making his effort, then he must slow down and take another breath to continue and is then able to accelerate again. The efficiency of a horse's lungs is the reason why some horses are fast over short distances and others can maintain their effort over a longer distance.

The act of inspiration with closed larynx is called wind-sucking and when the horse closes his teeth on an object while wind-sucking it is referred to as crib-biting – both

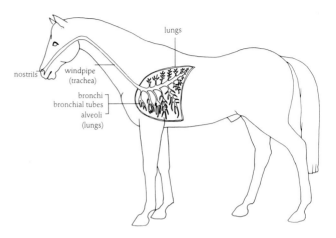

RESPIRATORY SYSTEM

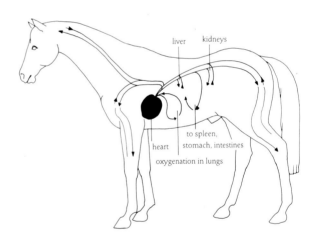

CIRCULATORY SYSTEM

are considered vices and are very difficult, if not impossible, to cure. These activities impair the performance of the horse and reduce his stomach capacity, thus contributing to lack of condition. They must always be disclosed when selling a horse – if this is not done the sale is not legal.

Expiration with a closed larynx is used for defecation, urination and parturition.

The respiratory rate of the mature horse is 8-16 per minute and that of a foal 16-32. The fitter the horse, the lower the respiration. Very fast respiration often indicates pain, although fear will also increase the rate.

Haemoglobin or red blood cells absorb 97% of the oxygen and carry 20% carbon dioxide back to the lungs. White blood cells are the front-line defence against disease and multiply considerably when the horse is sick or injured.

CIRCULATION

The circulatory system is closely associated with the respiratory system. It is made up of a series of arteries and veins of varying sizes. Arteries carry the blood from the heart which has received it from the lungs reloaded with oxygen. The function of this blood, which is dark in colour, is to transfer nutrients and oxygen to the body cells. Veins return the blood, which is bright red in colour after dispersal of the oxygen, to the heart and lungs, carrying cell waste to the kidneys and liver on the way. The circulatory system also conveys hormones from one tissue to another, helps to regulate the temperature, provides a buffer for all cell water and maintains cell pH balance.

The frog in the foot is also involved with circulation, as well as with concussion, and it is important that it is in contact with the ground at all times. The outer tissue of the frog is fibrous and insensitive but the inner tissue resembles a sponge and soaks up the blood as it travels down into the foot. Each time the horse places his weight on his foot, the sponge is squeezed and the blood returns upwards through the veins in the leg. A series of valves close after the blood has passed, preventing it from returning to the foot. Once the blood has cleared the leg, it runs back to the heart, then to the lungs to be replenished.

Injuries which sever an artery are far more serious than those which sever a vein, although both must be dealt with before too much blood has been spilt. The action of the heart will cause the blood from a severed artery to spurt some distance, while that from a vein will flow freely but will not spurt. The colour will also give a clue to whether an artery or vein is involved. When injured in this way, the quieter a horse can be kept the better, as movement accelerates the pumping or flowing action.

The heart, which is a double action pump, is responsible for keeping this circulation in motion. The heart rate of the horse at rest is about 32-34 beats per minute. The fitter the horse, the slower the rate and the younger the horse, the faster the rate. Exercise accelerates the beat, and how soon it returns to normal depends upon the amount and strenuousness of the exercise and the fitness of the horse.

The circulatory system of the horse carries 240-320 litres of blood and takes 31 seconds and approximately 27 heart contractions to complete a round of the body.

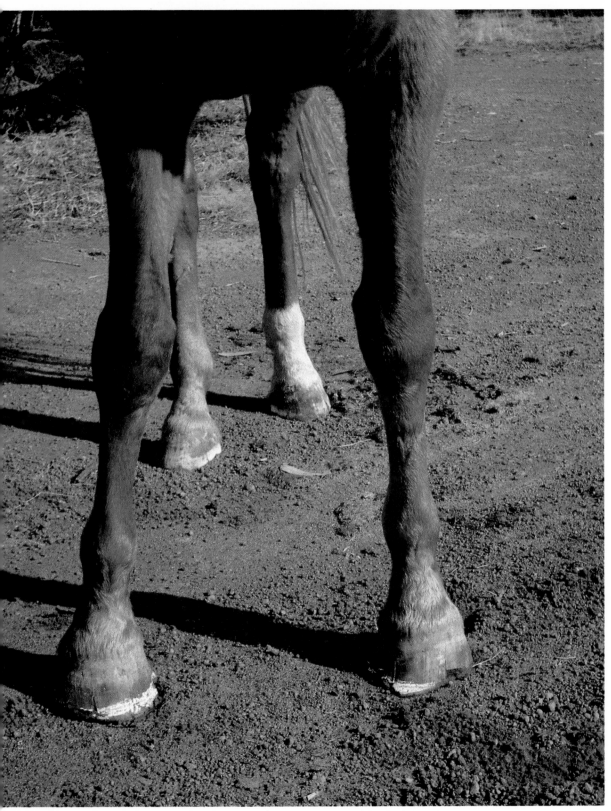

Some horses are pigeon-toed (see photograph on page 41) but the defect can be corrected. Here the feet have been marked with white chalk by a farrier, indicating how they should be trimmed to improve their angle. Page 36 shows the trimmed feet ready to be shod. Photograph by Bill Roper.

Improving pigeon toes: here the feet have been trimmed according to the farrier's instructions (see page 35) and are ready to be shod. The fault has been considerably improved although it will return as the foot grows and will need to be corrected at each shoeing. Photograph by Bill Roper.

CHAPTER 4

CONFORMATION

The word 'conformation' refers to the way the horse is put together. It covers not only the body structures individually but also refers to the overall build of the horse. The horse is described as having good or bad conformation according to his general appearance.

Harness horses are judged by different standards from the riding horse and good conformation in one may not be good conformation in the other, although many of the good and bad points apply to both.

The first consideration in assessment of conformation is the shape, size and physique of the animal. A horse which is badly or incorrectly put together can become unsound very early in its career because of conformational defects, yet others with the same problems complete their working lives without succumbing to trauma. This is often the result of careful husbandry. On the other hand, a horse which is of good conformation may also succumb to trauma due to accident or bad management. However, if there is a choice, good conformation should be selected, while excellent conformation would be a bonus.

LEGS

Although the horse's 'engine' is in the rear (all horses are Volkswagens!), a greater amount of weight is carried on the forehand than on the hindquarters. For example, in the canter, the whole weight of the horse and rider comes down on one front leg, and when jumping the weight comes down on the two front legs from a great height. So it is the front legs which are exposed to greater trauma than the hind legs.

When a horse takes a step forward, the weight of the horse is first taken on the foot. This is the first shock absorber. As the foot lands on the ground, the frog and the plantar cushion are compressed and will spread the heels and the lateral cartilages apart. The size of the feet must be suitable to the horse, and both front and back feet should match each other. The horn of the outer hoof and the sole must be strong and not shelly. Brittle horn breaks away and soft soles are prone to bruising; both problems can result in sudden cessation of work at an inopportune moment. Careful shoeing and choice of working surfaces can help to prevent injury.

The heels must be able to expand and they cannot do this efficiently if they are high and narrow (contracted heels). Equally, they will not be able to absorb sufficient shock if they are low and too wide (flat feet). If they do not expand sufficiently they allow much of the shock to travel further up the leg; the structures of the leg are designed to accept just so much stress and may break down if extra stress is applied over a period of time.

The correct angle of the foot is important, but as this can so easily be altered by incorrect shoeing the expertise of the farrier should be taken into account when studying this point. Even naturally incorrect angles can be improved by knowledgeable farriers. The recommended angle for the front hoofs is about 58° from the front of the hoof, at the coronet, to the ground, and in the back hoofs about 70°. The front feet should be neatly rounded while the back feet are slightly elongated.

Under the foot is the frog, a rubbery kind of tissue which is insensitive. Directly above the frog on the inside of the foot is the plantar cushion which is made of a spongy sensitive tissue. The plantar cushion has another function, as well as being a shock absorber. It is employed in blood circulation, returning venous blood back up the leg through a series of valves each time the horse puts his foot to the ground.

Above the plantar cushion is the pedal bone, which is roughly the shape of a paper dart, and behind this is the navicular bone, which functions as a pulley wheel and is involved in navicular disease. Above this again is the lower pastern bone. All these structures are deep within the foot and protected by the horn of the hoof, which makes them difficult to treat when things go wrong.

The deep flexor tendon runs under the navicular bone and is attached to the pedal bone. The extensor tendon runs down the front of the foot and is attached to the front of the pedal bone.

Behind the foot, at the heel, the lateral cartilages enclose the foot on each side but do not join together, as they must spread apart as the foot takes weight. Injury or stress in this area causes the cartilages to calcify and instead of being pliable they become stiff and unyielding – referred to as sidebone.

Around the top of the hoof is the coronet where the leg ends and the hoof begins. It is only a very narrow band and is hardly visible, but it is from the coronet that the horn of the hoof is produced and any injury to the coronet will affect the growth of the horn, either temporarily or permanently. This is where pressure is applied in the disease ringbone and it causes considerable pain. The coronet approximates to the quick or cuticle of the human finger.

The lower pastern bone (os coronae) fits into the pedal bone and its upper end fits into the higher pastern bone (suffraginis). This joint occurs at the level of the coronet and stress in this area causes the bone to ossify – (make more bone). This increase in bone formation, which is quite rough and not neatly covered by smooth membrane, pushes out against the coronary band causing excruciating pain, particularly when it is forming.

The upper pastern bone fits into the cannon bone at the fetlock joint. This bone is also subject to ringbone but, unless ossification directly affects the joint or the tendons and ligaments, this high ringbone is merely unsightly and not as restricting as low ringbone.

The absorption of stress continues up the legs, reducing as it travels upwards. The fetlock joint is the second line of defence against shock; it absorbs the shock by flexing strongly. The amount of flexion in this joint is influenced by the length and angle of the upper pastern bone. The longer this bone is,

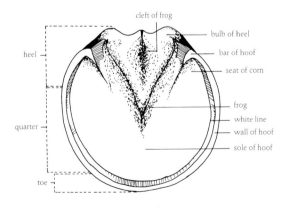

STRUCTURE OF THE HOOF (fore)

the greater the flexion (and, incidentally, the more comfortable the ride), **but** an excessively long pastern bone is not good for the horse. It takes up more than its share of shock and often allows the back of the fetlock joint to touch the ground, injuring the ergot (the small hard core found among the fetlock hair at the base of the fetlock joint).

At the back of the joint there are two small sesamoid bones which act as pulley wheels over which tendons pass. These bones can also be injured if the fetlock joint flexes too much. Too short a pastern bone makes for very uncomfortable riding and less absorption of concussion in the fetlock joint, thus weakening the whole structure of the leg. This is a major cause of the diseases ringbone and sidebone.

The length of the cannon bone below the knee should be much shorter than the length of the forearm above the knee. In fact, it is almost (but not quite) impossible for the cannon bone to be too short. Under the knee and running down each side of the cannon bone, roughly halfway, there are two small bones referred to as splint bones. These are the residual bones of the extra toes of the prehistoric horse. They have not disappeared completely because they help to support the knee.

Many horsemen and women live in fear of their horses throwing up a bony formation (also known as a splint) but, in fact, splints strengthen rather than weaken the legs unless they appear too close to a joint and cause that joint to function less efficiently. Legs that do not require the assistance of this bony formation are, of course, to be preferred.

The third point of stress is the knee itself and if the first two (foot and fetlock joint) are not efficient this joint is in serious trouble. The knee of the horse is equivalent to the

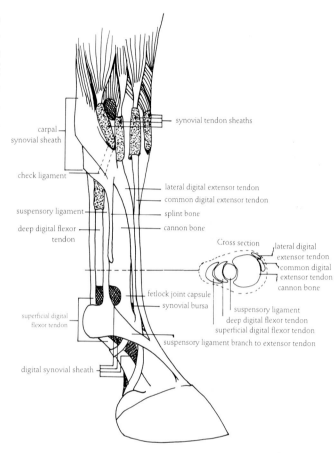

STRUCTURE OF THE LOWER FORELEG

human wrist and there are seven bones involved which can be damaged individually or together. Chipped knee bones are common in young racehorses especially if the first two bastions of defence are not fully developed and sufficiently strengthened before fast work is carried out.

The knee should be as large as possible without appearing too cumbersome; the front of the knee should be flat and the outer side straight, with no suggestion of roundness here. The bone behind the knee (the pisiform bone) has a channel through which the tendons and ligaments pass. There should be no suggestion of tightness here, a condition referred to as 'tied in below the knee' and characterised by a sharp bend inward immediately below the knee. The correct shape is a gradual reduction of size flowing into the back of the cannon bone.

The width between the knees should be the same as the width between the feet below and the top of the legs above. If this width is not maintained the resulting appearance is referred to as 'base wide' or 'base narrow'.

The cannon bone itself should be placed directly beneath the knee; it should not appear a little behind the front of the knee, a little in front of it, or set a little off-centre, a condition known as bench knees or off-set cannons. Being 'over at the knee' causes less trauma than being 'back at the knee'.

Young foals often appear to be over at the knee as they grow because they have to bend their knees and keep them bent in order to crop the grass, an activity which often begins a few days after birth. The knees will straighten later as the foal grows and is able to reach the ground comfortably.

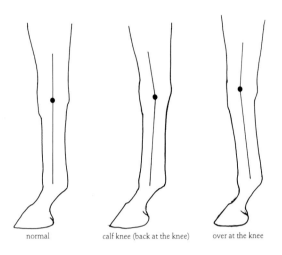

normal   calf knee (back at the knee)   over at the knee

GOOD AND BAD CONFORMATION
forelegs from the side

Not only is it necessary that the base structures of the leg be described, but the tissues which are attached to the bone of the leg, or run down close to it, are also important. They supply the motive power and must be as strong as possible. In most cases, if the conformation is good and the horse is sound, well fed, and has had a trauma-free upbringing, these structures will be as strong as they were meant to be, but any of the above problems may have an adverse effect on the leg tissue.

The extensor tendon, in its sheath, runs down the front of the cannon and spreads across the front of the foot, fastening to the bones of the foot; it is employed in lifting the toe. The cannon bone itself is covered by a very fine tissue called periosteum which can shatter, rather like a pane of glass, and cause severe pain if it is damaged, as in too early work. This is known as being 'shin sore'. Pain is felt when the front of the leg is touched and when the horse puts his foot to the ground, thus discouraging him from a desire to move fast. In America it is known as 'bucked shins'.

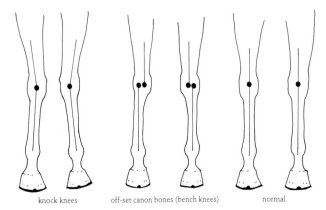

knock knees   off-set canon bones (bench knees)   normal

GOOD AND BAD CONFORMATION
forelegs from the front

Coming from behind the knee and joining the check ligament on its way is the extensor tendon of the cannon bone, which actually runs down the side of the leg and attaches to the fetlock joint. Behind the leg are the deep flexor tendon (which is also connected to the check ligament) and the superficial flexor tendon, both of which pass over the sesamoid bones and continue down into the foot. Both the knee and the fetlock joint are wrapped with a tissue called the synovial membrane, and when preparing a horse for work it is just as essential to develop strength and toughness in this membrane as it is to develop the muscles of the body. This is done by slow work, such as walking and trotting.

When a horse is said to have broken down, damage has occurred in one or more of these leg structures. If severe, the whole structure has parted, if less severe only threads have torn or the sheath only has been damaged. All are disastrous but some more than others. The tendon sheaths can become inflamed from undue friction but this usually only requires rest.

The synovial membrane which wraps itself around the knee also holds the tendons and ligaments which pass over the knee or around it. The usual joint buffers in the form of the bursa and its lubricant fluid are within this membrane. Leakage of fluid from either the bursa into the membrane or out of the knee structure is considered to be severe damage; although it may be possible to plug the leaks, the joint will never be as strong again. The outer skin of the horse's knee has no flesh beneath it, and this is why knee injuries are potentially serious and always require the attention of a veterinary surgeon.

The long forearm (radius and ulna bones) and short cannon allow the horse to stride

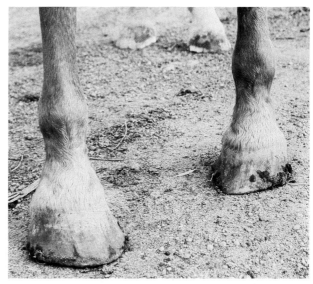

This horse is naturally pigeon-toed, a fault which places most of the weight on the inside of the foot. It is often the cause of damage to the other leg, when struck by the inside edge as the other foot moves through. Colour photographs on pages 35 and 36 show how the defect can be improved. Photograph by Bill Roper.

well forward and to use the shoulder muscles to their best advantage. At the top of the forearm is the elbow joint, which corresponds to the human elbow. If all functions below are working correctly, the major stress of weight will be dissipated by the time it reaches here. However, even if everything is not functioning perfectly, the elbow can sustain considerable shock without undue trauma provided the shoulder is well laid back. If the shoulder is at all upright, however, it will be more vulnerable to stress. The elbow should work straight ahead and not bend inwards or outwards and there should be plenty of room between the ribs and the elbow when the leg is fully stretched backwards.

The upper arm appears to join the shoulder at what is referred to as the 'point of the shoulder' but this point is, in fact, a tuberosity and the joint itself is deeper into the body.

The tuberosity is, however, very vulnerable to injury when passing through doorways or turning sharply when incorrectly flexed. These traumas usually occur when the horse is being led in a negligent way or when he is free and running away either in fear or in play.

The angle of the shoulder, from the point of the shoulder to the centre of the withers (the highest point), should ideally be about 43°, but the actual angle is decided by the length of the upper arm. The closer the shoulder is to the upper arm when fully flexed the better. A good shoulder allows freedom of movement – this will be better understood after reading the chapter on education.

Unless there is freedom in the shoulder the horse cannot work to maximum efficiency, despite the fact that the motive power is in the rear. A correctly sloping shoulder nearly always goes with a correctly sloping pastern. However, if the shoulder is nicely sloped and the pastern is straight, this is much better conformation than a sloping pastern and a straight shoulder.

The front of the horse is slung between the two front legs and is attached only by muscles, as the horse does not have a collarbone. These muscles are developed by good nutrition and the use of special lateral exercises.

On the underside of the shoulder close to the body are muscles which allow the horse to move laterally (sideways) and assist in lateral flexion. They need special exercises to improve their suppleness and to allow the horse to use them efficiently. Shoulder problems can be very deep-seated and cause considerable difficulty over a long period of time. Unfortunately, these problems often occur at a crucial stage of the horse's preparation.

There are a great many muscles involved with the movement of the forelegs, but it is sufficient for our purposes to recognise those directly involved with the tendons and ligaments of the lower legs.

In the forearm, the superficial muscles which are connected directly to the tendons are the extensor metacarpi magnus, from which the extensor tendon of the foot

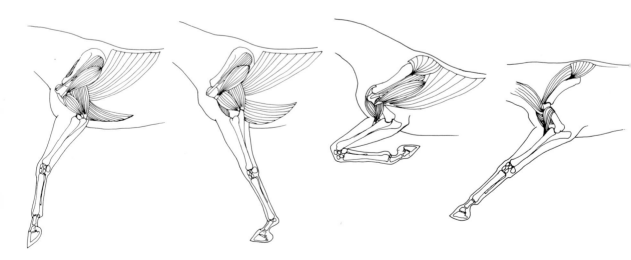

EXTENT OF FORELEG FLEXION

departs, the extensor pedis, which is involved with the extensor tendon of the leg, and the flexor metacarpi from which the flexor tendons depart. The muscles which attach the forearm to the upper arm and the upper arm to the shoulder are the biceps and triceps, which should be well developed and as wide as possible.

A line dropped from the point of the shoulder should find the centre of the knee and the centre of the hoof. Any deviation inwards or outwards of any of the bones or joints places increasing strain on muscles, tendons and ligaments, sufficient to cause temporary or permanent breakdown.

The lower legs of the hindquarters are the same as the forelegs until they reach the hock, except that the hind hoofs are slightly more elongated. None of these structures is prone to the same amount of stress as those of the front legs until the hock is reached.

The hock is a very complex joint; in fact, it is two joints and can be compared with the human heel and ankle. It is often considered to be the most overworked joint in the horse's body and is certainly very important to the rider. It stands up well to its task if correctly conformed. The angles of the hock and the stifle joints are closely connected and if there is too much bend at the stifle, the hock will also be too bent; if the stifle is too straight, the hock will also be straight. These joints – together with the hip joint – are the joints involved in 'engagement of the hocks', one of the most difficult exercises for the horse to accomplish efficiently with a rider on his back, and one which is directly affected by a too straight hock and stifle joint.

The hock itself should be large, but not so large that it looks unwieldy. The width should be sufficient to absorb the shock of

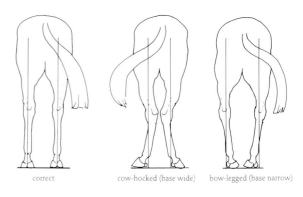

correct   cow-hocked (base wide)   bow-legged (base narrow)

GOOD AND BAD CONFORMATION
hindquarters from behind

landing for that particular animal and the joint should be lean and flat-sided in appearance. The whole joint should be quite long from the upper end to the lower end; if it is too short the hock cannot be engaged sufficiently.

'Sickle hocks' are curved towards the front and do not stand directly under the horse, 'cow hocks' bend inwards towards each other, and 'bowed hocks' bend outwards giving a bow-legged appearance. All these positions place extra strain on other joints and are, therefore, not recommended, although sickle hocks are sometimes preferred by jumping riders.

Straight hocks are becoming fairly general among Thoroughbred horses as there is a belief that they help the horse to move faster. Yet any deviation from the correct angulation places strain elsewhere, and unless there are compensating factors it is dangerous to depart from what has long been considered correct.

A line dropped from the point of the buttock should touch the point of the hock, then lie against the back of the cannon right down to the fetlock joint. If the distance between the feet and the distance between the hocks is not exactly the same, the fault is referred to as 'base wide' or 'base narrow'.

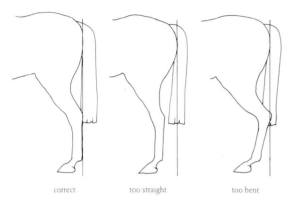

correct   too straight   too bent

GOOD AND BAD CONFORMATION
hindquarters from the side

The second thigh or gaskin (tibia and fibula bones), like the forearm, should be well muscled and as wide as possible. These bones should be as long as possible (described as 'well let down'). As in the foreleg, the gaskin should be long and the cannon short. If lined up with the front leg, the point of the hock should be roughly in line with the 'chestnut' of the front leg.

The gaskins carry the powerful muscles which lift the horse off the ground when leaping and galloping and there should be plenty of width for them to develop. If the hock and stifle are straight these muscles will be restricted to a certain extent. Therefore, straight legs are not recommended for jumpers. A good wide second thigh, together with a good wide forearm muscle, will ensure strength for any kind of work.

The stifle is equivalent to the human knee, complete with patella, and is subject to all the same stresses, including cartilage trouble. It has two joints – a hinge joint and a ginglymoid joint. This makes it quite a strong structure and a well-made stifle, unless directly injured by kicks or wounds, seldom causes trouble.

However, a very straight stifle can 'slip' (luxate) very easily. Slipping stifles in young horses may improve if the animals are allowed to rest and mature before work is commenced; it is necessary to insist that they refrain from their own playfulness for a considerable time and this is not an easy task. Stifles which dislocate are not so easily handled and you will need the attention of a veterinary surgeon to replace them.

The lower head of the femur connects to the tibia and forms the stifle joint. At the other end the femur fits into the pelvis bone and a protuberance behind this joint forms the 'point of the buttock'. Ideally, this point should be directly above the hock. The hindquarter joints are well covered by strong muscles and seldom cause problems except in the case of accidents.

The upper end of the pelvis construction locks into the sacrum and a protuberance from this bone forms the 'point of the hip'. The hip joint itself is deep within the body. This protuberance is usually referred to as the hipbone and is vulnerable to damage by swinging gates and doors, kicks, or knocks of any severe nature. Such injuries can knock the pelvis structure out of place and/or chip pieces of bone off the hipbone.

The inside muscle of the thighs should be sufficiently developed to join both legs well down and any suggestion of space high up under the tail (cat-hammed or cut-up behind) should be avoided.

The muscles of the hind leg are different from those in the front leg but still attach to the tendons which run down the leg to the feet. The major muscles involved are the extensor pedis and the flexor metatarsi (which also has a fibrous tendinous portion called the Achilles heel). The muscles run down the inside of the gaskin from stifle to hock. The muscle which is attached to the point of the hock and the upper end of the femur is called the gastrocnemius muscle, and the gluteal and visti muscles are involved with the stifle to buttock joint. As in the forelimbs, there are many more muscles involved but it is not necessary for the layman to know them by name.

Above the knee and the hock, damage to muscles is easier to deal with than in the structures of the legs below these joints. Muscles can, of course, be stressed but they usually only need rest and a good constitution to improve them. The deep shoulder and hip muscles can usually withstand considerable stress but some of them are very deep and impossible to treat directly. For this reason, injuries to the shoulder and hip are not as easy to diagnose and mostly require long rest to repair.

The tissue around all joints, especially knees, fetlocks, stifle and hock, is rather like a thin plastic, but it has more elasticity than plastic and will become even more elastic with judicious work. But it may stretch and not contract quickly enough when the horse is tired or unfit, thereby causing the joint to be stressed.

Head
Starting on the body at the head, we find that is the best place to assess the temperament of the horse. The eyes, the ears, and the nostrils are all very expressive to the knowledgeable

Floppy ears – lack of a muscle in the area allows the ears to stand out at the side. The author's Welsh grandmother used to call them 'douk ears'. Photograph by C. Lade.

horseman or woman. The head is also very important to the balance of the horse and affects his ability to carry himself correctly. Present-day judges often prefer small heads, but there is a danger in them becoming too small. Ideally, the head should look in proportion to the rest of the body and the skull bones should be neither too heavy nor too light.

The ears should be neat – not too long or too short – nicely spaced and mobile. They should prick forwards more often than backwards. Ears that lie flat against the neck are threatening dire consequences to anyone or anything which dares to come too near; when in full flight, it indicates maximum effort. Lop ears are sometimes seen; they are often inherited and indicate a lack of nerve control in that area. There is widespread belief that lop-eared horses often become good jumpers, but the reason for this belief is obscure.

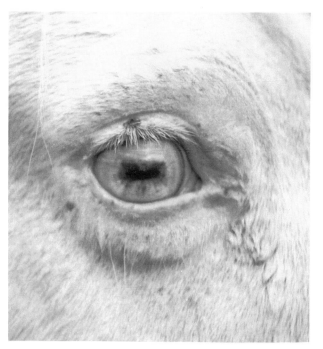

Wall eye: a condition where the whole eye (or most of it) has no colour. This one was caused by an injury but some horses are born with a wall eye. Photograph by S. Sobey.

The forehead of the horse should have width and be reasonably short, but if too wide it sets the eyes too far apart. The space between the eyes should be flat and not raised. Some people consider this rise to indicate bad temper or an obstinate streak.

The eyes themselves should be large and clear and of slightly rounded appearance, set as close to the front as possible. Small eyes set too far to the side are not considered to be good conformation, as they affect the ability of the horse to see correctly. Eyes set too close together are often small and 'piggy'; they are undesirable because of the restrictions placed on length and field of vision.

Other problems can arise from eyes which stand too far out, although a 'full eye' is considered desirable. Excess sclera (except in the Appaloosa breed) and 'wall' eyes present problems of sunburn and possible poor vision. A horse which shows the white of the eye is considered to be untrustworthy by many old-time horsemen.

A long narrow face is not conducive to efficient breathing or mastication so, although the face narrows beneath the eyes, it should do so gradually. A Roman nose is considered ugly and suggests the animal concerned is obstinate. A 'dished' face is an undulating frontal bone and indicates the presence of Arab blood.

The muzzle should not be too fine – often associated with Arab blood also – as the ability to breathe correctly is inhibited if the nostrils are very pinched. Nostrils should be large and able to flare with exercise.

The horse's jaw must not be undershot (bulldog jaw) or overshot (parrot mouth). Both are considered to be inheritable and therefore quite unacceptable in breeding animals. It is not necessary to open the horse's mouth to determine the shape of the jaws – a finger run over the surface of the front teeth will discover whether the jaw is level or not. If the upper teeth do not meet the lower teeth exactly, the jaw is more or less under- or overshot. These disfigurements cause problems with mastication, uneven wear of teeth and the introduction of bits.

Different horses have different sized mouths and they do not always conform to the standard 'pony', 'cob' or 'horse' measurements of the bits. A large mouth may not be very beautiful but neither is a very small mouth – the size is usually in accordance with the breed. In a small mouth the tongue can be squeezed into too small a space, making a bit uncomfortable in the mouth.

The set-on of the head to the neck is very important when looking for good conforma-

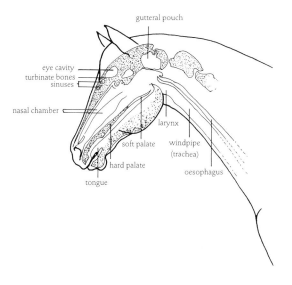

STUCTURE OF THE HEAD AND NECK

Diagram labels: gutteral pouch, eye cavity, turbinate bones, sinuses, nasal chamber, larynx, soft palate, windpipe (trachea), hard palate, oesophagus, tongue

'Skipper', at Illilangi Equitation Centre, South Australia, makes a lovely pony head study. Note the small, neat ears and correct placement of the eyes. 'Skipper' is an intelligent looking pony, calmly assessing photographer and camera.

tion and when choosing a horse for dressage. Too close-coupled and the horse cannot flex correctly, too loosely coupled and the flexion can quickly become 'overbent'. A good rule of thumb is to be able to place four fingers in the space between the back of the jawbone and the upper end of the jugular groove. If they fit nicely the head and neck can be said to be correctly coupled.

NECK

The neck is the most important barometer of correct movement and the set-on of the neck to the shoulder is one of the more important details in good conformation. Correct conformation requires a neck of good length without its being too long, and the width of the neck should increase gradually until it joins the withers and the lower shoulder, where it should blend gracefully into these positions. Too long and thin and the horse will never look balanced, and too short and thick and his ability to flex correctly will be greatly impaired.

A neck which appears to be set on 'upside down' is known as 'ewe' neck – this may be entirely due to poor conformation or the blame may be laid at the feet (or rather hands) of the rider.

The neck should bend at the poll (the atlas) and any suggestion of a bend further down the neck (swan neck) is undesirable because it also restricts the neck from carrying out its correct function as a balancer.

The cervical bones of the neck do not form a straight line from the poll to the wither but curve gently downwards and then turn upward again to join the body at the withers. Recently, it has become obvious that the horse has as much trouble with his backbone as humans do and often needs a physiotherapist to put him right. The first two bones of the neck, the atlas and axis, often need attention as does the point where the neck joins the withers.

This 6-week-old foal shows a basically good bone formation and strong growth. His friendly temperament is demonstrated as he greets his breeder – no tidbits, no food, just happy to see her. Photograph by G. Simpson.

BACK

The dorsal bones at the wither are long and point backwards, gradually decreasing in size and becoming more upright. This is the strongest part of the back, and the part with the least flexion, because the ribs interlock with the backbone here and form a fairly rigid base on which the rider sits. Riders should never assume this formation was made specifically to allow the horse to be ridden, but it is fortunate for them that this strength appears at the spot where they must sit.

The withers themselves may be 'high' or practically non-existent if the neck is not correctly connected. Both cause problems with saddling. The high wither will be pinched or rubbed if the saddle does not fit or is not placed far enough back, and the low wither will allow the saddle to slip forward and place the rider's weight on the forehand. Often, horses which are too fat lose the definition of the wither and they, also, are hard to fit with a saddle. The ideal wither is one where the third dorsal bone is set at the centre and just a fraction higher than the shoulder blade, while the following bones reduce gently in height to blend into the dorsal bones at the loin.

The back must not dip too sharply from the withers (sway back) or remain straight (roach back). The ribs should swell out gracefully from the backbone, tending slightly backwards. Too steep a fall gives a narrow appearance (slab-sided). This narrowness causes a narrow breast and in extreme cases the front legs appear to be coming out of the same hole. This places the legs so close together that they 'brush' each other and cause injury. A too-wide breast, although not as detrimental, detracts from the appearance and encourages the horse to 'paddle' or 'plait' (throw his feet outwards and then bring them in again before landing).

The front and hind legs should be directly in line and if there is sufficient breadth of chest the horse is said to 'stand over a lot of ground', usually a plus mark. There must be ample room for lungs and heart, so a good 'spring' of ribs is essential.

The long back makes it difficult to carry equal weight on all four legs, especially with a rider on the back. A roach back stiffens the back and makes it more difficult for the horse to flex along his full length. A sway or 'swampy' back places excess strain on the part of the back where the rider sits.

LOINS

The loins are perhaps the most vulnerable area of the whole horse as there is no protection immediately below, except for the dorsal bones, and the loins are literally slung between the back and the hindquarters. However, if the horse's muscles have been developed to their maximum potential, this makes for good strong loins.

They should be wide and rise gently towards the sacrum where the pelvis joins in. Weak loins – that is, loins which appear lower than the back and the croup – do not allow the horse to use his powerful hindquarter muscles to their maximum efficiency. Loins which are raised above the croup and connected to a roach back will be narrow and weak. A good strong loin is raised and broad; when the muscles are well developed they fill out the back of the saddle and riders are able to feel what is happening beneath their seat. It is here that the correct swing of the back begins when the horse is trotting.

Hindquarters

The croup should be the highest point of the hindquarters, but it should not rise abruptly from the loins or fall abruptly behind the join at the pelvis. A sloping croup detracts from the appearance but, unless excessive, is not necessarily undesirable. A croup that remains completely straight is usually associated with Arab conformation, but to provide a well set-on tail and nicely rounded hindquarters there should be a slight drop towards the rear. It can be said that neither the 'goose' rump nor the Arab hindquarters are bad conformation; they are a matter of personal preference. Some jumping riders definitely prefer the goose rump.

The quarters themselves are the big muscles which form the larger portion of the hindquarters. They should be nicely rounded and slope gently downwards to the thigh. Looked at from the rear they should meet in the centre and although not joined together should be closely associated all the way down towards the gaskin. Horses in poor condition often appear to be cat-hammed or 'cut-up behind', but when properly conditioned this effect disappears. If they are still cat-hammed when in good condition this is a conformation fault.

Quarters such as 'apple quarters', 'pencil' or 'square' quarters are a matter of personal preference and not necessarily bad or good,

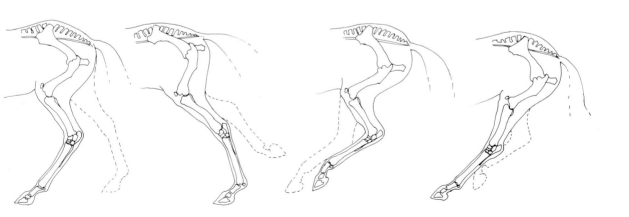

EXTENT OF HIND LEG FLEXION

as long as they are well muscled.

The set-on of the tail is very important to the appearance of the horse and the bony dock at the top of the tail is a continuation of the backbone. If the tail is set too low the horse does not have the elegant appearance which is obtained by a high tail carriage. On the other hand, the very high-set tail of the Arab is not to every horseman's liking. The way the tail is carried is a very clear indication of the state of the horse's back; the tail carriage and the head carriage are so closely connected with the flexibility of the back that all horsemen and women should be certain to assess both very carefully.

If the back is stiff and inflexible, the tail will stand out behind almost straight and the head carriage will be high, held up by the muscles at the bottom of the neck instead of those at the top. If the back muscles are unfit, the tail will hang down close to the quarters or may even be clamped into the buttocks. As the back muscles become stronger, so the tail carriage will become higher. If the back muscles are soft and flexible and the correct neck muscle is carrying the head, the horse will carry his tail most elegantly.

As far as facility is concerned, the goose-rumped horse can get his hindquarters much further under himself. The too high croup means that the hind legs are left too far out behind and the horse has difficulty getting them under his body.

MUSCULATURE

The muscular structure of the horse is not as well known as the other structures of the body. This is strange because all the work we do in educating and exercising the horse is aimed at developing and disciplining these muscles, to ensure that the horse is able and willing to carry out our requests. If the muscle potential is not there at birth it will never be developed during life. Only those muscle cells that are already in existence can be developed. So when assessing conformation the main muscles should be in evidence even if they are not yet fit for work.

The muscles of the neck with which the rider should be concerned are the splenius, serratus magnus, rhomboideus, trapezius and the mastiodo humeralis. If the horse is ewe-necked or becomes ewe-necked when ridden, it is the mastiodo humeralis muscle which is overdeveloped. The muscles which should be developed in order to obtain correct head carriage are the splenius and the serratus magnus. The rhomboideus is the crest which should be developed, but not overdeveloped.

Over the withers the trapezius is attached to, or works with, the supraspinatus, the infraspinatus, the deltoid and the triceps muscles which work the shoulder. Over the back the latissimus dorsi is responsible for joining the back and front of the horse and, when the horse is being ridden, it is directly involved in carrying the rider. It should also be noted that the rider's latissimus dorsi is one of the more important muscles.

The deep abdominal muscles of the horse lift his middle piece to allow room for the hind legs to come further underneath, and when these muscles are in use a line beneath the ribs along the flank area is visible. The gluteal, tensor, biceps and triceps muscles must be more or less developed in the hindquarters to allow the horse to carry out the work required.

CHAPTER 5

HORSE BEHAVIOUR AND PSYCHOLOGY

A knowledge of behaviour patterns is essential for any person dealing with horses. It is just as important to the rider as it is to the handler, if not more so. Knowing how a horse can be expected to react under certain circumstances will often make the difference between success and failure when educating or competing on the horse.

The age-old urge to run away from danger, or from a situation which is new and potentially dangerous as far as the horse is concerned, remains the first defence of the horse, and this should be kept in mind by the horse rider in all dealings with the animal. If he cannot run, the horse's next line of defence is to kick or bite, or both, and this reaction must be accepted as a possibility from a young horse. As the animal gets older, however, and becomes more used to his handlers, such actions become known as vices.

As a young animal the horse's reluctance to be caught stems from his fear of the unknown. Some youngsters which have been brought up to depend on humans for their very existence will remain shy of the physical touch of man until they are quite mature; others will be friendly from the very beginning and will trust man from a very early age. Knowing the difference between the two types of horse and treating them correctly is the art of horsemanship. It is an art which is acquired only by constant observation and analysis and close proximity to many horses over a long period.

The horse could be described as defenceless, timid, sensitive, alert, intelligent, agile and speedy. He desires to please, is easily trained and educated, and provides mobility for man.

The characteristics required of a good horseman and horse rider are strength and sensitivity, intelligence, courage tempered with caution, sympathy, understanding and determination, as well as observation and dedication. Without these attributes man becomes the dictator or the slave and misses the experience of man and his friendly servant.

Let us take a closer look at each of the characteristics of the horse.

We have already considered his lack of defences, remembering that from time immemorial his best means of defence has been to flee, and that this is still his first reaction to pain or fear. A vicious jab in the mouth from a too thin bit given by an unsympathetic hand, even if unintended, may produce anything from a mild trot away to a mindless bolt at full gallop. The act of running past a jump he has just refused is often the horse's defence against the punishment he expects to receive. A refusal in front of the jump, without the attempt to run past, might indicate that the horse considered he was justified in refusing and expected his rider to agree with him. The thinking rider will not automatically raise the whip to every stop but will quickly analyse the reason for the stop before taking action.

Because of this constant necessity to flee from the unknown or painful, the horse remains in a timid state. He can be induced to suppress this timidity by correct handling but it is always just below the surface. Most

'Reggie' seems slightly nervous of the cameraman. His expression seems to say: "What's going to happen now?" His ears are twitching nervously and he has an apprehensive look in his eye. 'Reggie' ('Regal Painter') belongs to Kate Rice. Photograph by Keith Stevens.

horses are timid until they get to know their handlers; even horses which are getting on in years and have travelled widely need time to adjust to new places and strange faces. Some remain timid all their lives and new situations are quite traumatic for them.

The horse's natural instinct when danger threatens is to run away, but his assessment of what is dangerous will be quite different from that of a human. Our superior intelligence may tell us that the situation is not dangerous.

Humans set great store by courage, but the horse cannot afford such luxury or he would long since have disappeared from the earth. To refer to the horse as 'chicken' or 'brave' is misleading. The very bold horse across country is not necessarily showing his bravery – he may just be running away in his own imagination – and the horse accused of being 'chicken' is probably exercising his sense of self-preservation.

Although the horse is known to have a very small brain and cannot reason in the same way that man does, he is still intelligent within the limits of that brain. For example, he can associate good behaviour with pleasant results from his handler or rider, and learn that bad behaviour results in inconvenience to himself. Most horses have a strong sense of fair play – if he is punished for something he knows to be against the rules he will accept the punishment philosophically, but if his sense of justice is violated a brave-spirited horse may retaliate.

Anyone who has had dealings with a large number of horses will know that the vast majority of them have a desire to please which is only suppressed by bad handling. We must remember, however, that horses are animals and, like the human animal, genetic misfits and physical accidents can occur to change this situation. Thus, the occasional horse does not fit this pattern.

As much as we would like to believe otherwise, the horse is relatively unintelligent when compared with other animals, such as the dog, for example. In spite of stories and films on the subject it is very unlikely that the horse would be instrumental in saving the life of his owner, or anyone else, except by accident while trying to preserve his own safety.

In the case of a bad fall and consequent injury to the rider, the horse may do one of

When galloping free, the horse often negotiates curves by flexing to the outside, thus unbalancing himself in a series of jerky movements. Here 'Zamazaan' shows perfect balance and correct flexion while galloping free in his paddock. His diagonal pair – left hind leg and right foreleg – is landing together, while the right hind leg is pushing the horse's body forward. (Note that in the gallop the hind leg lands slightly in advance of the foreleg giving the four-time beat.) Photograph by Martin King.

A natural wall eye, as opposed to showing the white of the eye. Photograph by Mitsuaki Iwago.

two things. He may move off at whatever pace seemed to fit the need of the moment. In this case, anyone finding the unridden animal would start looking for the rider and perhaps be in time to help. On the other hand, if the horse is particularly attached to his rider, he would most likely remain quietly grazing or standing in the shade, waiting for the rider to get up and remount.

If the horse was at all concerned for the safety of the rider his actions would be more likely to cause greater injury. He would very likely strike at the inert figure with his front feet, trying to inspire it to action as he does when a foal lies dead or a companion has gone down for the final time.

If a horse is able to stay on his feet when desperately ill, it gives him hope for recovery, but should he have to go down at this stage he will most likely give up the fight as hopeless; and because of his limited intelligence he would expect the same kind of reaction from his rider or handler.

Unlike other animals, however, the horse uses what little intelligence he has to learn effectively what is good and what is bad for him and to retain this knowledge. He learns at a similar rate from the day he is born right throughout his life and never forgets what he has learned. Thus, young horses exposed to skilful handling appear to be easier to train than those which have not been handled. However, the accent is on the skill of the handler and unskilled handling can have quite the opposite effect.

Many horsemen and women have been amazed that a horse which has never been handled before turns out to be very easy to train. This is because, having never been mishandled, he has no knowledge of man's good or bad habits and if treated well he is quite prepared to co-operate.

When he first entered a school of instruction, 'Rocket' was terrified of the instructor and refused to allow her to come within ten metres of him. He would not halt anywhere near her. But after five or six lessons, confidence was achieved and the instructor was able to stand this close to correct Colin's leg position. 'Rocket' now greets her with friendly confidence. Photograph by S. Sobey.

There is no doubt that the horse is agile and speedy. Those who own polo ponies, stock horses and show jumpers can vouch for that. But this does not mean that the horse needs no preparation for the work he is expected to do. When taking part in these activities he is just as much a sportsman as human swimmers, runners and footballers and needs his muscles, heart and lungs prepared just as human athletes do.

Not only does the horse have to carry himself, he must also carry a rider, and in these activities the effort is sustained for much longer than the effort to avoid danger.

Therefore, it is again stressed that the

'Bold Eagle' is not a very bold horse, despite his name, and he allows 'Follyfoot' to boss him. 'Bombalo' has to be isolated because he challenges 'Follyfoot' for top position and injury could result. Photograph by Cindy Lade.

horse must be treated as an athlete and correctly prepared for whatever work he is asked to do.

The horse has a relatively short attention span and all educational work should be restricted to short periods of a maximum of six minutes, when the subject should be changed. Fortunately, a change of subject can be a change of direction or pace, but more on this subject in Chapter 10.

The ability of the horse to learn depends on the strength of the stimulus. Unlike humans the horse cannot rationalise but learns from past experience. He tends to repeat behaviour which brings a favourable response and avoid behaviour which evokes an unfavourable response from the rider or handler. If a change is desired once a pattern of behaviour has been learned, the trainer should allow time for the new pattern to take shape before demanding too precise a performance.

The horse's desire to please is a very important aspect of his training – perhaps the most important – and any action on the part of the trainer which reduces this desire must in the long run work against the trainer. On the other hand, should the horse get the idea that his trainer is subservient to him, the trainer will have great difficulty in controlling

the horse. The horse's subsequent behaviour is referred to as bad manners.

Horses, like children, react favourably to discipline so long as the discipline is applied consistently and fairly. Good discipline at all times is the basis of good horse training.

The horse's behaviour is largely controlled by his senses rather than by reasoning, although he has a very limited ability to think things out. The senses involved are vision, hearing, smell, taste and touch.

The horse will also assess his rider's status within the equine hierarchy (the 'pecking order'), particularly in relation to himself, and this understanding of their relative 'social' standing and power has a very strong influence on his habits, especially when free in the paddock. The rider should never forget that the horse is always aware of who really has the upper hand, even when the horse is being ridden. The rider's status will take precedence if the rider is in charge, but if he is not, the actions of the horse when being ridden can cause considerable embarrassment and often danger to his rider, other people and horses, or property.

The horse's eyes are set wide apart and to the side of the head, resulting in a wide field of vision. With the head in a grazing position he can see around almost 360°. The only

'Bold Eagle' and 'Bombalo' at play. Photograph by Cindy Lade.

limitation is straight ahead, where his vision is blurred up to 3 metres and he is virtually blind some 120 cm directly in front. This is why the horse throws his head up and moves backwards when a stranger approaches with outstretched hand directly in front of his face.

Experts think that the horse sees only in black and white, their reasoning being that the process needed to be able to see colour is missing from the make-up of the horse's eye. This information is difficult for the horseman to believe, especially when the horse reacts to brightly coloured objects such as painted jumps or vehicles. There appears to be evidence that the horse can distinguish bright colours, but whether he actually sees them in colour or just recognises the deeper or lighter tone is debatable.

Due to poor peripheral vision, caused by the imperfect surface of the cornea, the horse must centre his vision. To observe distant objects he raises his head (binocular vision) and for close objects he lowers it (monocular vision). This is because the lens of his eye is inelastic and he has a sloping retina. His eyes are made this way to enable him to use his speed to advantage in flight – to do this he must see danger as early as possible and must also be able to see while grazing. Because of his small stomach the horse needs to graze constantly over a long period. In the wild, if he could not keep a constant vigil while grazing, he would soon starve to death or become a victim of his enemies.

What the horse lacks in vision he makes up for in hearing, which is very acute. He can detect sounds inaudible to the human ear and often, when he seems to be watching something in the distance, he is actually listening.

The horse pricks his ears towards the

'Crown Law's' attention has strayed from the rider's influence to watch young horses cavort in the paddock ahead. Note the ear trumpets pricked forward, eyes looking ahead and nostrils dilating, all straining to pick up the sounds, smells and pictures presented by the youngsters. The rider, Erica Taylor, is trying to regain his attention and keep him on a course to the right by increasing the pressure of the right hand and leg – revealed by the bar of the bit beginning to show and the spur coming into use. Photograph by Keith Stevens.

'Crown Law's' attention has returned to the rider and he is using his hindquarters to good effect in preparation for a halt from the trot. Note the lowering of the hindquarters and the jaw relaxing to the half-halts being applied. Erica appears to be standing in the stirrups a little, rather than sitting deep, probably due to her previous efforts to get his attention. Photograph by Keith Stevens.

sound, as one would direct a hearing trumpet, to concentrate on the noise. A blind horse can compensate for his lack of vision by constant movement of the ears, enabling him to pick up minute sounds. It is possible for a blind horse to move around his normal surroundings as easily as the sighted horse, and it is only when taken out of this environment that his blindness troubles him.

A nervous horse is characterised by continual movement of the ears and it is possible to assess the state of the horse's nerves by this fact alone. All horses are nervous on windy days, much more so than when the air is still, and some riders will not ride on windy days. The reason for this nervousness is probably not that everything is moving; it is much more likely to be that the horse cannot hear as well with the rush of wind past his ears. He cannot pick up the usual sounds and he also hears many sounds that are unfamiliar to him.

The mobility of the ears on a working horse whose attention is on the rider should not be mistaken for nervousness. If the rider has the horse's full attention the ears will be moving gently backwards and forwards in the centre of the head, sometimes together and sometimes singly, giving the horse a very intelligent appearance.

A nervous horse will have a raised head with both ears travelling well forwards and right back, or with one forward and one back, or constantly changing position. Often the head will be to one side.

The horse's fine sense of smell and his acute hearing make up for any limitation in his vision, but both also add to his nervousness, especially in unfamiliar surroundings. When using his sense of smell the horse's nostrils dilate widely and are pointed towards the source of the smell.

Horses often dislike other animals such as donkeys, pigs and camels, not only because their form is unfamiliar but more likely because their strong smell is new to the horse. Once the horse has become familiar with these animals, he will take no further notice. One of my horses left home when a donkey was introduced temporarily to the property, and he was only induced to stay at home when the donkey was removed.

The tongue is a muscle with taste buds incorporated over its surface area. These are used to recognise different tastes in different areas and also in the tongue's relationship to the bit. Sweet and salt are recognised by the tip of the tongue, sour tastes are recognised at either side of the tongue and bitter tastes are recognised by the back of the tongue. This information is very useful in our attempts to get the horse to take something which will be good for him but which he does not like.

The horse's preferences differ from ours and quite often from those of other horses. Some love sugar, others will not even try to taste it. Apples, carrots and salt are other delicacies that we expect the horse to like, but the occasional horse will not accept them. Sometimes it is because he has never been offered them before and he does not know the taste, but a few horses just do not like them.

These four items, together with bread, are the usual titbits offered to the horse in the form of bribes. In moderation they can do no harm, but if used in excess they can upset the horse's digestion. It is preferable to offer a small portion of his usual food if a bribe is offered at all, but a kind word and a pat, or cessation of the exercise being performed, is better understood and appreciated by the horse.

When a bridle is put on a horse, the bit rests on the top of the tongue. Its strength and flexibility help in keeping the bit in the correct place. If the horse will not accept the bit on his tongue, problems arise which are difficult to overcome, so it is expedient to take great care when bitting a horse for the first time.

When accepting the bit the tongue lies flat and relaxed, allowing the bit to rest on the bars of the mouth on each side. When the horse gives with his lower jaw to requests from the rider he readjusts the bit in his mouth with his tongue. A horse 'on the bit' should be gently moving his tongue, lifting and lowering the bit and producing saliva to keep his mouth wet. If the horse's mouth is fixed and 'dead' it will be dry and the presence of the bit in his mouth will be an inconvenience. How he reacts to that inconvenience depends upon the nature of the horse.

If the bit is fitted too loosely, the horse will get his tongue over it; this will place greater pressure on the bars of the mouth, causing increased pain, and his reaction to pain might be to run away, buck, rear or simply refuse to move. If the bit is fitted too tightly he may object in the same manner, so it is important for the rider to make sure the bridle is correctly fitted.

Occasionally, a horse will be found to have an abnormally thick tongue which will need special consideration, such as a mullen-mouth snaffle instead of the standard broken-mouth snaffle. A too thin tongue might also become a problem. These body defects are rare, but should be considered when unexplained problems arise.

Most of the horse's body is relatively insensitive to touch except for a blanket area covering the withers to loins and down over the ribs. This area has a subcutaneous mus-cle layer rich in nerve endings, known as the panniculus muscle. This allows the horse to feel such things as flies landing on his hide, and to react immediately by 'shivering' the hide to dislodge the offending insect. The tail does the same chore for the hindquarters area and the mane and forelock take care of the head and neck area. Although this high-density nerve area was not designed for our specific use, it does come in handy for the rider, because the rider's legs occupy some part of this area.

Tactile hairs (that is, hairs with nerve endings) are found around the muzzle, flank and fetlock areas. The muzzle hair nerves let the horse know when his muzzle is near to the ground or the bottom of his feed bucket. He cannot see this area because of the angle at which his eyes are set. The nerve endings in the fetlock hair warn the horse of unstable ground and keep him informed of possible danger in soft going. Because of this, some horses object to entering water, but a tactful approach and constant practice will overcome this fear.

The nerve endings of the hair in the flank area warn the horse that he must clear his hindquarters before turning sharply while passing through restricted spaces. The handler should always look behind when leading the horse through a door or gateway to make sure the hips are clear of the posts before turning sharply.

Although some horses give the impression that pulling their mane or tail hairs is painful, this is not so as they have no nerve endings in this area. It is possible that the pulling sensation upsets them, while other horses will take no notice at all. Often a horse which objects to the pulling at first will eventually cease his objections after it has been persevered with over a period of time.

CHAPTER 6

GAITS

Good instructors will always question their pupils about the way the horse moves. If they cannot answer, the instructor should go into detail about these movements. The reason for this approach is that the horse moves quite differently in each gait, so it is necessary for riders to adjust their balance to maintain the equilibrium of the partnership in all gaits. To be able to do this they must first understand how the horse moves and then learn to feel the movement through their bodies.

Very few horse riding pupils can answer correctly and it is quite possible they wouldn't be able to answer the same questions about their own movements. However, these questions put to a professional athlete would probably get an immediate and accurate answer. Such knowledge is a necessary part of their training, since they must be able to develop the muscles connected with their particular activity.

When a rider sits on a horse's back, the horse becomes an athlete and it is important that the rider understands how the horse moves in order to be sure the horse is moving correctly. If he is not, the rider can then give maximum assistance to enable the horse to carry out his duties in the most efficient way. In the same way, the rider should also become an athlete, developing the body muscles required to stay in the saddle and to direct the horse.

It will probably be known that the horse walks in four-time, trots in two-time, canters in three-time, gallops in four-time and reins back in two-time, but few riders will be aware of the significance of this knowledge.

THE WALK

To move forward at the walk, the horse should lift a hind leg and move it forward; the front leg on the same side is picked up to allow the hind leg to make its maximum stride, which should be well beyond where the front leg was standing. As the first hind leg comes to the ground, the opposite hind leg is lifting and moving forward; then the other front leg moves on out of the way and completes the cycle.

A horse which is moving freely forward will overstride the front foot mark by many centimetres (depending a great deal on the conformation of the horse) and should move each leg exactly the same distance, in exactly the same time. Occasionally, the horse will lift the opposite front leg first, but the better trained he is, the less often he will do this. The horse's head will nod slightly with the movement of the body; the more relaxed the horse, the more the head will nod.

To understand what happens to the horse's body while he is progressing is important in developing the rider's ability to remain in balance and to know when the applied aids will achieve the best results. As the hind leg is picked up, the hip, stifle and hock joints are engaged and the back on that side lifts up a little and moves upward and forward. Then, as the leg is landed, the back straightens again. At the same time as the back lifts fractionally, the ribs on the opposite side bulge outwards slightly.

This action is repeated to each side as long as the horse continues to walk. If the horse wishes to quicken his pace, he does not naturally go faster but takes a longer, lower stride. Conversely, to go more slowly he should take a shorter, higher stride. The time taken to make each stride is the same whether it is long and low or short and high.

Only when a rider sits on his back does the horse tend to go faster and continue to do so, sometimes getting quite out of control, until he is trained to work more efficiently by a knowledgeable and capable rider.

THE TROT

The trot is a two-time movement in which the horse moves one hind leg and the opposite front leg together; then the other diagonal pair move forward together. There is a short period of suspension as one set of legs is landing and the other set is lifting. This suspension is quite obvious when the horse is extending his stride to the fullest, or when correctly collected, and gives the appearance of floating above the ground, but it is hardly visible at medium and working paces.

When trotting, the horse's back should tip slightly to the opposite side as each set of legs moves forward. Observers should be able to see the swing of the horse's back from the loins and the hips – while watching from the right side they should be able to see the hip on the right side but not the hip on the left, then with the next step the left hip rises into sight to be a fraction above the right hip. The horse's tail should swing from hock to hock rather than up and down. If the back is not swinging correctly the tail will bounce up and down and the hindquarters will appear to be left behind and will not swing.

Again each set of legs should take an equal stride and an equal amount of time to complete the stride. Lameness and uneven rhythm become obvious when one leg is taking a shorter stride than the other three and is usually more noticeable at the trot than at either the walk or the canter. As in the walk, the horse should not go faster or slower but will take either longer, lower strides or shorter, higher strides to increase

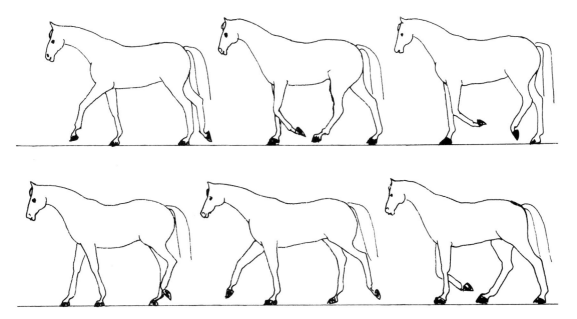

SEQUENCE OF THE FOOTFALLS AT WALK

or decrease the amount of ground covered. It must be remembered that the horse cannot put his front feet down beyond his nose so if his frame, including his neck, is not allowed to extend, the horse cannot extend his stride.

What he will do when asked to extend without the ability to stretch his frame is to take his front legs forward, then bring them back a little distance to put them down. The hind legs will either trail behind or step outside the front hoof print. This is not a correct extension and prevents the horse from using himself fully, invariably resulting in shorter strides from the hindquarters. Extending the frame should not be interpreted as extending or poking the nose. At the trot the head should remain steady.

THE CANTER AND GALLOP

To canter or gallop, the horse starts the movement with one hind leg which, if correct, will be the opposite hind leg to the direction in which he is moving; that is, if he is going to the right the first step should be taken with the left hind leg. Next, the opposite diagonal pair, in this case the right hind leg and left foreleg, move together and land, then the leading leg lands, in this case the left foreleg. The horse's body moves over the

The walk sequence. In the top picture the horse's left hind leg has moved forward to land beyond where the left foreleg was standing, the left foreleg is moving forward and the right hind leg is preparing to lift. At this moment the right foreleg is taking most of the weight (free walk).

In the second picture, the left foreleg is preparing to land and the right hind leg is moving forward. The weight is being taken on the diagonal pair, left hind leg and right foreleg (extended walk).

The third picture shows the right hind leg still moving forward and the right foreleg preparing to leave the ground. The weight is being taken on the left hind leg and left foreleg (collected walk).

Finally, the right hind leg has landed and the right foreleg is preparing to land, while the left hind leg is moving forward to repeat the sequence. The weight is again on a diagonal pair – right hind leg and left foreleg (medium walk).

These photographs were not taken in sequence, but each represents one of the four walks of the horse as well as the steps taken. A study of the rider's position at each moment will reveal – by her body position – the particular problem being encountered. Photographs by Keith Stevens.

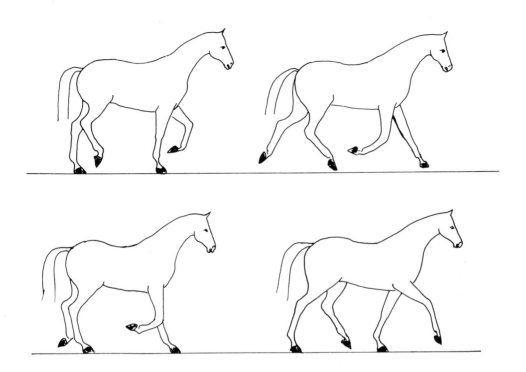

SEQUENCE OF THE FOOTFALLS AT THE TROT

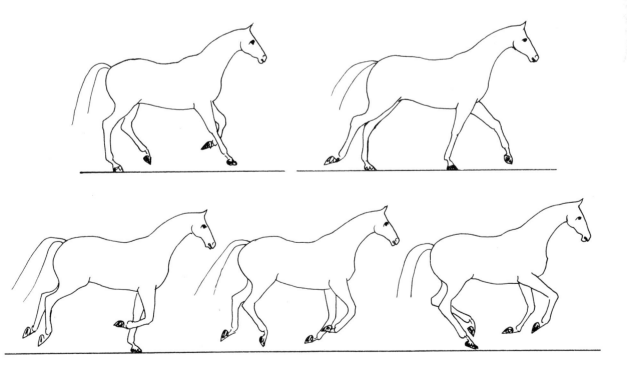

SEQUENCE OF THE FOOTFALLS AT THE CANTER

leading leg which is taking the complete weight of the horse, then there is a moment of suspension when all four legs are off the ground as the body is propelled forward. Then the stride is repeated.

The movement of the horse's body in the canter is thus: both sides of the horse's back move forward, raising the back upwards and forwards, then the back stretches out again very much the same as it did at the walk except that both sides move together.

The only difference between the canter and gallop is that the diagonal pair land separately, the front leg a fraction after the hind leg, making the fourth beat of the gallop. In both the canter and gallop, the neck moves forward and back with the movement of the body; the neck is more or less stretched according to the length of the stride which, as in the other gaits, is either higher and shorter or lower and longer.

THE REIN-BACK

To rein back, the horse moves backwards from the halt in two-time using diagonal pairs of legs, as he does at the trot, but at a walking pace. The rider must not force the horse backwards from the front or he will become unbalanced and either move to each side alternately or 'run' backwards. When the number of strides backwards is com-

The canter sequence: top picture shows the first step of the canter right. The left hind leg is about to take the weight and thrust the horse forward, the diagonal pair (right hind, left fore) are moving forward and the leading leg (right fore) has not yet left the ground. In this, the collected canter, the moment of suspension is practically non-existent. Note the rider's body remains upright, not leaning forward.

The second beat of the canter shows the diagonal pair taking the weight. The leading leg has left the ground and is moving forward to take the next step. Note the engagement of the hindquarter joints under the horse, especially the stifle, hock and fetlock joints. Note also the position-right of the rider, shoulders still, not swinging back and forth.

In the third picture, the right leading leg is taking the weight. After the moment of suspension, the left hind leg will begin another sequence.
Photographs by Keith Stevens.

THE REIN-BACK

pleted, the horse must be ridden forward immediately without hesitation.

THE HALT

When coming to the halt from any of these paces (except the rein-back) the horse should begin to stop with his hind legs first: that is, at the walk the hind leg should be put down and should stay there; the front leg on the same side should be the next to stop; then the opposite hind leg should be set down alongside the first; and the final leg to stop is the opposite front one. At the halt, each leg should carry its correct amount of weight and the horse should give the impression of having a 'leg in each corner'.

When first in training, it is permissible to carry out all transitions progressively, even to halt; that is, through the trot and walk from the canter and through the walk from the trot. Later, the horse will find it easy to make all transitions from the gait in which he is travelling to the halt without moving through the gaits. The ultimate correct halt is not obtained in the first lessons and it can be continually improved throughout the horse's working life.

Pick up any book or listen to any instructor and at some time you will hear the statement: "The horse's hind legs must always follow truly in the path of the forelegs except in some lateral movements." Yes, this is so, **but** it is not the front leg which decides where it is going to be placed. It is, in fact, the hindquarters which should decide where the front leg will land and then proceed to follow it.

Having studied the gaits and understood their sequence of movement, it is necessary to give consideration to the change from one gait to another. These and the changes within the gaits are known as transitions.

The halt from trot sequence: the first picture shows the diagonal pair (left hind, right fore) 'putting on the brakes' and transferring weight from the forehand to the hindquarters. The horse is beginning – a little late – to relax his jaw to the rider's request.

Centre photo: the left diagonal has continued the braking action and stopped. The right diagonal comes to a halt alongside. The horse has lowered his poll and is showing less resistance.

In the third picture the horse has come to halt, but is not squarely placed and is slightly on the forehand. (Note how the front legs are a little far back, preventing his weight from being evenly distributed over all four legs.) Many riders would be happy to achieve a halt as good as this in two strides. The horse's slight resistance throughout is probably due to the forward thrust of the rider's weight, which is being placed on the toes rather than the heels. This pushes the seat forward rather than letting it down into the saddle. Photographs by Keith Stevens.

TRANSITIONS

The aim throughout the training of the horse is forward straight, in correct rhythm and with perfect balance. Transitions must be fluently forward. Evasions, or resistance from the horse, outright disobedience and unsteady riders will affect the rhythm and balance of all forward movement and, in particular, the transition. At no time should the horse be allowed to 'hurry' forward.

In the rules of dressage the different paces within the gaits are referred to as :

Walk – collected; medium; free and extended

Trot – collected; working; medium and extended

Canter – collected; working; medium and extended

Although the gallop is not included in dressage movements, this gait has its own identification terms in other sports and in this book the following terms will be used:

Gallop – hand; three-quarter pace; evens; full gallop.

The difference between them all is the height and length of the stride. The movements should never be considered faster or slower, although they will appear so to the uninitiated. The horse does, of course, cover more ground when he increases his stride, but it should not be because he is moving faster.

The rhythm and balance of the horse remain the same throughout each gait. The changes from one gait to another and to halt and up again (transition) should be smooth and forward-going. There must be no jerky movements or a show of temperament from the horse.

It should be mentioned here that there are other gaits performed by specialist horses, but apart from the 'pace' (which is a trot where the horse moves both legs on each side together), all other gaits are artificially produced.

Halt from walk. Photograph by Keith Stevens

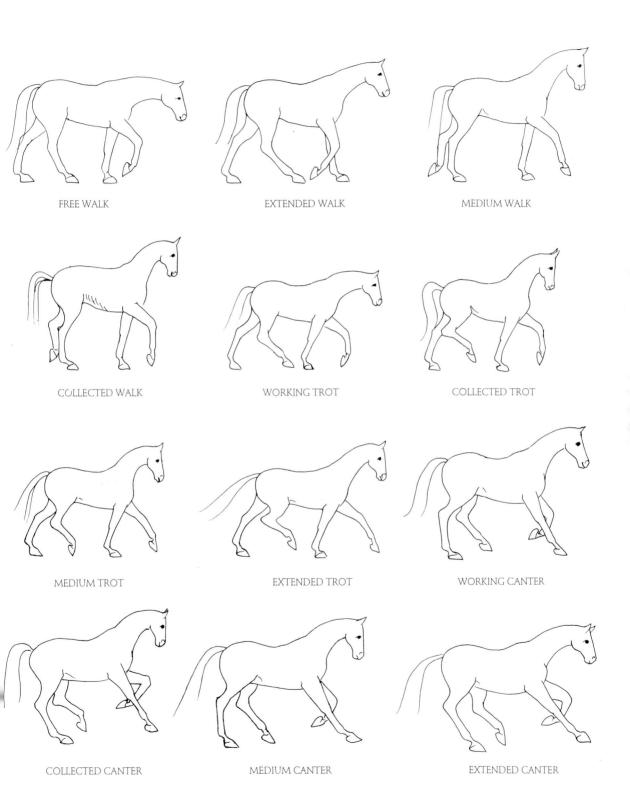

FREE WALK

EXTENDED WALK

MEDIUM WALK

COLLECTED WALK

WORKING TROT

COLLECTED TROT

MEDIUM TROT

EXTENDED TROT

WORKING CANTER

COLLECTED CANTER

MEDIUM CANTER

EXTENDED CANTER

CHAPTER 7

THE HORSE'S POSITION UNDER THE RIDER

When being ridden, the first and most important requirement of the horse is that he should go forward, straight, no faster than the rider wishes him to go and in the same balanced form he used when unmounted. He is also required to stop when asked to do so.

When free, the horse uses his head and neck to balance himself, raising and lowering it and turning it from side to side as necessary. In his natural state, he carries his weight balanced among all four legs and seldom finds it necessary to do other than travel straight. Therefore, what we ask of him is quite natural except that it has been made more difficult by adding weight to his back – an unnatural 'head and neck' above his back over which he has no control.

STRAIGHT HORSE

Most horses seem to believe they must travel faster than they normally would to accommodate this extra weight and the rider's task is to convince them that this is not necessary. The rider must always be aware that the horse's 'engine' is in the rear and that he moves himself forward with his hind legs where the major power is generated, only using his front legs to assist when he requires maximum effort.

To assess the extent of the horse's problem, let us examine our own reaction to weight. No matter how light the load, it makes a difference to our posture. Even under a small weight, we will adjust our position from the upright and lean more or less forward. If we get down on all fours and place a weight on our back, we find we must lengthen our neck and lift our back in the middle to enable us to carry the weight. The heavier the weight, the more difficult it is for us to carry – but the more practice we get in carrying the weight, the more efficient we become.

As the horse is built to move on four legs, he is able to adjust his weight more easily than we can. Even a very light weight will make a difference to the horse's ability to move correctly with that weight until he has had sufficient practice, but if he is able to deal with this weight by adjusting the position of his head and neck (assuming he is allowed to do so by the rider) he becomes increasingly efficient at this task.

However, he cannot adjust that extra 'head and neck' that he carries on his back. This must be done by the rider, either by keeping quite still so that the horse can maintain his equilibrium, or by the rider adjusting his/her weight to stay in balance.

To be able to carry the rider's weight and perform his duties with maximum efficiency, the horse must learn to transfer some of his own body weight to his hind legs so that his own weight, and the extra weight of the rider, can be distributed equally over all four legs. This, in turn, will free his shoulders so that they do not impede his efforts to propel himself forward.

At the same time, he must be encouraged to raise his middle part (in the same way that we have to do when down on all fours trying to carry a weight). When the rider over-weights the forehand and does nothing to help the horse to readjust his weight, the horse is anchored to the ground in front and is said to be 'on the forehand'.

The main problem for learner riders who wish to become expert is to learn to control their own balance so as to allow the horse to carry them efficiently. To do this, they must keep their weight and hands as still as possible so as not to interfere with the horse's efforts. At a later stage, the rider actively helps the horse to adjust his balance by continuing to maintain his/her own balance over the horse's point of balance at all gaits. At no stage can the rider balance the horse – this can be done only by the horse.

Now it can be seen why it is not practical for a beginner rider to start on a young uneducated horse, no matter how quiet that horse might be, as the horse must first learn from an educated rider how to adjust his weight.

During early efforts to develop the hindquarter muscles of the young horse, the rider should allow the horse to lengthen his body and lower his neck and head so that there is roughly a straight line from poll to croup, while still carrying his middle piece upwards and not letting it hollow out (long, low outline). Progressive exercises in lengthening and shortening the back muscles help the horse to develop them quickly and correctly.

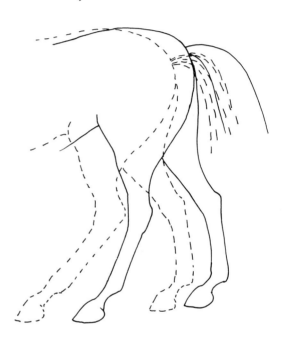

LOWERING OF THE QUARTERS IN COLLECTION

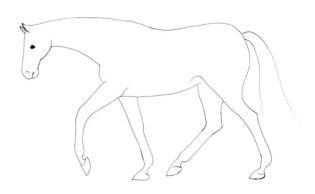

LONG-LOW OUTLINE AT THE TROT

Collected trot: an active, forward trot, shown here with left hind leg and right foreleg at the same height and flexion, returning to the ground. The horse's tail is swinging, indicating the swing in the horse's back. The left hip is correctly lowered by the lift of the left hind leg. The rider is sitting lightly to the trot.

Working trot: a longer, lower stride (the right hind and left fore are still lifting in this shot). A horse cannot put his front foot down beyond his nose, so he must be able to lengthen his neck (not his nose) to enable him to take a longer stride. If the horse takes his foot beyond his nose, he must bring it back to put it down and thus his action is not correct. The rider's hands must allow the horse to lengthen his neck sufficiently to take the length of stride required.

Medium trot: more length is apparent in the stride already, although the legs are still travelling forward. The horse's neck and his whole frame have lengthened to enable him to increase the length of stride. The extended trot (not shown) is longer still. All can be ridden at rising (posting) or sitting trot. Photographs by Keith Stevens.

As the horse's ability to carry weight improves, the muscles of the back and legs will become stronger and more supple. The neck muscles will develop sufficiently to allow the horse to raise and lower his neck and head and to adjust his balance within the tempo at which he is moving.

Riders who insist on shortening the horse's frame from the first moment they sit on his back not only prolong the work of developing the hindquarter muscles, but also develop them incorrectly and impair the horse's efficiency – perhaps for all time. The horse should not be asked to shorten his outline until he can do so while transferring weight to his hindquarters and lifting his middle piece (with the rider's weight added). Shortening the outline, by forcing the head in before the muscles are properly developed to carry weight, will result in the horse using incorrect muscles to hold his head and neck in place and in over-weighting the forehand and leaving his hindquarters behind.

As already mentioned, the horse in his natural state is seldom required to do anything other than move straight ahead. Circles, turns and sudden stops are rarely necessary and when they are required it is usually only once or twice at any one time. Therefore, the horse's body is not the most efficient instrument for carrying out these exercises.

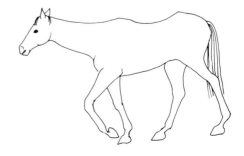

INCORRECT LONG-LOW OUTLINE

Przewalski horses: baby talk practised by all baby equines when being chastised or threatened by older animals. Photograph by David Langdon.

A veterinary surgeon checks a competing horse's respiration at a check point during an Endurance Ride. The horse must recover a more normal heart rate within the rest period time before it is allowed to continue in the competition. The recovery rate depends on how hard and fast the horse has been ridden and its state of fitness. Photograph by Keith Stevens.

To enable the horse to be used for playing games such as polo, and sport such as show-jumping, he must be able to circle, turn and stop, accelerate and decelerate efficiently without endangering his own body.

Let us look at the body positions the horse must adopt to carry out these exercises. To stop correctly and efficiently, the horse must bring his hind legs further underneath the body and stop himself with the powerful muscles of the hindquarters. When he does this he is balanced and poised ready to move forward again at whatever gait and tempo is required. The faster the stop required, the further under the body the hind legs must reach.

The least flexible part of the horse's back is the centre where the rider sits. This is because the ribs, expanding from their inter-locking position with the backbone, join the breast-bone under the horse's chest, thus discouraging the act of bending. The fact that the ribs and backbone are made up of separate bones (the ribs joined by tissue) does allow some closing and opening of the spaces to enable the horse to turn. The muscles required to make these turns, how-ever, have to be developed gradually and progressively so that the animal does not damage his back.

A

B

C

D

The rein-back.

A
Halt in preparation for a rein-back should be square and balanced. 'Crown Law' is a little on the forehand, but otherwise he is attentive and ready to obey his rider.

B
The first step back has been taken with the diagonal pair, right hind, left fore. The horse is resisting, causing the rider to use too much hand (or vice versa).

C
The second step has been taken with the left hind leg and right foreleg. Resistance has decreased but the rider is still pulling slightly.

D
The right hind and left fore, which lifted to continue the rein-back, are now on the way forward as the rider has asked the horse to proceed in a forward movement. Photographs by Keith Stevens.

To turn his body effectively, he must step further underneath himself with the hind leg on the side to which he is turning and shorten the whole of his body slightly on that side, lengthening the whole of his body slightly on the outside to correspond. The hip, stifle and hock joints must become engaged under the body and take much of the weight of the horse as he turns. If too much weight remains on the forehand, the horse will progressively unbalance himself on to his forehand through the turn, thus swinging his hindquarters out.

Turns and circles should be large until the horse has developed the ability to carry the weight of the rider in a straight line and adjust his own weight backward through the turns, at the same time remaining upright and not leaning into the turn. Work on the lunge without a rider on the back, if correctly carried out, will help the horse to develop the necessary muscles to enable him to bend, but ridden circle work should be reduced to a minimum until the horse is able to go forward straight, lengthen and shorten his outline while increasing and decreasing the length of his stride on a straight line (using the correct muscles) and transfer some of his own weight on to his hindquarters.

If sufficient time is allowed for this outline to appear, the rider will have no difficulty in getting the horse to perform correctly when asked to circle and turn.

A recent incident will illustrate how easy it is to develop muscles incorrectly. A yearling filly severed a shoulder muscle while trying to negotiate a fence without jumping it. The fenceline included star pickets and one of these entered the shoulder behind the muscle. The filly pulled back and the muscle tore away. The bottom half of the muscle was still attached to its ligament and moved sickeningly within the wound; the upper half disappeared up into the shoulder itself.

The layman owner was quite certain the filly was finished and would have to be put down; instead the veterinary surgeon cut away the remaining muscle, treated the wound and pointed out that there were three or four other muscles in the area that would take over from the injured one. If it is as easy as that, how many 'wrong' muscles are being developed in the education of horses owned by uninformed riders?

Words that come easily to the tongue of the educated rider are 'on the bit', 'flexion' and 'collection', but they are not always clearly understood.

A horse cannot be collected unless he is flexed correctly and is on the bit, but he can be on the bit without being flexed or collected, and he can be flexed without being collected, but not without being on the bit. So although all three are most important, they must each be understood separately as well as collectively.

Let us start with **on the bit**. The horse does not need to be collected or flexed to be on the bit. It simply means that the horse's mouth is in contact with the rider's hands and remains so regardless of the length of the rein. He is offering his lower jaw to the rider, which will enable him to accept every message given with the hands.

It is never correct for the horse to be 'above' or 'below' the bit, as to get into these positions he must have lowered his middle piece and left his hind legs behind. Both these positions can develop into permanent evasions and are difficult to correct.

Sometimes it is acceptable, for a brief period, for the horse to be 'behind the bit' (overbent) when the rider is striving to teach the horse what is meant when he is asked to

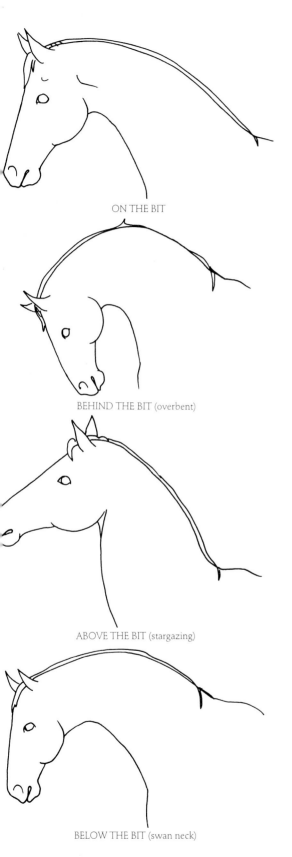

ON THE BIT

BEHIND THE BIT (overbent)

ABOVE THE BIT (stargazing)

BELOW THE BIT (swan neck)

accept the bit. Also, it often helps to develop the back muscles by stretching them, for the horse must lift his back to come behind the bit. When behind the bit the horse has over-flexed his neck but still has his middle piece lifted and his hindquarters engaged.

Flexion refers to the bend of the whole horse in the direction to which he is moving. To be correctly flexed, the horse must be symmetrically bent throughout his whole body. There must be no more flexion in the neck than in the middle or rear part of the horse.

The least bendable part of the horse is his back where the rider sits. This is because the rib cage is attached to bones above and below. To be able to turn correctly (that is, without damaging his back) the horse must be slightly bent, or flexed, throughout his whole body before he increases this bend to make a turn. The turn may be a long continuous one or a short sharp turn before returning to a straight line.

Flexion improves throughout the horse's education and the rider should not expect the same degree of flexion from a young or untrained horse as one would from an animal with more advanced training. At first, the young horse is asked to flex lightly on corners, turns or circles, and remain straight on straight lines (but definitely never flexed the wrong way). Later the horse will be expected to maintain a very slight flexion in the direction to which he is working, increasing it for turns, circles and lateral work and for all collected work.

Collection is the term used to refer to the form of a horse which is completely given up to the rider. That is, the horse is engaging his hind joints underneath his body, is supply flexed in the direction in which he is moving and is on the bit. This is a very advanced out-

Flexion left or bend to the left: 'Crown Law' is on the bit with hindquarters engaged and swinging nicely. The bend is correctly under the rider's seat and the neck muscles from shoulder to poll are carrying the neck and head correctly. A clear gullet line from throat to chest shows that no lower neck muscle is involved. The rider is correctly positioned to the left, but is leaning slightly in that direction instead of maintaining an upright position.

Straightening the horse before the change of flexion. 'Crown Law' relaxes his jaw to the rider's half-halts in preparation for the change of flexion.

Flexion right. The horse is on the bit with correct muscles in use. The rider's bad habit of dropping her inside hip is clearly seen here.
Photographs by Keith Stevens.

line which should not be asked for until the horse is physically capable of maintaining this position. Dressage riders will know that collection is not required before Elementary tests.

The aim of every rider should be to educate the horse so that he is at all times using himself in the most efficient way. This will increase his strength, and enable him to work for longer and be less tired.

The muscles that move the horse forward run from poll to hind feet, travelling under the rider's seat, which is where the rider eventually maintains maximum control. If you visualise these muscles in a simplified form as 'pulley belts' it may be easier to understand their working.

Imagine two sets of pulleys on each side of the neck and back, one above the other. To propel himself forward the horse uses one set of muscles to lift the legs and the other set

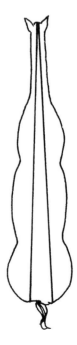

PULLEY BELTS

A medium canter to the right in Novice/Elementary outline. The horse is engaging his hindquarter joints sufficiently for his standard of education and is on the bit (not collected). He looks quite happy in his work and is attending to the rider. Photograph by Russell G. Griffiths.

Long-low outline: note poll and croup at same height. The horse is walking into his bit and taking strides of equal length. The lightest of contacts ensures that the horse carries his own head, but does not poke his nose. Preliminary work in this position at the walk and trot, before starting an educational session, will help to develop the top-line muscles of the horse – muscle work starting at the hindquarters, up through the loins, back and neck. Photograph by Keith Stevens.

When the horse is correctly on the bit (that is, working up from his hindquarters), the neck muscles will be developing along the top-line of the neck from wither to poll. The lower muscle just in front of the chest will be correctly relaxed, showing a clean gullet from throat to chest – as is seen in this photograph. If too strong a hand is used to pull the horse into this position, the neck will thicken and bend in the centre, increasing the size of the crest and giving a 'cramped' look to the neck. Photograph by Keith Stevens.

to let them down. It will be appreciated that these pulley belts must be moving freely without restriction unless they are required to slow down or stop.

An unnaturally high head carriage and the consequent hollow back will severely restrict the pulley's ability to move the legs forward in easy rhythm and balance, whereas a very low head carriage will restrict the length of the horse's stride. The ideal is a correctly raised middle piece and unrestricted hind leg drive which will automatically place the head and neck in the correct position, and the horse will be on the bit.

So it is necessary to look to the 'engine' (the driving force) first, before thinking of head carriage. In fact, if the horse works correctly from behind, it is not necessary to study head carriage because it will always be correct when the horse's muscles are sufficiently developed and quite supple.

The muscles working the front legs are attached to the pulley belts and are influenced by the drive from behind – if this is correct the shoulders will be seen to be working correctly too.

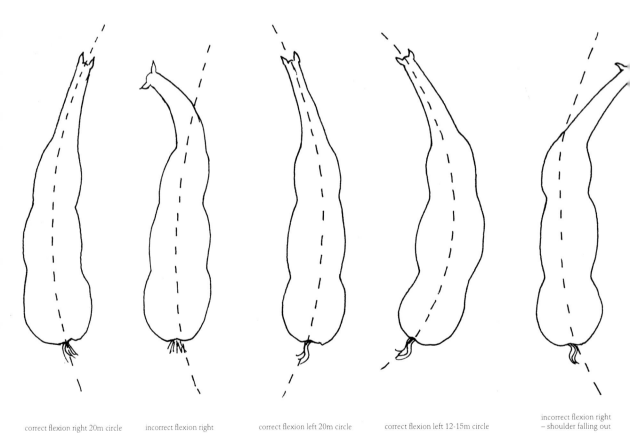

correct flexion right 20m circle   incorrect flexion right   correct flexion left 20m circle   correct flexion left 12-15m circle   incorrect flexion right – shoulder falling out

FLEXIONS

CHAPTER 8

THE RIDER'S POSITION ON THE HORSE

The art of expert riding is to be able to sit in a position which will not impede the horse's movement but will assist him in a practical way to continue to move as easily and efficiently as he would without a rider on his back – as he would when free in the paddock. Anyone can sit on a horse and stay with him while he carries out the movements required (if the horse is co-operative), once the art of balance on a moving horse has been mastered, but if the horse is expected to work at maximum efficiency the rider must do more than sit on him.

To be able to do this, the rider must first know how the horse is put together and how he uses himself, then understand what the rider must – or must not – do to help the horse maintain his correct balance, rhythm and posture. Then he/she must work towards maintaining this position at all gaits. Not as easy as it sounds!

In his natural state the horse's most efficient means of defence was to flee – straight and truly forward. Any change of direction would consist of a sudden turn or veering around a large circle. To turn this

In unison: a pair of riders who have been able to get their horses working together in a perfectly matched stride. Both horses are about the same size and have the same length of stride, but such perfect balance and rhythm is unusual. Photograph by Steve Lovegrove.

circle, quite often the horse will bend his body to the outside and come around like a boat but, if he turns like this with a rider on his back, he risks damaging the vital mechanics of his legs and back. He is not built to maintain a steady pace and move around freely in a small space – activities which are necessary if he is to carry a rider on his back. He cannot do this efficiently, and compete or perform effectively, without lengthy training and many suppling exercises.

To assist the horse, the rider must be positioned so that he/she appears to be part of the horse. The rider must sit over the horse's point of balance, which is just behind the withers, (moving slightly forwards or backwards of that position depending upon the gait at which the horse is travelling), and should give the impression that his/her seat is growing out of the horse's back.

When the horse is moving freely he uses his own head and neck to balance himself, raising or lowering his neck to suit the situation. A rider sitting on his back provides that extra 'head and neck' over which the horse has no control, so the rider must control his/her body as the horse does his neck, and remain in balance with the horse.

Beginner and inexpert riders are unable to maintain this position at first – or even at all – no matter how desperately they wish to do so. But if they will strive diligently for control of their own muscles in the early efforts to ride and not try to change the horse to suit themselves, they will, after a time, be able to move with the horse. Much more importantly, they will be able to remain still when necessary.

Saddles are made wide at the back and narrow at the front to enable riders to adjust their seat to this position – wide at the back where the two seat-bones sit squarely on either side of the centre of the saddle and narrow in front where the upper thighs close on the front of the saddle at the waist. Knees (the back of the side of the knee) and thighs (the inside of the thighs and not the back of the thighs) should be resting on the saddle.

The reason for the wide cantle on the saddle is to accommodate the swelling of the horse's loin area as the horse lifts his middle part and fills the seat of the rider.

Karen and 'Bobby' at the beginning of their work together. Many faults are noticeable: Karen has straight arms and flat hands, and she is standing rather than sitting in the saddle, with her weight on her feet. This is probably caused by forcing her heels down instead of letting them drop naturally. 'Bobby' is on the forehand and a little above the bit. His top-line muscles are not developed and as a result there is a peak in the centre of his neck. Photograph by V. Smith.

Karen and 'Bobby' three years later present a much more pleasing picture. Karen's arms are now where they should be – at her side. Her hands are softer and her seat lower in the saddle. (She is shown here in the act of rising to the trot.) 'Bobby' is no longer above the bit and his top-line muscles have developed nicely; his rhythm and balance are very good. Photograph by Steve Lovegrove.

The make and shape of the saddle has a big influence on the position of the rider and a great deal of thought and experiment should be put into the choice of a saddle.

Firstly, it should fit the horse and, when this has been achieved, it should also fit the rider. A saddle which tips the rider forwards or backwards is unsuitable, as the rider will have to use muscles to maintain the correct position, instead of allowing the saddle to provide a comfortable base for his/her seat. The muscles needed to keep the rider in place on a badly fitted saddle will then be tense and stiff, whereas they should normally be relaxed and supple.

The saddle chosen should allow the rider to sit comfortably in the deepest and narrowest part; it should not rise too steeply in front nor slope backwards without support for the seat-bones. A high pommel will be most uncomfortable at the rising trot unless the height is obtained gradually. A sharply rising cantle will cramp the seat forward instead of letting it sit comfortably forward, and a saddle with no rise at the cantle will allow the seat to drop backwards.

To be in balance with the horse, the rider's shoulders should rest squarely above the hips and be sufficiently supple to follow the movement of the hips without getting in front of or behind them. The legs of the rider follow the shape of the ribs; that is, the thighs bulge outwards, the lower leg following the slight backward tip of the ribs until the leg itself is directly under the hip of the rider. The front of the knee should point in a diagonal line to the ground.

A plumbline dropped from the rider's ear should pass through the centre of the shoulder joint and the hip joint and down to the ground through the heel joint.

Many riders will dispute this instruction and say they have always ridden with their lower legs forward on the horse's shoulder. If they will place their hands on either side of a friend's arms, close to the shoulders and

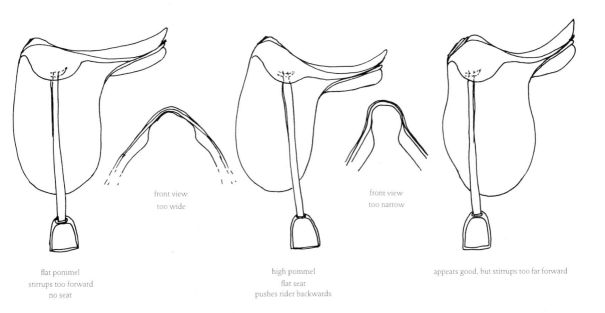

front view
too wide

front view
too narrow

flat pommel
stirrups too forward
no seat

high pommel
flat seat
pushes rider backwards

appears good, but stirrups too far forward

SADDLE PROBLEMS

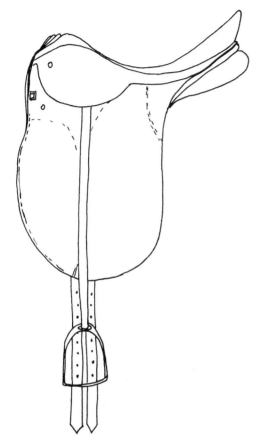

A GOOD FLAT-WORK SHAPE

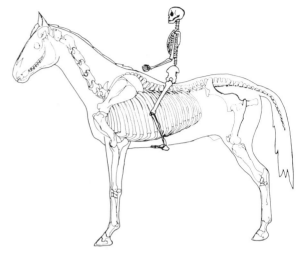

HORSE AND RIDER IN SKELETON FORM

your legs you would fall on your knees – not on your face or back. The weight of the whole body should be on the saddle. The weight of the leg only should be down through the heel. None of the weight of the body or the leg should be on the toe in the stirrup.

In theory, if the body is balanced in this way, the rider could not fall off unless the horse fell. In practice, of course, any slight change of balance will overweight one side or the other, when you can easily fall unless you have control of your balance.

The position of the stirrup bars is also very important. If they are too far forward, the legs will have to be either held backwards or allowed to ride forwards on to the shoulder, both positions which are detrimental to a balanced seat. The ideal position for the stirrup bar is at the top of the thigh of the rider so that the stirrup leather hangs down straight from the bar under the rider's thigh and, when the foot is in the stirrup iron, the stirrup leather hangs naturally straight down.

incorporating the rib area, they will discover how hard it is for the friend to bend to left or right. This also applies to the horse when the legs are held forward on the shoulder.

The rider's weight should be evenly distributed not only on either side of the saddle but also between front and back. In other words, the rider should not be sitting forward on the crutch or backward on the coccyx. When in a perfectly balanced position, while the horse is at halt, you should feel that if the horse were taken away from between

Leathers which have to be held backwards or pushed forwards make the rider tense and use muscles which should be relaxed.

Stirrup leathers and irons are a part of the mounts on all saddles but they are there for one purpose only: to carry the toe and enable the rider to keep the heels down.

If there is one single thing more than any other that enables the rider to remain balanced, it is the act of keeping the heels lower than the toes, softly down, not forced down. Should the heels be held up higher than the toes, or inadvertently lose their downward position, the seat of the rider is instantly loosened. Keeping the heels down is not difficult. The problem is keeping the toes up for, without the assistance of the stirrup irons, they quickly become tired and droop down, allowing the heels to rise.

At no time should stirrups be used to help the rider rise to the trot. If they are so used, they immobilise the leg as an aid. The ankle must remain supple to allow the leg to apply the aid and if the heel is forced down or the toe forced up the ankle cannot rotate as required. It is immaterial to accomplished riders whether they ride with stirrups or without, rising or sitting.

Learning to sit in this position and being able to maintain it will take a long time and considerable practice. No one can be an expert at riding just because he wants to be, any more than a cricketer can be an expert bowler just because he wants to be. Firstly, there must be talent and then the prospective expert must spend time and effort over many years learning the expertise and perfecting his ability.

There is no substitute for time in the saddle; although expert tuition is also necessary, in the long run only the rider can do the work needed to become an expert.

Rider's position at canter.

Top picture shows the horse cantering to the right, so the rider is sitting in a right position. She allows her seat-bones to follow the movement, but keeps her shoulders above the hipbones to restrict the 'rocking horse' movement which inexperienced riders often obtain. The rider's position is correctly to the right, that is, right seat-bone forward and left shoulder forward, but hands are a little flat. The toe is turning out because she is using her spur.

The second photograph shows the rider's seat in the relaxed position after the forward thrust. There should be no more movement in the shoulders than can be seen by comparing the two pictures. In both shots, the rider is looking ahead, planning her next move. Photographs by Keith Stevens.

Rising trot: here Erica is showing several of the faults that can creep into a rider's position, and these should be corrected by an instructor. She is rising too high, thus straightening her knee and causing her to stand in the stirrups. Her hands are flat and she is looking down with her right shoulder drooping. She should rise no higher than the horse's hind leg sends her, and the rise should be forward into a bent knee. No extra weight should be taken on the stirrups. As the horse takes the next stride, the rider should sit lightly in the saddle, ready to be thrown up and forward again. Note also that Erica is riding on the left diagonal, but riding to the right. Photograph by Keith Stevens.

Circle to the left: the horse is stepping under the body with his inside hind leg, which keeps his hip position slightly to the right; thus, the rider's inside seat-bone must be forward. The bend to the left starts under the rider's inside seat-bone, continues through the horse's shoulders and up through the neck to the poll, placing the shoulders slightly to the left – so the rider's right shoulder must be forward to put her shoulders in line with those of the horse. The rider's position should be: inside seat-bone forward, inside leg on the girth, outside leg slightly behind the girth (to hold the horse's quarters in place) and outside seat-bone centred on that side of the saddle. The rider's outside shoulder should be forward and the head straight on the shoulders, eyes looking in the direction of the circle. The hands hold the bit to direct the horse on the circle and determine the size of the circle. Here, the rider's hand is incorrectly moving in towards the wither, thus allowing her elbow to move away from her side.

Straight ahead: the horse is moving forward straight but with the slightest flexion in the direction to which he will make his next turn (left), so the rider is also straight. Seat-bones level, shoulders level, hands level and legs level. Here, the rider is looking down instead of forward and as a result the horse is a little on the forehand.

Free walk: 'Crown Law' is preparing to turn or circle to the right and is tracking correctly. The rider's raised heel is causing her to drop her shoulder and collapse her left hip and shoulder. Her left hand is correctly moving away from the wither to direct the turn, but the elbow could remain closer to the body. Photographs by Keith Stevens.

Until now, the universally accepted one-sidedness of the horse has not been mentioned. My theory is that the horse at birth is no more right- or left-sided than humans are, and that the handler and/or rider is entirely responsible for any increase in resistance built up in the horse's body.

In other words, it is the rider who is predominantly one-sided and unconsciously increases the resistance of the horse on the side which is difficult for that rider. Why else would a horse ridden by a left- or right-handed person be soft or hard on one side, yet change dramatically when permanently ridden by a rider who uses the opposite hand?

Let us give this subject a little more thought. When asked to kick a ball, a right-handed person will kick it with the right foot, if given a choice. There is no problem – the foot lifts, kicks and goes back to the ground with no difficulty. But if asked to kick the ball with the left foot, he must rebalance himself on the right foot, pick up the left foot and kick the ball (which will not travel nearly as far as when kicked with the right foot). Then the left foot regains the ground and the person must rebalance himself. It is not disputed that this performance can be improved, but he would have to work at it over a period of time to become equally proficient with both feet.

A person – or a horse, for that matter – cannot change muscle reaction permanently just by asking the muscles to change. The muscle mechanism ensures that once a certain procedure is established the muscles will continue to react in this way until the mind has actively thought of the new way to react, and concentrated hard on making the muscles react in the new way. Repetition over a period of time is necessary to ensure the change is established. At first, as soon as the mind leaves the subject, the muscles return to their old way of working, changing only gradually with much practice.

This is why an instructor can become frustrated when a pupil appears to be quite unable to obey the repeated instruction to keep the heels down. After a few such directions, an added suggestion that the rider "talk to the heels" and tell them to "stay down" will make the pupil think more positively about them.

How many riders take the trouble to strengthen their weak side before using their own body to obtain results from the horse? Making the rider's body muscles independent of one another is the basis of good riding. It is just as important as suppleness in the horse's back and limbs, and should be established in the rider before trying to obtain suppleness in the horse.

Another human habit which affects the results obtained from the horse is that of using the hands for almost every task in daily life, using the legs only minimally in comparison.

Put a beginner on a horse and ask him/her to close the legs firmly in the aid to go forward and the hands will automatically copy the action. It will take some hours in the saddle and considerable effort on the part of the rider before this automatic reaction of the hands can be stopped.

When the rider is using the legs, the hands must be able to remain quite still or be working under their own instruction, either together or singly or opposing each other. To be able to do this the upper body must be quite independent from the waist up.

Teaching muscles to work independently is a long hard chore, and is the reason why European instructors put riders on the lunge without stirrups for many hours before letting them ride alone.

The rider's arms should hang down from the shoulders in a relaxed position with the elbows bent and the forearms dropping towards the horse's mouth on each side of the neck. A straight line from bit to elbow should be maintained. Under normal circumstances the rider's elbows should rest alongside the point of the hip and should

Erica is showing how not to rein back. Her heels are lifted, thus shortening the legs and pushing the knees forward, hands are flat and pulling backwards. Her seat is being forced down, which will prevent 'Crown Law' from lifting his mid-section correctly to allow his legs to lift up and take a backward step in comfort. Note the horse's resistance in the head and neck and the ensuing twist of the hindquarters. This will result in a step to the side instead of straight backward.
Photographs by Keith Stevens.

Here Erica demonstrates the up-forward position of the rising trot. The push of the horse's right hind leg has sent her forward and the left hind leg will take the saddle forward under her seat, so that she will sit without moving her body backwards. The rise should not be any higher than the horse throws the body upwards; Erica is rising a little high here to show the position required. Note that she is rising on the left diagonal, i.e. rising as the left foreleg and right hind leg are on the ground. This is considered the correct diagonal for trotting to the left.

never be held forward or pulled backwards.

The hands holding the reins should be held with thumbs uppermost, an observer being able to see the back of the hand and the knuckles only. The fingers should close over the reins, which should be held in the palms at the bottom of the fingers.

If the rider holds the rein contact between the thumb and forefinger – the rein passing over the joint of the forefinger – this contact can be maintained steadily. The lower fingers (except for the little finger which should be on the outside of the rein) can increase or decrease pressure as required and apply half-halts as necessary.

The power that controls the hands for normal activities moves progressively up the arm muscles as increased power is required, but the rider should make superhuman efforts not to allow this to happen. The reins should be held and controlled by the hands themselves and not by the arm muscles. Any extra power needed should come from the shoulder girdle which has the ability to limit the strength to the exact amount required

HORSE AND RIDER 'IN THE FLESH'

and is able to release the power instantly.

Experiment off and away from the horse, preferably with an elasticised rein, and discover how sensitive the hands can be.

It may be asked why all this is necessary since people have been riding all their lives without giving it a thought. The answer is, of course, that it is possible to ride in almost any form, but a stiff rider makes a stiff horse and a stiff horse cannot carry out any of the sophisticated activities required in modern horse sports. It is highly likely that certain riders have achieved these aims without even realising that they have done so and, therefore, wonder what the fuss is about.

Having got this far, the rider should now remember the 'pulley belts' and realise that he/she is sitting right above them. Remembering also that the 'engine' is in the rear, the rider should realise that he/she is **sitting** on the 'controls', not holding them in the hands. However, the hands should not be dismissed as they also play a role in correct movement.

Before the rider can use legs on the horse to ask him to go forward, it is necessary to teach the horse that that is what he is required to do when the legs are closed on him. This should be done when the horse is broken in. The panniculus muscle, which is the muscle that 'shivers' the flies away, makes it easy for the horse to feel a light or heavy pressure and to distinguish between them. This is another reason for carrying the legs in that area.

The greatest value of the pulley belts is discovered when the rider wishes to halt or half-halt the horse. The weight of the rider coming directly onto both belts presses them together, and has much the same effect as pulley belts on an engine which are fouling each other. That is, they reduce the forward drive of the engine and ultimately stop it.

The rider should follow the movement of the horse's back at the walk. If this is not done, it has the effect of restricting the pulley belts and thus shortening the stride. This movement should be with the seat-bones only, and is facilitated by a supple waist. The rider's shoulders should remain almost still but must not be stiff. If the rider's mind is directed to the hips and their movement, the shoulders should automatically remain balanced over the hips and relatively still.

It may not have occurred to novice riders that each gait is ridden differently. They ride in one form at the walk, two different forms at the trot and another form at the canter.

At the trot the rider may maintain one of the positions, either sitting or rising (posting). Both should be equally comfortable to horse and rider, but this will depend on the expertise of the rider to a large extent. It also depends on the standard of education of the particular horse – young horses, and those beginning their education, should be ridden predominantly at rising trot until their muscles are sufficiently developed to carry the rider sitting.

The sitting trot will be the most difficult to master, but it is important for the rider who wishes to be an expert to be able to sit to the trot comfortably. It is the method most often called for in dressage tests, especially in the more advanced tests, and it is invariably required in rider classes. Many accomplished riders find it easier to ride sitting than rising, as they are more able to feel what is happening beneath their seats.

At the sitting trot the rider must keep the hipbone and, therefore, the pelvis upright and the body straight, with the weight evenly placed on both seat-bones and the crutch. Two-thirds of the weight should be on the seat-bones and one-third on the crutch. The loin muscles must be relaxed; together with the stomach muscles, they give and take to absorb the thrust of the horse's hind legs, which is upward and forward. The rider's movement should be for-

This rider has a good basic position but is a little stiff in the back, no doubt because he is trying too hard to maintain it and is forcing his heels down, instead of lowering them with a flexible ankle. Bill should widen and relax his shoulders so that they rest above his hips without tension. His tenseness has caused the horse, 'Follyfoot', to over-bend. Photograph by S. Sobey.

This rider is leaning back behind the movement, placing undue weight on the horse's propelling muscles – note the look of discomfort on the horse's face. The rider needs to take his hipbone backwards (stomach to backbone) instead of his shoulders. Photograph by S. Sobey.

ward and back without leaving the saddle.

There may be a temptation to ride the horse at a slower tempo when sitting, to enable the rider to absorb this thrust more easily, but this must be resisted. The four trots should be ridden at the same tempo whether sitting or rising.

To begin rising from the sitting trot, the hipbones are tilted slightly forward and the rider allows himself to be thrust upwards and forwards by one diagonal pair of legs and to regain the saddle on the next diagonal. It is not necessary to rise more than a few centimetres in the saddle and the lift must not come from the stirrup. The shoulders remain still and poised over the seat-bones, never behind or in front of them.

When regaining the saddle the rider should not sit down but should just touch the saddle with sufficient weight to receive another thrust forward from the horse. Hipbones remain in the forward position, with the shoulders balanced above them. The upper torso should not 'swing' to the trot.

A forward-moving horse whose rider is correctly looking ahead and riding the horse on, while planning the next moves. Note the relaxation in the lower hand of the rider, while the thumb and index finger still maintain the contact. The horse's attention is completely on his rider. Photograph by S. Sobey.

The legs should remain in place on the horse's sides and must not swing backwards and forwards.

As the seat is thrust forward the knee and heel should lower, not rise, and as the saddle is regained they return to their former position. This is a small movement of only a centimetre or so. While the rider is in the forward position, the horse's second diagonal pair of legs move forward and place the saddle under the rider, so there is no need to sit back. The sequence of the movement is up-forward-down, not up-forward-back.

As the horse's head remains almost still at the trot, the rider's hands must also remain still and not move up and down with the body. It is absolutely imperative that the rider does not use his/her hands to help in rising and that the rider keeps a regular rhythm, employing a mental metronome to do so.

When wishing to rise to the trot, riders should regularly change the diagonal on which they are rising. It is standard practice to change diagonals when the direction is changed during educational sessions, but if riding on a straight line for any length of time the diagonal should still be changed regularly.

In the chapter on gaits it is explained how the horse's back swings at the trot, and it will be remembered that as the right diagonal (left hind and right fore) moves forward the back lowers a fraction on the opposite side (right side). If the rider is riding on the right diagonal, the left side of the back always receives the weight as it returns to the saddle.

Unless the diagonal is changed regularly, one side of the back will be massaged by the rider's seat, while the other side will not and will, therefore, be less supple.

It is quite a simple matter to change the

Erica Taylor and 'Crown Law' in collected canter during a dressage test. Note the transfer of weight to the hindquarters, giving the forehand an upward lift. This position is obtained only after many months or even years of hard work. Photograph by Stephen Shaw.

A collected trot beautifully illustrated by Erica Taylor on 'Crown Law'. Note the horse's back swinging to the left as the right hind leg is brought forward. The lift and angle of the fetlock joints of both hind and front leg are identical, the neck is bent at the poll and the head is in the correct position. Photograph by Stephen Shaw.

diagonal; it merely requires the rider to sit for one extra beat, then continue to rise as before. However, the longer the rider has ridden on the one diagonal, the less amenable he/she will be to the change. The horse will often put the rider back on the original diagonal himself because his muscles on the other side are not as strong and supple. Changing diagonals regularly after having ridden for years on one diagonal will be uncomfortable, but it should be persisted with until it is equally comfortable on both diagonals.

Dressage experts from different schools of thought argue the case for releasing the inside shoulder of the horse as opposed to his outside shoulder when negotiating turns and corners. There is a good case for both arguments, but the best reason for riding on a particular diagonal when under instruction, or competing, is to allow the judge or the instructor to check whether in fact the diagonal has been changed.

It is said to be 'correct' to rise on the inside diagonal, that is, to rise as the inside front leg comes to the ground, but as long as a change is made when the direction is changed there should be no penalties for 'wrong' diagonals.

At the canter the rider's seat should never leave the saddle and the shoulders should remain above the hips. They must not lean further forward than the hipbones. When the horse leaves the ground in the moment of suspension, both seat-bones follow the forward movement of the horse's back and the knees and heels lower a fraction. As the horse's initiating hind leg comes to the ground, the seat relaxes deep into the saddle and the knees and heels regain their position.

Any lift of the seat from the saddle means there will be a bump on the horse's back when the saddle is regained. This will disturb the horse's balance and may also trouble his mind sufficiently to make him fractious.

The hands follow the head as it moves forward and back, while maintaining steady contact with the bit. Some riders at canter have a very bad habit of going against the horse with the hands. That is, bringing the hands back towards their bodies as the horse's head goes forward and letting them go forward as the horse's head comes back. This unbalances both horse and rider and also makes it difficult for the horse to move correctly.

A young rider who has collapsed in the middle, raised her heels and is looking down. This position causes the horse to hollow his back, raise his head by the lower neck muscle and leave his hindquarters trailing. She should sit tall above the saddle and stretch softly down into her heels. She would then be able to use her legs, seat and weight effectively. Photograph by S. Sobey.

Only when the horse moves into gallop should the rider be a little more forward with the hips. As in the trot it is the hips which lean slightly forward and not the shoulders, although the shoulders remaining over the hips will appear forward. Even at full gallop the rider should be balanced with the shoulder, hip and heel in line. A supple waist is imperative.

There are several problems which beset most riders at one time or another.

Head tilted to one side or the other, or looking permanently down or to one fixed spot. As the head is the heaviest part of the body, it must be held squarely between the shoulders, with no tension at the base of the neck or in the chin. "Chin relaxed" and "neck in the back of the collar" should be in the rider's thoughts. One of my favourite sayings is: "Look where you are going and the horse will go where you are looking." Evasive or bloody-minded horses will sometimes be an exception to this rule, but mostly it works.

Shoulders rounded or collapsed forward. The old-fashioned exhortation to "Throw the chest out of the window" may be an over-correction, but if the rider can think of stretching imaginary muscles sideways and closing the shoulder blades closer together, the correct position will be achieved quite easily without tension.

Stiff upright back or collapsed rounded waist. Both are equally incorrect. The back muscles are very important when giving aids and they must always be upright and supple. A rounded back, or chair seat, can be corrected by thinking "waist to pommel", while a rider on the crutch can correct this by thinking "stomach to backbone".

Collapsed hip – often the result of a regularly incorrect position when seated. Sitting on one hip while driving a car or sitting at a school desk and leaning on one arm can cause major posture faults. A rider who allows the hip to collapse to one side makes it difficult for the horse to move correctly, and is a major cause of crookedness in the horse.

To correct it, try to remember to sit straight at all times and, when riding, make sure the leg muscles are strong enough to carry out their tasks so that the temptation to augment their power with the hip muscle does not occur.

I once had a pupil, a man in his fifties, who wanted to improve his riding sufficiently to accompany his daughter and compete in shows with her. In the process of making his living he drove a tractor with an implement behind, down narrow rows between vines, day after day for many months of the year. Because of the limited space available he had to sit to one side, watching in front and behind at the same time. This had been going on for many years. He sat exactly the same way on his horse and could not change no matter how he tried. Consequently, his horse moved reasonably well towards one direction but was quite unable to perform on the opposite rein.

The moral of this story is to sit straight whenever you sit down and you will find it easier to sit straight and evenly balanced in the saddle.

To sum up, the rider's body should be in three sections which are able to work separately or together as necessary. The most important division is the seat, which can be likened to the 'keystone' of the whole body and includes the area from below the ribcage to about halfway down the thighs. The upper body should be centred above this keystone at all times and includes the ribcage, shoulders, arms and head. The third section includes the legs from halfway down the thighs to the feet, which should be centred below the keystone.

Not only must the body be equally divided on both sides of the saddle but it must also be equally distributed from front to back. If the rider is not balanced the horse cannot balance; the rider cannot balance the horse just as a load cannot balance the carrier!

Under normal circumstances there is no grip in riding. The thigh and the side of the knee (not the point) should rest on the saddle, touching without gripping. If grip is needed when a horse is misbehaving it can be applied by the upper thighs into the throat of the saddle. Together with lowered heels and upright body, this will be sufficient to allow the rider to remain in the saddle unless the horse falls or stumbles badly.

The point of the knee must not be turned into the saddle, as this forces the lower legs away from the horse's sides. The ball of the foot should rest on the stirrup, allowing the rider to raise the toes. Heels higher than toes

loosens the seat. The temptation to carry the foot 'home' in the stirrup when riding fast may be too strong to resist, but it should be remembered that in the case of a fall the feet may be difficult to remove from the stirrups in a hurry. This position also loosens the seat slightly.

It is imperative that the ankle is not held rigidly in position, but kept supple like all other important points. The foot should be placed more or less in the direction to which the horse is moving, neither turned out away from the horse's side nor forced inwards. The weight of the foot should be on the outside to enable the ankle joint to rotate when applying the aids.

Sometimes, riders find that they have abnormally long or short arms, in which case no attempt should be made to force them to hip level. The rider should allow them to rest where they fall naturally. A short-armed person will need to carry the hands a little higher and the long-armed person a little lower, to be able to keep the straight line from elbow to horse's mouth.

To suggest, as some instructors do, that

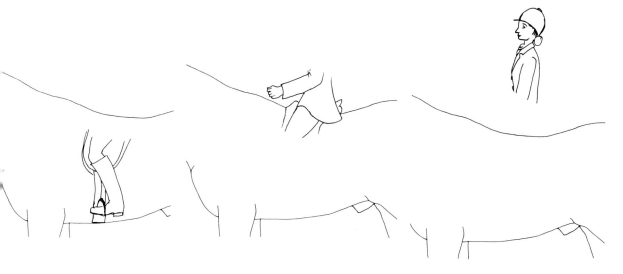

BUILDING THE RIDER'S POSITION, BLOCK BY BLOCK

the hands should be so many centimetres above the withers and so many centimetres apart, is absurd. This may be the ideal when everything is absolutely correct, but how often does this situation occur in any moving combination? Maybe at the halt, but certainly not on the move.

When walking, a person will incline the body in the direction in which he is moving; that is, an onlooker can clearly see that the pedestrian is going to move to the right or the left by the position of the body. This small inclination should be obvious when watching a rider. When turning to the right, the right leg is applied, the right seat-bone is pushed slightly forward and the outside shoulder is also forward, making it clear to both horse and observer that the rider wishes to go to the right; and vice versa. This does not infer twisting the seat around in the saddle – the actual twist is in the rider's back muscles just above the pelvis.

The forward or floating seat. The rider's position on a horse that is jumping is slightly different from that used for flat riding. The rider must be able to alter his/her balance at the same time as the horse, and remain 'with' the horse in all his movements, which will be quickly changing over the jump.

It is important that the jumping rider shor-

The rider shows a typical example of a dropped hip and shoulder, caused here by raising the heel to apply the spur. In this case, it is reducing the length of the stride of the horse's right hind leg which is going to land before reaching the position where the front leg was standing – an action referred to as 'not tracking up'. Photograph by Keith Stevens.

tens the stirrup lengths to be able to maintain this forward seat. The number of holes to be taken up depends on the expertise of the rider and the height to be jumped. As expertise improves, the stirrups will be shortened four to six holes from the length used for flat work.

A jumping rider must have an adequate 'seat' that can remain in balance at all times. Unbalanced riders inadvertently try to maintain or regain their balance with the reins and there is nothing more calculated to stop a horse than the rider swinging on his mouth.

As a jumping course consists mostly of riding on the flat – twelve jumps will involve twelve jumping strides only – the basic aids will apply and the horse is ridden between the fences using the same aids as those used for flat work. However, from three strides before the fence the horse should be left to jump the fence himself, the rider moving in balance with him and asking only for forward impulsion if that is lacking.

The basic jumping seat is calf of the leg and thigh closer together, the seat further back in or just above the saddle, and the hips tilted forward. The waist of the rider will be closer to the pommel and the shoulders will be straight and wide, not rounded. The head will be up with the eyes looking along the track from between the horse's ears. Heels must still be lower than toes and the legs must not swing backwards or forwards.

The rider's knees maintain more contact in jumping but the weight still goes down through the knee to the heel. During jumping,

This rider is leaning forward and her legs are also forward, a position which does not allow the back, seat and legs to influence the horse. Her hands are her sole control. To maintain this position, the rider must grip with the upper thighs and stand in the stirrups, and she will be most insecure if the horse becomes restless. Note the pony's stiff back and apprehensive look. Photograph by V. Smith.

the body has something of a concertina effect, waist closing towards the pommel and up again, and the distance between thigh and calf opening and closing. The rider should have a backward pressure at knee and heel and a forward pressure at the calf to keep the leg in position.

It should be remembered that the horse is doing the jumping and the rider needs only to remain in balance over the jump. In other words, the flat ground belongs to the rider who should be in complete charge of direction and speed, and the last three strides and the jump belong to the horse who should be allowed to make his own arrangements.

CHAPTER 9

RIDING AIDS

Aids, or body language, in the equestrian sense, refer to the means of communication with the horse; they aid riders to convey their wishes to the horse. Aids are given with parts of the human body to parts of the equine body in a continual 'conversation'. The rider should think of them individually as letters of an alphabet which, when put together, make words and eventually sentences.

The communication between horse and rider should be cultivated from the first time the rider sits on the horse and maintained and perfected throughout their life together.

Learning to ride is a time-consuming and painful activity but when mastered it is infinitely more demanding and satisfying than swimming or any other athletic activity which is not performed in partnership.

The aim of the rider should be to produce a horse which is as active and supple under the rider as he is when free in the paddock, so that he can perform whatever activity is required efficiently and without stress.

The grace and beauty of the horse showing off in his paddock is like the grace and beauty of the model or beauty queen on the dais. Putting a rider on the horse's back is equivalent to asking the model or beauty queen to carry a rucksack on the dais, and puts the horse at an equal disadvantage unless the rider contributes by remaining in balance.

A fellow instructor is fond of reiterating that no one ever says they can swim when they cannot and yet, with very few exceptions, no one will admit to being unable to ride. These exceptions are usually people who can ride a little and have discovered for themselves how inadequate they are. So it is recommended that all would-be riders attend instruction before they attempt to ride on their own.

Any horse will go forward if he is kicked hard enough and stop (perhaps) if he is pulled hard enough, but his mind and energies will be elsewhere. If he is a lively type he will be looking for trouble, if lazy, he will be going to sleep.

However, if he is taught a 'language' he can understand which tells him exactly what is required, he will change his whole attitude and the rider will be transported from a passenger on a rather unpredictable vehicle to the dominant member of a pair working together.

Any person can sit on a horse and pull the rein for direction and kick with the heels for movement, but both horse and rider will soon tire and often become bad-tempered and fractious. Without complete understanding and obedience, the horse cannot follow a polo ball, or jump a course, or carry out any of the other activities required of him. It is a measure of his desire to please that he continues to make the attempt, even when the rider is bumping around in the saddle saying "go" with the legs and "stop" with the hands at the same time.

Not only does the rider have to know this language of the body, but the horse also has to be taught it before he can understand what is required; he is not born with this knowledge, as some unthinking riders seem to assume.

There are a very limited number of letters in the alphabet of this language and the learning and teaching of it may not appear too difficult, but in practice it is an art which takes time and effort to perfect.

The letters themselves are: **head, legs, seat and back, weight, hands** and **voice,** sometimes assisted by the 'artificial' aids **whips** and **spurs.** Riders can do without these artificial aids, as the name suggests, but the whip does assist the early understanding of communication, and the spurs are helpful later on.

The **head** is at the top of the list, not because it is the top of the body, but because it is the most important aid. It enables the rider to think about, understand and co-ordinate all the other aids. Without an actively thinking brain the rider is always at a disadvantage, being unable to assess correctly what interpretation the horse is putting upon the 'conversation'. This the rider does by feeling through his/her own body and analysing in the mind.

Legs are the next in importance and it is incidental that they are at the other end of the body. The rider's legs control the horse's legs. Without control of the horse's legs the rider has no control at all. The rider's legs initiate all movements including direction and transitions, that is, forward, backward, lengthening, shortening, turning and halting.

The **seat,** which incorporates the **back** muscles, helps the leg aids to improve the forward drive of the horse – or impulsion, as it is called in dressage. The seat aid needs to be used with tact and understanding and should be minimal until the horse clearly understands the language of the leg aids.

Weight is a mighty aid, as the horse must remain under the weight if he is to retain balance. The rider's weight is a magnet to the horse and if it is placed to the right the horse will move to the right and vice versa. Because it is so important, it is very easy to use incorrectly and the horse is often abused by the rider's weight, used consciously as an unnecessary aid or unconsciously as a bad habit. Yet used judiciously it is a very important aid indeed.

The **hands** are probably the most often misused aid of them all. They are placed near the end of the list to play down the effect

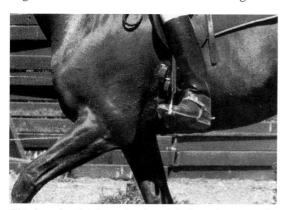

This shows the rider's leg used on the girth for forward movement, the calf of the leg giving the aid. Photograph by Keith Stevens.

Here the rider's leg is behind the girth for lateral (sideways) movement. She is using her spur and this action has drawn her leg up. The aid is usually given with the calf of the leg unless there is resistance from the horse, when the spur or whip can assist. Photograph by Keith Stevens.

of their natural superiority in most other human activities, and to remind riders that the hands are intended to **support** the other aids. They are used to indicate the direction and designate the actual moment of halt and extension or reduction of stride, and not to initiate these movements. The rider should think of them as 'punctuation' marks in the sentences.

The **voice** has a limited use which is usually confined to the early lessons and to practice sessions (its use is not allowed in dressage tests), but the voice can quite often prevent disasters in any form of riding at any level if used judiciously. The horse, of course, does not understand the words, but the tone of voice is well understood by him.

The **whip** should be carried at all times, not to be used to punish the horse, but to be there when needed. If a whip is needed, either as a stimulant for the leg or a deterrent for misbehaviour, it is needed instantly; minutes later is too late as the horse will not connect the action of the whip with his earlier actions. It should be used with tact

The rider carries her whip correctly across her thigh, ready for use behind her leg when necessary. When used as a training aid, it should only touch the horse lightly as an incentive to 'listen to the leg', but is available for heavier use if required. A whip is an incentive to attend to the rider, not an instrument of punishment; the horse should respect it but not be afraid of it. This also applies to the use of spurs. Photograph by Keith Stevens.

and not wielded as would a slave driver.

Spurs should be kept for horses already educated to the leg aids, as then they become a very subtle aid. Spurs should not be worn by riders who use their heels habitually, as they will then be used indiscriminately and their advantage is lost. Again, they should not be considered punishment, but rather an encouragement to move forward. Spur rowels must always be blunt; sharp rowels will disturb the horse's concentration and are not allowed in competition.

To be able to use the aids correctly and successfully, the rider must have complete independence of each of the three parts of the body mentioned in the previous chapter – the seat, the upper body and the legs. This is achieved only by practice, practice and more practice, hours in the saddle over many months and in some cases years, until the aids are thoroughly understood by both horse and rider.

During this practice the rider should, preferably, be on a quiet, well-educated mount on which the rider can think and feel without the intimidation which results from riding uneducated or volatile horses.

Riders should imagine they are trying to communicate with a blind, deaf and dumb creature and act accordingly. Of course, the horse will not actually have any of these afflictions but he can be considered blind because he cannot see the rider and so is not in a position to see and recognise any signals the rider might be giving. He is deaf in the sense that he cannot understand the spoken language (the fact that he can react to the tone of voice and recognise a few words helps, but is not sufficient to depend upon); and he is dumb, because he cannot ask what is meant by a particular aid and must experiment to ascertain whether the aid really did mean what he thought it meant.

Unless the rider is thinking and feeling he/she will miss the little experiments the horse makes to help him understand what the rider requires.

The rider should think of the leg aids as the gist of the sentence, the seat as the emphasis on individual words and parts of sentences, and the back as advising the urgency of the instruction. The hands supply the punctuation marks and the weight adds further explanation if required.

A study of the art of basic dressage will give riders insight into a body language which the horse can easily understand and obey, no matter what activity they plan for themselves and their equine partners – hacking, jumping, eventing, ridden games or western riding.

It is not necessary to aspire to advanced dressage movements – which is art for art's sake – but an understanding of basic dressage movements will be invaluable.

Dressage training provides a system which allows the horse to perform whatever activity is required of him efficiently and without stress, because he has already been taught what is required at home in a peaceful atmosphere. This presupposes that the trainer is himself capable, by prior knowledge and riding ability, of carrying out this education. All riders can become knowledgeable trainers by working on their own ability to ride and by using a very active brain.

It is recognised that almost any form of communication can be used to advise the horse of the movements required. The aids could be completely reversed or completely changed, if desired, but the horse's ability to carry out the specialised movements required might be impaired because of loss of balance, and the language would not have the advantage of being universal.

The success of dressage training lies in the fact that, if both horse and rider are correctly taught, any rider anywhere in the world can ride any horse, if the expertise is there.

The argument most often heard against dressage is that it requires so much time to learn and to teach, but no other method yet devised can achieve in less time the same results as those achieved by standard dressage training.

The rider who uses knee pressure instead of leg pressure gets results by continually unbalancing the horse in the direction he/she wants him to go; the horse has to go in that direction to regain his balance. The rider who carries the legs forward on the shoulder prevents the horse from bending his body and forces the horse to make turns like a boat, that is, continually bringing the hindquarters into line with the rigid forehand, instead of being able to keep his front legs in line with his back legs with a supple middle piece.

The fact that horses trained in dressage are often found wanting in other areas, such as the jumping arena, is not the fault of the system. It can be firmly laid at the feet (or

On the bit and collected: 'Crown Law' is correctly flexed at the poll, with the face just beyond the vertical. Note that the distance between cheek-bone and gullet is decreased, the lower jaw is relaxed to the rider's hands, and his whole bearing shows that he is 'listening' to his rider's aids. Photograph by Keith Stevens.

legs) of the rider who has either misunderstood the method, or not given sufficient time to early education to ensure the horse knows exactly what is required. Or the rider has simply forgotten the language and been struck dumb, leaving the horse stranded.

The horse does not have the benefit of walking the course or assessing the problems beforehand as the rider does. It is acknowledged that jumping horses need to use more individual initiative, but correct dressage training and a thoughtful rider will teach the horse how to accept the initiative when necessary.

Every sport has its expertise and horse riding is no exception. To swim competitively, the swimmer must learn to breathe correctly, to move arms and legs in a particular way and to practise regularly in a dedicated manner. Without this dedication there is little success and this applies equally to equestrian competitors.

APPLYING THE AIDS

The most important moment in any movement is the rider's preparation for that movement, which should be started before reaching the actual spot where the movement is to be performed.

Although the movement itself should not be anticipated by the horse, he should be warned through the aids that he is to be ready to do something. Because of the horse's desire to please, he does anticipate, but by tact and firmness the rider can ensure that the horse waits for the vital instruction before he attempts to obey. By thinking and feeling and deciding in advance where the movement is to begin, the rider can forestall any undesired movement, but he/she cannot do this unless there is complete understanding of the way the horse moves, and complete independence of each of the rider's muscles with which the aids are given.

The leg aids are applied at the girth for forward movement and a little further back for lateral (sideways) movements. They are mostly directed to the hindquarters, which is the horse's 'engine'.

The rider's seat should be deep into the saddle, with the legs in the correct position (see Chapter 8) and in contact with the horse's sides. The heels should be lower than the toes. To apply the legs, the heels are fractionally lowered and closed by moving the toe in towards the horse and rotating the ankle. Each application is released immediately and applied again in a continuous 'conversation' with the horse.

The legs must remain touching the horse's sides and when the aid is released they are not removed from that position – the muscles applying the aids are relaxed, **not** the legs from the sides. When the heel is lowered, the knee moves slightly backwards and downwards with it. Any attempt to bring the leg up to apply the aid should be resisted.

The bulkier calf muscles come into contact with the horse's side first and this is usually sufficient to convey the necessary messages. If not, the heel is applied, but the heel should be thought of as a 'reproving' voice. Liken the pressure to a low conversational voice, a louder 'requesting' voice and finally a raised 'demanding' voice. Return to the requesting voice after each demand until the horse responds: ask, insist, demand.

The rider's knees must relax to allow the calves to close the contact but they should not leave the saddle completely. Remember, thighs and knees rest on the saddle but do not grip.

When teaching the horse, after each application there should be a slight pause in which the horse should start to obey. If he does not actually do as requested, the aid may be reapplied.

Remember that, having closed the legs, the message has to be received by the horse's nerves and transmitted to his brain; the muscles must receive the message to comply from the brain (or auto-nerve), and then must comply. So there will be a lapse of time between application and compliance which will decrease as the horse becomes familiar with the meaning of the aid, until it appears as a reflex action, exactly the same as any other voluntary activity in man or beast.

The rider's legs are the most important aid – in fact they are so important that this chapter should have been called 'Legs, legs, legs'.

Back and seat aids are introduced only after the request by the legs has been taught by the rider and understood by the horse. They are not used a great deal in the early lessons, but as the horse begins to understand the language of the legs, the back applies sufficient forward urge through the seat to enable the horse to move forward with the required energy. The muscles of the lower back increase the urgency of the seat as necessary but should be used only sparingly until the horse fully understands the language of the legs.

Careful consideration of the use of the rider's back and seat aids will prevent many problems from arising when training a horse. Over-zealous seat aids are the most common cause of sore backs, and 'electric' bottoms cause uneasy and often fractious horses. Rarely is it the leg aid that upsets the horse; it is more often the unconscious severity of the seat and back aid.

The seat and back aid is used in rhythm with the horse's gait, that is, alternate influences on the seat-bone as it follows the back at the walk, equal influences on both seat-bones in two-time at the trot and in three-time at the canter. Legs and seat used in two-time at the canter produce an incorrect four-time beat or a break back to trot.

Weight aids are in the seat-bones and come from within the body. They are not in the shoulders or any other part of the body. The upright position of the rider's back should never be altered to apply weight aids. The seat-bones themselves need only increase the weight slightly in towards the centre of the saddle, which results in increasing the weight on the other side, forward towards the pommel (for turns and circles), or deeper into the saddle to influence the equilibrium of the horse.

Try changing direction or riding a corner with the inside seat-bone forward and the outside shoulder forward – the ease with which the horse turns will astound most novice riders.

This must not be interpreted as moving around in the saddle as such movement is unnecessary and will unbalance the horse. The rider should always sit still and use only the influences from within the body to apply the seat aids.

To apply the hand aids, the reins should be held in the hands – not the fingers – the rein crossing the palm of the hand after entering between the little finger and the third finger. The aids are applied by the fingers themselves and do not need the muscular power of the arms. The thumb and first finger hold the reins at the length required and, by locking the thumb over the first finger with the rein between, can prevent the horse from forcing the reins out of the hands. The hands remain in control whether the reins are long or short, and move backwards or forwards to shorten or lengthen the horse's frame.

Only when the rider wishes to ride on a loose rein are the reins allowed to slip through the fingers. The horse should never be allowed to take control of the length of the rein, except when requested to do so by the rider.

The third finger of each hand is the most important, initiating the opening and closing of the fingers to apply the 'punctuation marks'. The other fingers must, of course, also open and close with them but it is the third finger that decides the amount of give or take of the reins. The horse itself should maintain the contact with his mouth by moving forward into the bit when asked to do so by the legs of the rider.

At no time should the rider hold on to the horse's mouth; it is the horse himself who holds the rider's hands.

Force should never be applied, except occasionally when the actions of the horse make this unavoidable, and even then it should be ceased as soon as possible. The ideal contact is a reciprocal hold by the rider's hands and the horse's mouth, with the horse willingly relaxing his lower jaw when the rider applies a half-halt. This ideal situation is developed over the years of education and cannot be expected to appear without many months, or even years, of work.

All the aids must be synchronised to give the horse as clear a message as possible. In the initial lessons, the aids should be likened to the kindergarten letters being learned in preparation for reading, and progressively developed until the horse is 'reading' the messages; meanwhile, the rider is correcting the 'spelling' and 'punctuation' and the horse's understanding of the 'words' is being formed.

When teaching the horse the rein aids, the direct rein should be used; that is, when wishing to go to the right, the right thumb is turned over to the right and the rein leaves the neck a little. The left thumb remains upright and the rein touches the neck as the horse flexes towards the direction in which he is asked to move, the left hand giving a little so that the contact of the right hand is slightly increased.

Neither hand must cross the withers, or indeed come close to the withers. The direction of the contact should be from horse's mouth towards rider's hipbone and thus to horse's hind leg.

Once the horse understands the direct rein aid and obeys it automatically, the indirect, or rein of opposition, can be taught. That is, when a right turn is required the left hand maintains contact and helps to keep the horse's head and shoulders in front of the rider, indicating the arc of the turn.

It would, perhaps, seem unnecessary to discuss the movements that require a horse to move forward, straight, but it will certainly make some movements a little clearer to the novice rider if this is done.

In all forward movement, the horse should remain straight with the hind legs following in the track of the front legs. However, the hind legs should first indicate where the track will lead so that the front legs know the direction. The front legs do not indicate the direction – this is the task of the hindquarters.

This track is first decided upon and indicated by the rider, picked up by the horse's senses and developed by his hindquarters. Forward movements include the obvious walk, trot, canter and gallop on straight lines. They also include these gaits on circles, serpentines, transitions (up and down), counter canter and, believe it or not, the rein-back.

Three very advanced movements which will not be described in this book include the passage (pronounced 'pass-arge') and piaffe. The first of these is a slow high-stepping forward trot and the second a trot on the spot – both forward movements. The third is the volte, which is a 6-metre circle; anything larger than that is described as a circle. These three movements are very advanced and are not required in dressage until the tests beyond Advanced.

MOVEMENTS WITH FORWARD INTENT

The following movements are common to all gaits and are used in conjunction with all other movements in walk, trot, canter and, in some cases, the gallop, as well as the lateral movements.

Aids can be likened to shorthand writing, which has a set of outlines to be learnt by the student. After learning these outlines and practising at speed, shorthand becomes a very personal thing and writers develop their own style, although writers of a particular shorthand method can read and understand other writers of the same method. So it is with aids in horse-riding.

Half-halts

To obtain: the half-halt is itself a preparation for other movements. Execution requires an increase of weight into the seat of the rider by lowering the heels and knees, widening the shoulders and closing the legs. At the same time, the hands momentarily block the forward movement by closing the fingers. The hand maintaining the flexion (usually the inside hand) prevents the bit from being moved through the mouth, while the outside hand exerts a little extra pressure momentarily. The horse's head must not be turned towards the outside and the whole exercise is finished almost as soon as it is begun.

Horse's reaction: the horse should feel the restricting seat and leg aids and lower his quarters and engage his hocks, stifle and hip joints ready for a downward transition. At the same time, he should relax his jaw to the pressure of the bit, bringing it in towards his chest a centimetre or two. The aids for the next movement having been applied immediately, the horse should begin to carry out these instructions. When the half-halt is applied within a movement the horse should continue the original movement on request.

When correctly performed it has the appearance of a momentary shortening of the frame of the horse and is used as a preparation for **all** transitions and **all** corrections. **Caution:** the legs, seat and back are the major aids in half-halts and the hands must not be applied until the horse has started to comply with these aids. Like all aids it is a momentary action and must not be maintained, but should be released and applied again as often as necessary.

It is not necessary to shorten the reins to apply a half-halt. As long as the horse is on the bit, the rein can be stretched and the rider can still apply a half-halt. There is no limit to the number of half-halts which can be requested; 17-20 in a 60-metre arena is quite normal.

Halt from walk

Preparation: decide well in advance on the spot where halt is to be obtained. The horse must be stepping forward with rhythm and balance and the amount of impulsion commensurate with the standard of his education. Use forward aids and half-halts to establish these conditions.

Request to halt: rider's body ceases moving with the gait, heels and knees lower, seatbones and shoulders widen and legs close against the horse. The resulting extra weight compresses the 'pulley belts' (see Chapter 8) and the hindquarters start to engage. Hands applied together in a blocking movement say "now".

Horse's reaction: as the leg, seat and back aids are applied, the horse heightens and shortens his stride, and lowers his quarters (more or less, according to standard of education). When hands are applied, the horse should stop one hind leg and then the front leg on the same side, then bring the opposite side legs in line, hind leg stopping first, then the front leg.

If the horse is allowed to bring himself to halt he will halt squarely with a 'leg at each corner'. If the rider forces him to halt by continuing the pressure of the hands, the horse will probably halt unbalanced. At the halt, the horse should stand quite still and remain on the bit until asked to step forward again or be allowed to relax.

Caution: in the early stages the horse should be allowed several strides to come to halt and if this is done he will progressively reduce the time taken to comply. The halt should be held motionless for 15-20 seconds at first to ensure it is sustained. If insufficient leg, seat and back aids are used, the hind legs will be left out behind and the horse will be on the forehand. If too much hand is used, the horse's back and front legs may be too close together. Hands **must not** pull horse to halt, but restrict forward movement with a take-give-take-give action.

Halt from trot

Preparation: as before; in the early stages, the halt may be progressive, through the walk, but as understanding is reached and performance improves the horse should halt in the trot stride. Rider should sit trot in preparation, if not already sitting, then apply the aids as for halt from the walk.

Horse's reaction: the horse will halt one diagonal pair of legs by engaging his hindquarter joints, then halt the second diagonal pair as they come alongside. The whole frame of the horse will compress and he will be collected at the halt.

Halt from canter or gallop

Preparation: as before. The initiating hind leg of the canter (the outside hind leg) will land as if to take another stride, but will remain on the ground and the other three legs will land together alongside their respective pair.

Horse's reaction: the horse will be in a very collected frame and will be flexed at the poll, relaxing the lower jaw and mouthing the bit. Halt from the gallop is usually only required in fast activities such as camp drafting and western riding and it is only a momentary pause. It is a very strenuous movement and the horse's muscles should be well-conditioned before it is attempted.

Caution: the halts from trot and canter or gallop are more advanced movements and should be obtained progressively through the walk until the horse is at least of Elementary standard. The horse should remain quite straight and must not swing his quarters to either side. If he does so, it suggests he is not yet ready to perform these advanced movements.

Contact

To obtain and maintain: reins should be held at a length which allows the horse to be comfortably contained. Shorter reins will be required for more contact but contact can still be maintained with longer reins. It is the horse that should maintain the contact and he will not do so unless he is comfortable. Contact should never be abandoned except for free walk on a long rein, when the horse is allowed to take the reins through the fingers and carry his head and neck as low as he pleases. The horse should be encouraged by continuous use of the legs and seat of the rider to maintain the contact with the rider's hands, with the reins at a length desired by the rider.

To regain contact after walk on a long rein or when first mounted, the rider should take up the slack in the rein until it is taut. Legs, seat and back aids are applied, but instead of allowing the horse to move forward the hands should retrieve the further slack which will appear as the horse's frame compacts. This subtle action continues until the rein is the length desired by the rider.

Caution: allow time for the horse to learn what is required of him and co-operation will become immediate. There will then be no need to keep repeating the aid as the horse will give the amount of contact required. Horses are normally so receptive to a soft hand that it is difficult to understand why some riders find it necessary to use strong-arm tactics.

Downward transitions

All changes are referred to as transitions. They can be the obvious ones from canter to trot or walk, or from trot to walk, or they can be the less obvious ones between collected, working, medium and extended gaits, lateral movements, etc.

Preparation: the rider decides well in advance where the transition is to take place and prepares for it by improving impulsion and rhythm to the horse's ability at that stage, applying the necessary half-halts to achieve this aim.

To achieve the transition: stop the aids for the movement being performed and lower seat, knees and heels, which will bring the rider closer to the horse. Widen the shoulders and as the horse lowers his quarters the

rider's hands feel for the change. These instructions take time to read, but the actions should be performed almost instantaneously and should be as smooth and flowing as possible.

The aids for the next movement should be applied as soon as the horse has complied with the request to stop whatever he was doing, continuing with the new movement without hesitation as the aids are applied.

Horse's reaction: as the aids for one movement cease and the aids for change are given, the horse should heighten and shorten his stride and take a step into the new gait, which may be higher and shorter or longer and lower in the same gait, or a complete change of gait. He should move on in that form without pause or hesitation.

Caution: the transition should be obtained by the rider's body aids, supported by the hands. The change is **not** obtained by the hand aids, supported by the body aids. In the early sessions of a horse's education, he should be allowed to take as many steps as he finds necessary to perform the transition, but as his ability increases the transition should improve until he is obeying the aids as they are applied. If this time is not allowed, the horse can become anxious and upset and his whole performance will deteriorate. All downward transitions should be considered forward – not backward – movements.

Flexion

To obtain and maintain: to obtain correct flexion the rider lowers the inside knee and heel and keeps the inside seat-bone forward, placing weight to the inside. The rider's outside shoulder should be more or less forward (depending upon the amount of flexion required). The influence of the inside leg is towards the outside hand; the outside leg's influence will be more or less backwards, communicating with the horse's outside hind leg and preventing the quarters from swinging outward. The thumb on the inside hand should be turned slightly in the direction of the movement (taking the wrist with it), putting the inside rein free of the neck. The outside hand will remain upright with the rein touching the neck (caused by the horse's slight bend of the neck), discouraging the shoulders from leaning inward.

Horse's reaction: the horse should be bent (more, or less, according to standard of education) around the rider's inside leg. The bend should be continuous along the horse's whole body, with no more at the neck or the hindquarters than that obtained under the seat of the rider. The bend increases as the horse's muscles become more supple and his understanding improves. When correctly flexed the horse should be stepping well underneath the body with the hind legs, following the track of the forelegs, the head straight (not tilted) and the neck flexed at the poll.

In the more advanced movements the horse's head will be lifted, the neck shortened (the shortening taken up in flexion, not in retraction of muscles), the lower jaw relaxed and 'giving' to the rider's hands, the mouth wet and the tongue playing lightly with the bit: collection!

Caution: it is important that the degree of flexion should be no more than the horse can cope with. In his early lessons there is hardly any flexion at all and the horse should be encouraged to remain as straight as possible. Gradually, as his muscles develop and his understanding improves, flexion is introduced and improved with special exercises. When changing direction, the flexion should be changed. This is done by straightening the

horse first then re-flexing him to the new direction.

Incorrect flexion is a major fault in all dressage tests and the movements in which it is most likely to appear are circles, changes of direction and canter movements. When changing direction diagonally across the arena it is important to prepare, straighten and re-flex the horse before the track is reached, so that the horse can turn on to the track and negotiate the next corner in the correct frame.

Impulsion

To obtain and maintain: the rider's legs, seat and back aids are used in the rhythm of the gait to create and sustain impulsion, which is harnessed by the contact with the horse's mouth and the rider's hands. This contact increases as education proceeds, but it never becomes a tug-of-war between horse and rider. The process should be likened to setting a spring, which must have a restriction at one end, while the other end is active if it is to work.

Impulsion is not speed; it is the creation of the horse's desire to move forward in the direction required in balance and rhythm and with correct tempo, without any sign of reluctance. The observer sees a lively, obedient animal, and the rider feels that the horse is ready to carry out his/her bidding without demur and with enjoyment.

Horse's reaction: the horse should move forward with energy, covering more, or less, ground with each stride by engaging (flexing) the hip, stifle and hock joints in his hindquarters and with freedom in his shoulders.

Caution: jigging, jogging and sidling around is not impulsion, neither is it impulsion when the horse is leaning on the bit and driving his forehand into the ground. His gaits should be light and airy and make very little

A promising junior rider in correct position.

A beginner rider on an experienced horse. Note the horse's developed top-line muscles and the activity of the hindquarters. The slightly hollow back and poking nose are the result of an unbalanced rider learning to trot. Photograph by S. Sobey.

sound as he steps in a lively manner over the ground.

On the bit

To obtain and maintain: the horse is considered to be on the bit when he is maintaining contact with the rider's hands and relaxes his jaw whenever the rider's fingers close on the reins to apply a little extra tension. The rider's leg, seat and back aids should be continually requesting the horse to remain forward and moving into his bit by applying them in the rhythm of the movement. They should be as strong as necessary but as light as possible. In the early lessons the legs only should be asking the horse to go forward so that he is not confused by seat, back and weight – one thing at a time. However, as soon as the horse is answering the legs, the other aids can be added when necessary to maintain the required forward movement.

Horse's reaction: the horse should step underneath himself with the hind legs (more, or less, according to whether he is being asked to work in extended, medium, working or collected gaits) with a raised middle piece and softly flexed neck muscles. A horse can be on the bit with the lightest contact and the longest rein, as long as there is contact between the horse's mouth and the hands.

Caution: if the horse resists the hands he will be either above, below or behind the bit. Increased leg, seat and back aids, without releasing the hand contact, are used to correct the problems. Incorrect positions above, below and behind the bit, as well as hard-mouthed or pulling horses, are invariably caused by the rider. It may not be the rider presently riding the horse who is guilty, but there is no doubt that the problems are caused by the human element.

When the horse is above the bit, he is evading it by raising his head and neck, often using the muscles in the lower part of his neck to hold it in position (ewe-necked). This problem may have arisen from an incorrect introduction to the bit, sore mouth from teeth or grass seeds, or an unrelenting demand from the rider's hands. It can also be caused by an ill-fitting saddle, one which is pressing on his backbone either at the wither, in the middle of the seat or at the cantle. This will make the horse hollow his back and therefore raise his head.

When the horse is below the bit he is stretching downwards towards the ground and leaning on the bit (over-bent). If allowed to become a habit it will put the horse permanently on the forehand. This means the horse will not be able to use his back muscles to carry the rider, or his hindquarter joints to propel himself forward correctly. So he pulls himself along with his front legs.

The action of coming behind the bit is often developed when the horse is first asked to half-halt. It is caused by the horse being unable to use his undeveloped back muscles efficiently and the action should cure itself as the strength of the back improves.

It must be understood that being correctly on the bit is not collection, although it is necessary to collection for the horse to be on the bit.

Collection

To obtain and maintain: to be collected the horse must be on the bit, correctly flexed and moving with energy (impulsion). Therefore, if worked correctly, the horse will himself become collected in due time. Any attempt to take a short cut and obtain a premature collection will present problems by the time the horse reaches Advanced Education. This is because the horse must develop the correct muscles and organise his breathing and lung performance to maintain a collected position for any length of time. Working a horse in tight side-reins and forcing a collected outline is damaging to the whole horse – the muscular, respiratory and digestive systems and, in some cases, his temperament as well.

What is required of the rider to obtain collection is progressively asking for a more shortened frame from the horse. This is done gradually over the months, using more legs, seat and back while maintaining a little more contact. As the contact is accepted by the horse, it is increased slightly. This work is continued until the horse is accepting the position throughout his body and can maintain it for longer and longer periods.

Horse's reaction: when collected, the horse is moving with his hind legs underneath his body, the neck raised and flexed at the poll but otherwise straight, and stepping forward with a lively tempo, perfectly balanced and in rhythm. This outline should not be maintained for extended periods, but should be interspersed with working, medium and extended gaits.

Caution: it is interesting to note that the FEI rule book for dressage covers the subject of collection in six separate paragraphs and yet uses only one or two paragraphs for other more advanced movements. Therefore, the rider should be warned to take care when asking for collection and never force it upon the horse.

To Ride Forward Movements

Preparation: from halt – lower heels and increase weight on seat-bones, close fingers on reins. On the move – decide well beforehand where transition will take place. Cease aids for current movement, deepen knees and heels and widen seat and shoulders, half-halt and apply aids for new move-ments in progressively flowing actions.

Horse's reaction: at halt – the horse's abdominal muscles contract upwards, hindquarters lower (more, or less, according to standard of education), the horse's lower jaw softens towards the chest (gives) and the whole horse is in a state of readiness. On the move – the horse's body will compact to a shortened frame by contracting abdominal muscles upwards, lowering hindquarters and giving to the reins, while the change is made to the new gait.

Request to move at walk

Close both legs with a light tap and lower the back muscles so that the seat-bones of the rider come into stronger contact with the saddle. Maintain, but do not increase, contact with the reins. If no reaction, repeat more strongly in the sequence "ask, insist, demand", returning to ask, then repeat, until the necessary response has been achieved.

Horse's reaction: one hind leg steps forward, followed by the front leg on the same side and proceeding to a four-time beat including all four legs in sequence – hind leg, front leg, hind leg, front leg. The horse should relax his lower jaw and give the impression of walking into his bridle, regardless of length of rein.

To maintain the walk: rider's left seat-bone follows the left hind leg until the leg comes to the ground when the seat-bone relaxes and the opposite seat-bone follows the right leg forward. Shoulders remain relaxed. Rider's left leg closes on the left girth area as the ribs bulge towards it, and the right leg closes on the right side in alternate tapping requests to "keep walking". The leg is applied by rotating the toe towards the horse, then relaxing it, so that the calf of the leg applies the aid, not the heel. Both hands follow the nod of the head without losing contact. This action will be more pronounced at more extended gaits than at more collected gaits.

To increase length of stride: increase strength of leg, seat and back aids, allow horse's frame to lengthen by relaxing hands slightly when asked by the horse as he reaches forward a little with his neck. Do not lose contact.

To shorten length of stride: increase strength of leg, seat and back aids, maintain contact and half-halt. Continue the walking action but the movement of seat-bones and hands will be less pronounced as the horse heightens and shortens his stride.

To walk on a long rein: relax contact and allow horse to take the reins down through the hands as low as he wishes to go. The four-time beat of the walk must be maintained with the rider's leg, seat and back aids, and the horse's frame will lengthen and he will relax his back muscles. This is a resting exercise. A long rein is required in Test relaxation, but a loose rein should be given from time to time during education.

Caution: if the horse becomes restive it may be caused by a squeezing seat, and this is why it is important to reserve seat and back aids until the horse has learned to obey the leg aids. To improve a squeezing seat, widen the buttocks across the saddle and lighten the weight slightly.

Request to move at trot

Preparation: decide well in advance where the transition is to be made, cease walk aids and movements, lower weight and half-halt.

From the walk: as half-halt is applied the horse's frame will shorten. At this moment the rein should be shortened and both legs closed together in a tapping motion (obtained by rotating the toe towards the horse). At the same time, involve the seat and back aids if necessary. Continue at sitting trot or

rise as the inside diagonal comes to the ground (inside front leg and outside hind leg). All early movements to trot may be progressively through the walk.

Horse's reaction: when the half-halt is applied the horse will shorten his frame fractionally (including his neck) and the rider shortens the rein to maintain this shortened frame. If this is not done, the horse may lengthen his neck again for a fraction of time, then shorten it again when he trots, leaving the rider with no contact. When contact is re-taken, the action may bring the horse back to the walk, particularly if the mount is young or uneducated. Horse should step into trot with a diagonal pair of legs, then follow with the other diagonal in two-time. As before, he should take the same length of time for each diagonal.

From the halt: prepare as before; increase urgency of leg, seat and back aids. Maintain contact with hands. The head should remain almost motionless at the trot. This is an advanced movement and should not be required until the horse is of Elementary level. But it does take time to perfect, so it can be attempted as soon as the horse is moving into trot smoothly from the walk.

To maintain the trot: the rider should close both legs on alternate beats of the trot (two-time). When rising, the legs are closed at the moment when the rider returns to the saddle, for the sitting trot, on every second beat.

To lengthen the trot: after the necessary preparation as before, increase leg pressure, allow horse to lengthen his frame by relaxing the fingers. This enables the horse to lengthen his back muscles and make his body slightly longer, allowing him to take a longer stride. Contact must not be lost and, when extension is being requested, contact should be maintained more strongly than is required for a long-low outline. It must be remembered that the horse cannot lengthen his stride unless he lengthens his frame, because he cannot put his front feet down beyond his nose.

To shorten the trot: increase leg, seat and back aids, while maintaining or increasing contact, and half-halt. Increased contact will be required for collection.

Horse's reaction: when lengthening the trot the horse must take the extra length in the first stride and must not go faster. This may take a little while to perfect, but the true movement should always be in the mind of the rider and in the feel of the body.

The same applies when shortening the stride. The horse should not just shorten the stride without raising the legs higher. He should take the same length of time to complete all the different trots, covering more ground with the longer strides and less with the shorter strides. The horse should never be asked or allowed to hurry forward.

Caution: Do not rise from the stirrups as this prevents efficient use of the legs. To prevent a squeezing seat, widen the seat-bones; to increase strength of seat, widen the shoulders. In early lessons, seat and back aids should be used minimally to enable the horse to learn the significance of the legs. Remember that there is an even longer stride after medium trot (extended), and an even shorter stride after working trot (collected).

Request to move at canter

From the trot: the rider must be sitting to the trot for all transitions up or down so, if not already sitting, this must be done before cantering. The rider should decide well beforehand where the transition is to be, and prepare by sitting down and deepening the seat and legs, and half-halting immediately before applying the canter aid.

To canter to the right: the right seat-bone moves towards the pommel of the saddle, maintaining the weight to the right. The left shoulder is forward (also putting the weight to the right) and the outside leg is drawn back by the knee to influence the horse's outside hind leg, which is the initiating leg when the horse is going to the right. At the same time, the inside hand of the rider maintains flexion to the right and the outside hand supports the outside leg. Both legs close together with the emphasis on the inside leg, the message being "With this leg, canter". The aids are, of course, reversed for the opposite lead.

From the walk: the rider ceases the walk aids, lowers weight to apply half-halt and gives the canter aid.

From the halt: prepare as for other gaits from halt, apply canter aids with increased strength (at first).

Horse's reaction: if the rider is able to recognise the correct moment to give the aid, there will be no hesitation on the part of the horse who will go into canter on the correct lead. Should the rider not be that expert and the horse is allowed to make the move himself, he will wait for the right moment and go into canter on the correct lead also; but if pressed by the rider for immediate action he may take the incorrect lead or canter disunited. There is only one moment when he can take the correct lead and that is when the outside hind leg is preparing to land.

The horse should remain straight and any attempt to canter with the hindquarters inwards or outwards should be corrected by the rider's appropriate leg behind the girth.

Caution: the rider must not lean forward, inwards or outwards, and the outside leg is not raised to give the aid but remains stretched downward. The leg is drawn back only a very small distance, just a few centimetres.

The canter from the walk and from the halt are both advanced movements which are not required until later in the horse's education. He should be established in rhythm and tempo and well versed in the aids by the time he is asked to perform these movements.

The major fault that creeps into the canter movements is an incorrect four-time beat, instead of the correct three-time beat. This is usually the fault of the rider, either by applying aids in two-time or not following the movement of the horse's back.

To maintain the canter: the rider follows the movement of the horse's back with both seat-bones (in much the same way as at walk but with both seat-bones). The shoulders remain over the hips and do not move with an exaggerated swing. The rider's hands follow the movement of the head which is forward and back (not up and down), and the leg, back and seat aids are applied in three-time during the moment of suspension, just before the initiating hind leg comes to the ground. This keeps the horse moving forward under his body and discourages any inclination to leave the hind legs out behind. On a circle, the inside seat-bone remains in a forward position with the outside shoulder, giving the rider's body a position to the inside – but the weight remains predominantly on the inside.

To lengthen the canter: prepare with a half-halt and increase the strength of the aids, at the same time allowing the horse to lengthen his frame by releasing some contact with the fingers.

To shorten the canter: increase the strength of the leg, seat and back aids, half-halt and increase contact slightly.

Horse's reaction: as in the other gaits, the horse lengthens or shortens his stride instead of going faster or slower. The rider must follow the movements through, and remain in an upright position with the seat firmly in the saddle.

Counter canter
When not required by the rider, a counter canter is referred to as a canter on the wrong lead (or leg), but when required it is a suppling exercise in the same bracket as leg-yields. The horse should always be specifically asked for counter canter and not just allowed to take it as he wishes. The horse must be thoroughly educated in correct and counter leads before being asked to perform flying changes, or the rider will find it difficult to maintain a counter canter.

Preparation: exactly the same as for normal canter, but with flexion and position to the outside, or away from the direction of the movement. So if the horse is going to the right and the left counter canter is required, the flexion must be changed before the aid is given. In other words, working to the right the horse will be on the right flexion, and this must be changed to the left by straightening the horse then re-flexing to the left. As before, the horse must be prepared by sitting trot and half-halt, to get the hind legs moving under the horse.

The transition: apply the canter aid with the rider maintaining left flexion and his/her own position to the left. The rider maintains the forward straight position with the eyes looking in the direction required, but with the body in the same form as that of the horse. The right hand indicates the direction without disturbing the horse's flexion to the left.

Horse's reaction: if the horse has been thoroughly schooled to take the required lead, there will be no difficulty in obtaining counter canter. In the above case, the horse should depart into canter with the right hind leg, followed by the diagonal pair (left hind and right fore) and, with the left fore leading, maintain the flexion to the left and move straight ahead or around to the right.

Caution: the exercise must eventually have the same rhythm, balance and impulsion as a correct lead canter and be carried out without resistance. Care must be taken to prevent the horse continuing the movement if he changes leads or becomes disunited. In either case, he should be brought back to trot and the exercise started again.

If it is difficult for the rider to maintain his/her position, try, in the first instance, to ride the horse in counter canter by first achieving the correct lead and then working on to the other direction while maintaining the same flexion. In other words, ride the horse on a shallow serpentine down the long side until the counter lead (which is in evidence as the horse comes back to the track) is established. Progressively increase counter work by deepening the serpentine loop until the horse can reach the centre line – and later the opposite side track – and return to the original track without breaking back to trot or changing leads.

When this is established the horse can be ridden on two circles, the first on correct lead and, when changing to the second circle, maintaining the original lead. If the circle can be ridden and the counter canter maintained, the horse is ridden forward on to the correct circle lead before being brought back to trot. However, if the horse changes his lead or becomes disunited, the exercise should be ceased and started again.

Simple change of lead

This change is called simple because it entails coming back to the walk before changing the lead, not in itself a simple exercise but simple in comparison with the flying change. In the show ring the simple change is often performed through the trot, but in dressage the correct movement is through the walk.

Preparation: ride the downward transitions through the trot and walk, maintaining rhythm, balance and tempo in each gait.

Request to change: as the horse takes his first walk step, he is straightened and the flexion changed to the other side, then the canter aid for the new direction is applied.

Horse's reaction: the horse should take progressively fewer strides at trot and walk as his expertise improves, until he can make the change with only one or two of each. This improvement will come only after many weeks or months, practising the exercise only two or three times to each direction on each occasion.

Caution: before the horse can be asked for a simple change he must be able to achieve a canter depart from the walk. It is important to achieve a change of flexion before the new canter lead is requested or the horse will develop a wrong flexion for cantering.

Flying change of lead

This is an advanced movement which should not be required until the horse is well and truly educated to lead correctly and to counter canter when required. If it is taught before the counter canter is established, the rider may have difficulty maintaining the counter canter. The rider must be competent and able to recognise the exact moment of each section of the canter stride.

Preparation: the only time the change can be achieved correctly by the horse is in the moment of suspension and the preparing half-halt should be in time to influence the last hind leg to reach the ground, that is, the hind leg involved in the diagonal pair.

To achieve: as the horse leaps forward with all four feet off the ground (moment of suspension), the rider smoothly straightens, then re-flexes the horse and gives the new aid in a progressive fluid movement. There must be no interference with the rhythm, balance or tempo of the canter stride and no restriction from the seat or weight aids as they change their position.

Horse's reaction: the horse should change his flexion and leg positions while in the air, ready to land on the new lead. This movement can be progressively developed until the horse is changing at every stride, but each step should be perfected before the next one is undertaken – for example, five or six strides, change; four strides, change; three strides, change, etc. – a lengthy process taking perhaps a year or more!

Caution: if the moment has been misjudged by either the horse or the rider, the horse will change in front and not behind, or behind and not in front (both incorrect), resulting in a disunited canter. Then again he may change half the stride in one stride and the other half in the next stride, also incorrect. A disunited canter is always incorrect and should be immediately recognised and corrected by the rider, usually by bringing the horse back to trot and reapplying the canter aid. If the temptation to teach this movement too early is resisted, no difficulty will be encountered when it is eventually taught.

Request to gallop

At the gallop the rider is much more forward than at the canter, so the simple act of leaning forward will prepare the horse for gallop from the canter. This lean should be from the hips of the rider, not from the shoulders, the back remaining straight. At the same time the horse must be allowed to lengthen his frame, so the hands move further forward with the head and neck.

It is usual to ride with shorter stirrups if galloping is to be the major gait, such as between jumps in hunting or across country, in novelty games and racing. The hand gallop from canter in a hack class will not allow time for shortened stirrups, so it must be carried out with the usual length of stirrup.

With the standard length or shortened stirrups, the heels must remain lower than toes for stability of seat; the upper thighs close more firmly and knees maintain a stronger contact. With the body leaning forward the seat will have less influence, so the legs are used more strongly to keep the horse moving forward. Horse and rider must increase the contact between mouth and hand, but the rider's position must not be maintained with the hands.

To gallop from the standstill, as in mounted games, the aids are the same as for canter from the halt.

A specialised seat and technique, and a professional rider, are required for race riding.

THE REIN-BACK

The ability to move the horse backwards is required almost as soon as the horse is ridden forward, yet to move back correctly the horse must be thoroughly trained in forward movement. Therefore, it is as well to avoid this movement as long as possible.

Although called a rein-back, the reins have only a very minor role to play and the movement should be achieved by the use of legs. **Preparation:** a correctly balanced halt should be ridden and momentarily maintained with the horse at attention, prepared to move forward immediately if required. Decide on the number of steps to be attempted, remembering the horse steps back in two-time, and ask for only one or two strides at first; never more than six when fully trained.

To move backwards: the rider maintains contact and, with lower legs, gives the horse an aid for forward movement. As the horse picks up a hind leg ready to move forward, the rider's hands discourage this movement and the horse should step backwards. As he moves backwards the hands relax a little to let the horse know his reaction was correct. Immediately the correct number of steps has been achieved or the horse stops stepping backwards, he must be ridden forward again.

Horse's reaction: the horse should remain at attention and, having picked up a hind leg to move forward, feels the restriction to forward movement and steps back instead, taking the opposite front leg backwards at the same time. The legs will land in that order, back then front, almost simultaneously. The opposite diagonal moves backwards, continuing until asked to move forward, when the hind leg in the air will go forward instead of backwards and the walk will continue forward. As the horse's competence improves, he can be ridden forward at the trot or canter.

Caution: the horse's body should remain quite straight and the legs must not move from side to side, but straight backwards in line. When teaching the horse, one or two strides is sufficient; even a tendency to place his leg backwards should be accepted until he fully understands what is required. In the early lessons, lighten the seat a fraction until the horse begins to understand. At no stage must the rider be tempted to pull the horse backwards, no matter how frustrating the exercise. Although moving backwards, the forward influence should still be in evidence and the horse should willingly continue on his forward progression as soon as the rider asks him to do so.

CIRCULAR MOVEMENTS

The decision to make the movement (whatever it may be) should be made some distance before the spot at which it is to commence. This involves the rider's mind and also the eyes, which should be looking towards the spot decided upon. The leg, seat and back, and hand aids are preparing the horse with a half-halt as the spot is reached.

Corners (quarter-circles)

Each corner of the rectangular working area should be ridden as a quarter-circle. As the horse's education and muscular ability increase he should be asked to go deeper into the corners. Franz Mairinger considered the riding of corners so important that he would say: "The way in which a corner is ridden is the measure of the ability of the rider."

Preparation: the rider prepares for each corner as it approaches by improving the horse's frame with half-halts and forward aids where necessary. The horse must be moving with the maximum amount of impulsion he can muster at that stage of his training.

To ride a corner: as the corner is reached, the rider applies a half-halt, lowers the knee and heel on the inside leg and applies a stronger aid at the girth area. The outside leg influence is backwards, ready to be applied with increased pressure to prevent the horse's quarters from swinging outward. The inside seat-bone of the rider and the outside shoulder are in a forward position.

This puts the rider's body in the shape the horse's body must be as he turns the corner. The inside hand turns the thumb over towards the inside (taking the wrist over with it), ensuring the inside rein is free of the neck. The outside hand remains upright and the increased bend of the horse's neck brings the outside rein against the neck. Neither hand should move inwards – towards or across the withers.

The outside leg and the hands return to their original position, straightening the horse as he leaves the corner. Another half-halt is applied if the horse tends to move on faster after the corner. Like all aids, these aids are applied in the rhythm of the gait being ridden.

Horse's reaction: the horse answers the rider's inside leg by lowering and engaging his quarters, taking his inside hind leg well forward and in towards the centre of his body. The inside front leg follows this bend by stepping forward and towards the direction required. Guided by the rider's hands, he should keep his shoulders upright. The outside hind leg follows the direction of the turn by stepping under the body (not stepping outside) and the turn is completed in more, or fewer, strides depending on the standard of education of the horse, his muscular ability and the size of the corner required.

Caution: when a horse's education begins he is allowed to make a fairly large quarter-circle to negotiate corners, but as his expertise improves the quarter-circles become smaller and the horse is able to step further into his corners. The horse should not negotiate the corner by taking his head into it then turning out again; he must step into it with his hind legs, keeping his shoulders in front of his hindquarters. The horse should not be expected to go well into his corners until he is physically able to do so.

Turns and tracks

In dressage the terms 'track right' or 'track left' and 'turn right' or 'left' are used. The track is ridden in the form of a quarter-circle or corner and a turn is made with a much more compact body.

To ride a turn: the horse should be flexed to the side to which the turn is to be made and the rider's inside seat-bone should be well forward, increasing the weight to the inside. The rider's outside shoulder is forward and the outside leg moved backwards (from the top of the thigh, not from below the knee) to prevent the horse's hindquarters from swinging outward. The rider's inside thumb turns the hand over in the direction of turn, and this position is maintained until the turn is complete, when the horse is straightened by the hand and leg aids. Half-halts are applied as often as necessary to shorten and heighten the horse's steps.

Horse's reaction: the horse answers the rider's inside leg by lowering and engaging his hindquarters, and taking his inside leg well under and well forward towards the centre of his body. The inside front leg follows the direction of the movement by stepping forward and slightly sideways. He is guided by the rider's hands and upper body position which should remain upright and not lean in the new direction. The outside hind leg follows the direction of the turn on to the new line. The turn should be negotiated in fewer strides than are necessary for a corner or 'track'.

Caution: the horse should be allowed to make wider turns at the beginning of his education, increasing the tightness of the turn as his muscles become more supple and able to cope. Neither horse nor rider should lean into the turn, nor should the horse's hindquarters swing outward.

Circles

The rider should decide on the circumference of the circle at the same time as thinking about the spot where it will begin. The eyes of the rider should pick out four points around the circle, each denoting the end of a quarter-circle, and should ride the horse round these quarter-circles to ensure the circle is round and of uniform diameter.

To ride a circle: prepare and execute as for the corner, riding each quarter-circle to the mental marker. As the horse's ability to perform a circle increases, the rider's weight can be used more actively to keep the circle correct.

To do this, the inside seat-bone (which is forward) can move towards the centre of the saddle. This will increase the weight on the outside as the outside seat-bone moves outward and consequently moves the horse outward if he cuts in. This will not only keep the horse out on the circle but will also help to prevent the inside shoulder from falling inwards. The inside seat-bone should not abandon the forward position when moving inwards.

If the horse is making the circle larger and/or of the wrong shape, the outside seat-bone can assist the inside leg by moving in towards the centre of the saddle. The inside seat-bone should not abandon its forward position but move a little away from the centre of the saddle, increasing the weight to the inside, in response to the inward movement of its fellow.

The leg, seat and back aids are not abandoned when weight aids are being used, so it is obvious that the rider must be quite expert in co-ordination of the aids. Any attempt by the horse to move faster or lose rhythm should be discouraged by the forward leg aid and half-halts.

Horse's reaction: the horse should step under his body with the inside hind leg and increase the flexion (bend) of his body (under the seat of the rider) to the circumference of the circle. The rider's outside leg should ensure that the horse does not drift outwards, and the inside leg, with influence towards the outside hand, will discourage the horse from making smaller circles. Although the hind legs must move in the tracks of the forelegs, it is the hind legs which must indicate the direction.

Caution: neither horse nor rider should lean into the direction of the movement (nor away from it, of course). The rider's natural desire to lean with the shoulders will be discouraged if he/she thinks of using the aids from within the body, through the seat-bone where it touches the saddle. The shoulder, when moved forward, is moved by the collar-bone, not the shoulder-bone.

Serpentines and figures-of-eight

These movements are variations of the circle and should be prepared for and ridden exactly as for circles. The only difference is in the change of direction. These movements are exercises to improve the horse's response to changes of direction and flexion, as well as to improve his expertise in circle work. In the case of the serpentine, this is a series of half-circle loops, connected by a straightening and change of flexion.

Having decided upon the number of loops to be performed (an odd number will maintain the original direction, an even number will change the direction), the rider performs the first loop. Approaching the second mental marker, the rider begins to straighten then re-flex the horse towards the second loop, and so on to the third (and fourth) loops. Serpentines, like circles, should be large at first and never less than 8 metres. They must be accurate half-circles and all cover the same amount of ground.

The figure-of-eight is two circles joined in the middle where the horse is straightened for a stride or two and re-flexed to the new direction for the second circle.

Horse's reaction: the horse should react exactly as he does for the circle, until requested to straighten, and then re-flex to the new direction. It may take several strides to straighten the horse at first (which will change the shape of the circle), but this straightening should be obtained before the horse's flexion is changed as it is part of the gymnastic exercise being performed.

Caution: the rider should be careful never to take either hand across the wither. The inside hand should be moving away from the wither towards the inside of the circle, but keeping the elbow in line with the hind leg and the straight line from mouth to hand. The shoulders must remain centred over the hips and not lean inwards or outwards. It should be remembered that the rider's left hand is communicating with the horse's left hind leg and the right hand with the right hind leg, through the horse's mouth. Therefore, the elbows should be alongside the rider's hipbones and in line with the mouth and hipbones of the horse.

The size of the circles and half-circles should be commensurate with the horse's ability and the impulsion he is able to maintain. He must not slow down to negotiate turns or circles and then speed up again on straight lines, or vice versa. It may be stating the obvious to mention that circles must be round, but so many ridden circles are anything but round that it is necessary to stress this fact.

Volte

A volte is a 6-metre circle and should not be ridden until the horse is fully collected and very well educated. It is ridden like any other circle but, as it is difficult to negotiate, it is considered an advanced movement. The hind legs must step well under the horse to negotiate this small circle and so the bend of the horse must be much more acute. The hindquarters must not swing round like a boat turning in the water.

LATERAL MOVEMENTS

Lateral movements require the horse to step sideways as well as forward. They are divided again into those in which the horse is flexed (or looking) away from the movement and those in which the horse moves in the direction to which he is flexed.

The first group contains suppling exercises which can be ridden before the horse is collected. They are turns-on-the-forehand, leg-yields and shoulder-in. The shoulder-in is a very useful movement for introducing collection. The second group, which should not be included before the horse is able to be ridden with some collection, includes renvers (pronounced 'ron-vair'), travers ('tra-vair'), pirouettes and half-pass.

There is another lateral movement, correctly called a full-pass but sometimes erroneously referred to as 'passaging', which can be used to manoeuvre a horse sideways when there is no room to move forward or backward, but this movement is not included in dressage performances. The **passage** (in dressage parlance) is a straight forward movement at a very elevated trot. As it is an advanced movement not required until after the Advanced test, it is not described in this book. The **piaffe** is also a very elevated trot, but performed on the spot, and is in the same category as the passage.

Turn-on-the-forehand

This is the first lateral movement to be taught. It is an exercise to teach the horse to move away from the leg, and the rider how to co-ordinate the aids.

Preparation: mentally determine the spot at

which the turn is to be made – it should be one horse's width away from the outside track (on the inside track). Prepare for a halt, obtaining a halt as square and balanced as possible for the standard of education reached. In this explanation the horse is on the right rein and the turn will be to the left. The aids are reversed for a turn to the opposite direction.

Having decided on the spot and halted the horse there, the turn should not be proceeded with if he is unbalanced or not straight. The rider should ride forward again and try for a better halt. Once a reasonable halt has been achieved, the turn can be made.

To make the turn: the flexion, which (in this case) is to the right at the moment of halt (inside leg and hand to the right at this juncture), must be changed to the left and the left side becomes the 'inside'. The rider changes the flexion, which places the left rein free of the neck and the right rein against the neck. The outside (right) leg remains in the girth area to help maintain impulsion, or slightly behind the girth to prevent the hindquarters from swinging outwards. The outside hand (right) prepares to discourage forward stepping. The rider's inside (left) leg should be drawn back and used behind the girth.

Horse's reaction: the horse should step under and forward with the left hind leg, picking up the foreleg and putting it down again on the same spot but at a different angle (marking time). The right hind leg moves forward and a little to the right, bringing the body back over both hind legs. The right front leg is picked up and put down in the same spot at a different angle.

Any attempt to step back should be discouraged by the rider's right leg but, if the horse does step back, the turn stops and the horse

is moved forward the same number of steps that he took backwards. If he steps forward, he should be halted. In both cases, the turn is continued as soon as the horse has been corrected. As the horse's ability improves he should step across in front of the outside hind leg in a continuous, rhythmic walking stride, maintaining his upright position but not gaining ground.

Caution: the purpose of the turn is to teach the horse to move away from the leg, so the rider must be careful not to use the hand to achieve the turn. The hand must not cross the withers, but should apply half-halts as often as necessary.

At first it might take several minutes to achieve the turn but, as the horse begins to understand, the time taken will be reduced until the horse will turn on the forehand without hesitation.

The horse's left hind leg should not step alongside the right hind leg, but across in front of it. As the horse is very quick to anticipate, the turn-on-the-forehand should not be repeated more than once or twice in any session, and once it has been learned there should be several halts between each turn.

If the horse does anticipate the turn, the exercise should be abandoned and the horse ridden forward to try again later. The horse should step neither forward nor backwards while making the turn, but if he has to move to regain his lost balance it should be forward – never backwards.

Leg-yields

There are several methods of riding leg-yields, some easier than others. The rider should begin with the easiest and progress to the harder movements only after the horse understands the aids. The easiest leg-yield, involving no change of flexion, moves the horse from an inner track to the outer track.

Another fairly easy leg-yield is used to increase the size of a circle. The most difficult for the horse is the leg-yield from the track towards the centre of the arena, or away from the wall or fence. This yield can be performed parallel to the track or to the centre line if desired.

Preparation: the horse should be moving forward on the bit and with a degree of impulsion, depending upon the standard reached. The rider decides well in advance where the exercise will begin and which exercise it is to be, and applies a half-halt immediately before commencing.

Request to leg-yield: inside track to outside track – while on the left rein and wishing to leg-yield to the right, maintain position to the left with the left hand in an upright position and the right-hand thumb turning the hand over to the right. Lower the left knee and heel and apply the leg in the rhythm of the gait (walk or trot). The seat-bones and shoulders of the rider should remain level and straight to the front. The influence of the left leg should be towards the rider's right hand.

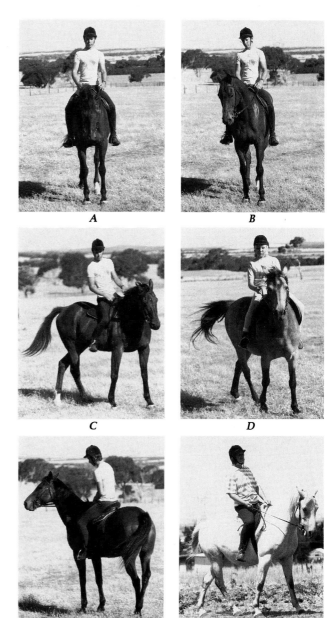

A

B

C

D

E

F

The turn-on-the-forehand is an important early exercise in the training of the horse, but it must be performed with care and accuracy to be of any value.

A
The horse is brought to a halt in as balanced and square a position as it is possible to obtain. Here the rider is sitting with his weight a little to the left, which will affect the horse's balance when the first sideways (lateral) step is taken.

B
Preparing the horse by requesting a bend to the left through the whole body. The rider could improve his position by keeping his head up and looking between the horse's ears. This would give him a better chance to balance himself and not drop his shoulder to the right.

C
The rider's faults are already affecting the horse's ability to turn to the left correctly. The horse has had to take a step to the right with his right front leg, instead of lifting it and putting it down again in the same spot but at a different angle. The rider's rigid right knee has prevented the horse from bending under the rider's seat, and the horse has compensated by bending too much in the neck and not engaging his right hind leg sufficiently to make a correct step.

D
Another rider takes the first step to the left, forward and under the body, correctly. The left front leg is in a better position and the young rider is sitting squarely in the saddle with a correct position to the right, which will allow her pony to continue the turn correctly.

E
Here the position of the first horse has deteriorated throughout the turn and he is now above the bit and quite unbalanced. The turn should have been abandoned before this state of affairs arose, and the horse ridden forward to another halt to try again.

F
In making an attempt to turn to the right on the forehand, this rider is using far too strong a hand. She is pulling the horse round, forcing the mare to retain her balance by stepping sideways with both front and back legs on the right. The rider is leaning too far back and using the back of her calf (instead of the side) to apply the aids, thus raising her knee instead of lowering it. Photographs by S. Sobey.

Horse's reaction: the horse should step forward and further under the body, crossing his inside hind leg in front of the outside hind leg in a forward and sideways step, in the sequence and rhythm of the gait. The front legs of the horse also cross, the inside crossing in front of the outside leg, with the horse's body remaining perfectly straight from poll to tail.

On the circle: the horse will be flexed in the direction of the circle. The aids are applied as above, moving the horse outwards to make a larger circle.

Horse's reaction: as above, except that the horse remains bent around the circle and does not increase the bend or allow the hindquarters to escape outwards. If this happens the rider's outside leg is taken back to hold the quarters in place.

Outside track inwards – (right to left). The horse will be on the left flexion when the decision to perform this movement is made, so this must be changed to the right by first straightening the horse, then re-flexing him. The former outside leg (right) becomes the inside or using leg, and initiates the movement sideways and forwards away from the track towards the centre of the arena. Both seat-bones and shoulders of the rider should remain level and facing forward; the left hand is turned towards the direction of the movement, while the right hand holds the flexion to the right. To make the movement in the other direction, reverse the aids.

Horse's reaction: again, the horse must remain perfectly straight from poll to tail and move sideways by crossing the inside legs in front of the outside legs.

The particular muscles of the horse which are involved in all leg-yielding are those beneath the shoulder blades, attaching the shoulder to the body, and the hip, stifle, hock

and fetlock joints of the hind legs.

Caution: only a few strides should be requested at first and the horse ridden forward again straight. If he tries to lead with either hindquarters or forehand, he must be corrected immediately or the exercise abandoned. This movement is only of value when executed correctly. Remember, the horse is being asked to use muscles which have not been used very much, and the following few days after first performing this work the horse will be stiff and sore, until these muscles loosen up. A few good steps are better than a dozen or so incorrect steps.

When leg-yielding from the outside track to the centre line or beyond, at the walk, there is room and time to re-flex the horse and remain on the original direction, but when performed at the trot (particularly in the early attempts) the horse should remain on the same flexion and be ridden a half-circle to go back the way he has come.

Shoulder-in

Preparation: the best place to begin to teach the shoulder-in movement is coming out of a corner (the horse should be working well into his corners by this time). Decide well in advance where the movement is to be performed – coming out of the short-side corner on to the long side would be an ideal choice. Start the movement at the walk, but once the horse has learned what is required it is best performed at the working or collected trot.

Ride the horse forward on the short side, using several half-halts to make sure the horse is well up to the bit. The ability to flex to the inside should be well established – if not, it is too early to start shoulder-in.

Request to shoulder-in: ride into the corner with as much flexion as can be obtained. Lower the inside knee and heel with the inside seat-bone and outside shoulder well forward. The inside thumb turns the wrist over sufficiently to take the inside rein away from the neck, leaving the outside rein touching the neck and the outside hand maintaining that position. The outside leg placed a little behind the girth prevents the quarters from swinging outwards. The rider's eyes should be looking out over the horse's outside ear, as the bend for the corner is maintained along the straight side.

At first a few strides only will be required before straightening the horse and riding forward again. A shoulder-fore position will suffice until the horse is able to be collected. Progressively increase the number of strides until the horse can negotiate the long side in shoulder-in position. The movement must be abandoned and the horse ridden forward if he loses his position.

Horse's reaction: the whole horse from poll to tail should be slightly bent throughout his length, with no more bend in the neck than can be obtained at the girth. The movement is performed on three tracks: the outside hind leg remains on its original track, the inside hind leg and outside foreleg move on the same track, and the inside foreleg moves on a track of its own just inside its original track. The horse must not move on four tracks.

To perform the movement correctly, the horse lowers his inside hip and engages his hip, hock and stifle joints underneath the body. His neck should be flexed at the poll, his lower jaw giving softly to the rider's hands as half-halts are applied as necessary to maintain the rhythm, balance and tempo of the gait. The movement should be performed along a wall or fence line with a 30° angle to the direction of the movement.

Caution: the movement is of no value unless it is performed correctly, and when it is performed correctly it is at first a very strenuous exercise, using muscles which have not been asked to do much until now. So, for the following few days, the horse will be a little stiff. Unless tact is used at this point, he will always be disinclined to perform lateral movements and thus there will always be stiffness.

The movement must not be continued if the horse loses his shape – he should immediately be ridden forward. The usual way the horse loses his shape is to put himself on a circle. If this happens, the forward straight movement should be on that circle, before the horse is asked to start the movement again.

The rider should be sitting with the flexion which is more, or less, according to the horse's standard of education. The horse will have only the slightest bend at first, but he will develop in flexibility as he practises the movement. It should never be more than 30-40°.

Turns on the hindquarters (pirouettes, half-pirouettes and demi-pirouettes)

This is quite a difficult movement to perform correctly and should not be expected until the horse is of Elementary standard or until he can perform the early lateral movements with ease.

The movement is performed at either walk or canter – never at the trot. The canter movement is considerably more advanced than that performed from the walk and is not required until beyond Medium standard.

Preparation – (at walk): the rider must plan well beforehand where the turn is to be performed and ride at good medium walk towards that spot. As the spot approaches, the horse should be put into collected walk (the spot can be approached at the trot and then a few steps of walk only will precede the turn). If on the right rein the turn will be to the right, and vice versa.

To ride the turn: rider places weight and position to the direction of the turn. Inside hip and seat-bone are well forward, outside shoulder forward and upper body maintained in the direction of the turn, until the turn is completed, when both hips and shoulders straighten to the new direction. The inside knee and heel are lowered and the inside hand turns over towards the direction of the turn and holds the rein free of the neck – leading the forehand around the turn. The outside leg is slightly behind the girth to ensure the hindquarters do not swing out and the outside hand prevents excessive bend and forward movement. Both legs maintain impulsion and both hands and legs apply the necessary half-halts to maintain rhythm and balance.

Horse's reaction: the horse steps inwards and sideways with his inside front leg, the hind leg on the same side having been picked up with engaged hip, stifle, hock and fetlock joint and put down again at a slightly different angle. Then the outside legs follow suit. The horse should step around in the rhythm of the gait without losing impulsion and without gaining ground forward.

Caution: the rider must make sure his/her seat does not slide outwards, as this will take the weight outwards too. As the hindquarters must remain under the weight, they will also swing outwards instead of staying in the correct place under the horse's weight. Leg aids for forward impulsion (not forward movement) must be continued or the horse will lose his balance. The inside hand must lead, not pull, the horse around. At first the turn may be on a larger arc than finally required, but this arc will reduce with practice, as long as correct aids are maintained.

Travers and renvers

Travers is often referred to as 'head to the wall' while renvers is termed 'tail to the wall'. This means that the horse is moving along flexed in the direction of the movement but with his hindquarters away from, or towards, the wall or fence. They are both advanced suppling exercises.

Preparation: the horse must be collected and should be moving forward in good form with rhythm, balance and correct tempo, as well as sufficient impulsion. The rider decides well in advance where the exercise is to begin and which one it is to be, and prepares for the movement with strong forward aids and half-halts. For the first few attempts the horse can be ridden along the wall of the indoor school or the fence line of an outdoor arena, but as soon as the horse is working correctly the exercise should be performed down the centre line or a little away from the wall or fence to discourage him from 'leaning' on the wall or fence.

To ride travers: maintaining flexion and collection with the inside hand and leg, the rider's outside leg moves backwards and is applied behind the girth, moving the horse's hindquarters on to an inside track. The forward impulsion is maintained with both inside and outside legs, seat and back aids.

Horse's reaction: the horse's outside hind leg crosses in front of the inside leg and the horse moves forward on three tracks. The inside front leg and the outside hind leg are on one track and the outside front leg and inside hind leg on their own separate tracks. The horse should be at an angle of about 30° to the direction of the movement.

Renvers: prepare as for travers but have the horse on the inside track, if moving along a wall or fence, and on the right or left of the centre line if working in the middle of the arena. Maintaining forward movement, straighten the horse, then change flexion towards the wall or track. Apply the 'new' outside leg behind the girth, bringing the hindquarters on to the line or track, and ride forward in that position. Again, the movement is on three tracks.

Horse's reaction: the horse's bend is first changed, then he moves his 'new' outside leg further under the body, crossing the 'new' inside leg and remaining flexed towards the direction of the movement. The angle should be no more than 30°.

Caution: early attempts should be restricted to one or two strides only, and then the horse should be straightened and ridden vigorously forward. When ridden at the trot in these early sessions, it will be practical to move on at medium trot after the movement, to improve the impulsion and forward desire.

Half-pass

The half-pass is a lateral movement wherein the horse goes forward and sideways and is flexed in the direction of the movement. This exercise can be performed at the walk, trot or canter, each gait being progressively more difficult. The movement should be taught from the walk and progressed to the trot and finally the canter. The half-pass is of Medium standard.

Preparation: The horse is ridden forward in a collected position. The rider decides where the movement is to begin and prepares the horse to move across the arena in a diagonal line.

To ride the half-pass: the rider's inside seat-bone and outside shoulder should be placed in a forward position. The rider's inside aids maintain the flexion, while the outside leg behind the girth asks the horse to move sideways and helps with forward impulsion. The inside hand of the rider turns in the direction of the movement, holding the rein clear of the neck. The outside rein will be touching the neck, controlling the amount of flexion. The rider's weight – on the seat-bone – will be placed towards the direction of the movement, and the knee and heel of the inside leg will be lowered.

When the movement is completed, the horse should be straightened and ridden forward on the line achieved; or his flexion can be changed and he can be ridden either straight forward, or in a half-pass to the other direction.

Caution: the rider's upper body must remain upright and not lean into the direction of the movement (or away from it). The eyes should be looking ahead in the direction of the movement. The rider's seat must remain in the centre of the saddle, weight being transferred from within the body and not by leaning. Neither hand must cross the withers and the direction of the inside hand should be away from and not towards the withers.

Only a few strides should be attempted at first until the horse understands the movement, and only one direction at a time. Do not change from right half-pass to left half-pass without a break in forward movement until the horse is fully conversant with the movement.

CHAPTER 10

EDUCATION, FITNESS AND EXERCISE

Because the horse learns from the day he is born and forgets nothing, all the good and bad things that have happened to him during his life are still remembered when it is time to break him in. No one – not even the breeder – can be aware of everything in the horse's mind. What has to be done at this time is to reinforce his knowledge of the good things and help the bad things to fade into the back of his mind, while at the same time instilling discipline.

Breaking-in is a job for the expert. A quiet, strong-minded, self-disciplined, non-aggressive persistence is the ideal temperament for the horsebreaker. Most human beings have the nucleus of a temper just below the surface, and ill-feeling often takes over when it is of least benefit. It behoves the horsebreaker to remember the late, great Franz Mairinger's words: "You cannot apologise to your horse; he will never understand what you mean." Because of the expertise needed, this chapter will assume that the horse is already broken in.

Time taken to teach the horse the meaning of the aids is never lost and subjects skipped over at this stage become obvious as lessons become more advanced. In other words, the horse should start his education at 'kindergarten', go on to 'primary school', then to 'high school' (or 'trade school', as it will be called here, since high school means something more advanced in equitation). He will then finish at 'college'.

The first lessons in kindergarten should include the meaning of the leg aids and direct rein aids, which should not be confused in the horse's mind by using strong seat and back aids. As understanding advances, the meaning of the different leg positions and the indirect rein aids are included. Later still, the influence of weight through seat and back aids is taught as well as the understanding of the co-ordination of these aids. In other words, teach him the alphabet of the aids, then teach him how words are put together and, finally, how words are put into sentences.

When this has been achieved, the horse can go to primary school where he learns to carry out the directions given by the rider, and maintain correct balance and good rhythm. He must learn to go forward straight, with a weight on his back, and to bend his body correctly for turns and circles. These lessons are learned by repetition and by using innumerable transitions through the different changes of pace, lengthening and shortening the stride, and including many halts. Lessons will now also include early lateral (sideways) movements.

At trade school, the horse must learn to improve his reactions to the aids and maintain his balance and rhythm through all transitions, including from halt to canter and canter to halt, without taking any walk or trot strides. He learns to rein back and to perform the more advanced lateral movements such as shoulder-in, travers and renvers. Here he can also begin his jumping lessons if he is to be a jumper, or racket practice if he is to be a polo or polocross mount, or any other specialised skills that his rider wishes to teach him.

When the horse is ready to go to college, he is at a stage where he can specialise and enter either 'commercial college' or 'university'. At this stage the horse's mental and physical responses should be tuned to their highest development but, like humans, all horses are not suitable for all types of specialisation. However, the rewards of such specialisation are great, as the horse gives the impression of being able to rationalise and becomes a most rewarding partner.

KINDERGARTEN

As in all forms of education, the pupil must be introduced to his lessons gradually. In the case of the horse this is doubly necessary because, to carry out his lessons, he must use muscles he may never have used before. He must also employ his limited mental processes to understand what is required. It is important to remember that the horse's maximum attention span on any one subject is about six minutes and at kindergarten stage is more likely to be nearer one or two minutes. Regular changes of direction and only short periods devoted to any one subject must be the basis of each educational session.

Early lessons should consist mostly of riding forward, straight, preferably in long straight lines and with very few circles. Although a horse naturally goes forward on a reasonably straight line, when a rider sits on his back it upsets the horse's natural equilibrium so much that he has to redevelop his ability to maintain a straight line under the weight.

The serious horse educator can appreciate the enormity of the horse's problem by experimenting with his/her own body. Try carrying a load on your own shoulders – if not used to carrying loads, you will find it needs continual adjustment until it feels comfortable. Regular load-carrying will improve efficiency and, if the load should be alive, balance will be found much more eas-ily and quickly if the load itself is evenly balanced and keeps still. So it is with the horse, and the responsible rider will learn to ride well before attempting to educate a young horse.

The area to be used for education should be a reasonably large rectangular space, preferably enclosed and with good footing. Slight rises and falls are probably an advantage at this stage, but rough ground is not recommended. A few poles on the ground or cavalletti scattered around singly or in pairs are very useful.

Although a dressage arena may be used (or an indoor school) it is, at this stage, better to work in a slightly larger area and out of doors. At a later stage in the young horse's education any of the above situations are suitable.

Whatever is chosen, the young horse's education should not be confined to this area alone. To enable him to learn and to handle different situations he must be exposed to new experiences. Almost everything is a new experience to the just-broken-in horse, as he is meeting it with a strange weight on his back and he will be quite unsure of himself. Thoughts running through his mind may be: Can I run away from danger? Will I be allowed to do so? What if my rider intends me to be harmed? What if my rider doesn't understand how I can be harmed? What if my rider doesn't care if I am harmed?

All these anxieties will be causing a nervous response, and sudden movements will invariably produce an instant reaction. The young horse's mental processes at this time will be rather like a highly nervous person watching a 'spooky' movie, when even the doorbell or the telephone elicits a startled reaction. As the animal settles down, his lessons can be intensified and an improvement in his concentration can be expected.

It is obvious that a nervous rider should not be involved in teaching young horses, as nervous reactions from the rider will only establish a firm belief in the horse's mind that there is something to be afraid of. Riders who are apt to scream when taken by surprise should never be allowed on any horse.

The educator should have a clear picture of the direction to take and should begin the work with a broad plan in mind. The fact that the plan may have to be changed or even scrapped altogether once the lesson starts is not important. The plan should be there to be scrapped. The dedicated educator may like to keep a daily diary of the plan and the ultimate result. Looking back over this diary is very helpful when things go inexplicably wrong, and could give a clue to the problem.

The horse is not born with a knowledge of the aids, so he has to be taught what is required of him. Showing him once only is not enough – the lesson must be repeated until a correct and automatic reaction is produced. Continued instruction will improve the performance. When it is remembered that the horse does not rationalise, it can be seen how long such a program can take, since each subject must be taught separately.

For instance, the horse cannot be taught to obey the leg aid to move forward while at the same time the rider insists that he only walks, and does not trot or canter. Should the young horse break into either trot or canter in response to the forward aid, he must be allowed to continue for a few seconds while his mind registers that 'move forward' was the correct reaction. Then he can be asked to come back to the walk and continue walking. When this has happened several times he will realise that he is expected to walk forward and not trot or canter.

A horse needs exercise daily for good health, especially if he is stabled. If he is in the paddock he will exercise himself sufficiently for his own needs, but if he is going to be ridden he must be given extra exercise to enable him to develop the muscles needed. This should not be so much that he is tired out. At the same time, it must be remembered that when the horse is taken out of his paddock it is his 'eating time' not his 'resting time' that is being cut short, as the horse will rest before he will eat.

Exercise aids digestion and circulation, but exercise on a full stomach should not be strenuous. Because of this, stabled horses need longer exercise time, preferably carried out before being fed, and work for the paddocked horse must be restricted if it is suspected that he has a full stomach. It is a mistake to confuse education with exercise. Education work is, of course, exercise but it is insufficient to get a horse muscled and fit, particularly in the early stages.

With work, the muscles will gradually increase in size and elasticity (but, as already mentioned, not in number of cells) and will enable the horse to perform more efficiently.

When a horse is started in work each day his muscles are 'cold' and must be 'warmed up' gradually, using exercises such as long striding walk or long-low outline trot, before too much strenuous work is requested. As the horse gets fitter, the warm-up can include cantering.

Muscles function by using energy to contract them; the by-product of the use of energy is lactic acid which is then converted back to energy. A fit horse has a very efficient energy cycle, whereas an unfit horse needs more energy and will, therefore, produce more lactic acid. Excess lactic acid cannot be dissipated and ultimately destroys muscle cells. Visible signs of this destruction are 'tying up' and azoturia. Therefore, feed, exercise and work should be correctly co-ordinated and, when stabled, the horse's energy-producing food must be withdrawn on non-work days.

The program towards fitness can also include basic education; the horse is then at primary school where the lessons he is taught improve his self-carriage and weight-carrying abilities. It is at this stage that his lack of natural flexion becomes obvious. His later education will include much more bending and circle work to improve his suppleness, but there should not be too much at this stage.

Unless the trainer is experienced it will be difficult to assess how much work and how much exercise should be given. Too little of either is almost as bad as too much. The horse will not progress beyond his kindergarten days if given too little education and will certainly not get full advantage from his schooling if he is worked too hard.

However, the horse gives very clear signs of having had enough long before he gets 'nappy' and refuses to move; which is what he will do if work is continued too long. A slight but quite clear loss of concentration will occur when the rider has been working too long at a given pace or exercise. The rider should not immediately stop the exercise, but should make a mental note and stop at the next convenient moment. If work is ceased immediately the horse will soon learn to anticipate and give the signs earlier each time.

Should the work go on too long the signs will become more obvious until eventually the horse will either refuse altogether or cease to co-operate. This will at best produce inferior performances and at worst antagonistic responses; 'shutting off' may occur, resulting in a complete lack of communication between horse and rider and loss of all the horse's desire to please.

Stumbling over his own feet, or joints giving way, are signs that the joint tissues are tired or not yet sufficiently fit to carry out the work required. Again, this should be noted and work slowed until the horse's legs have had a short rest, then work can recommence at the point where it was discontinued. For instance, if the horse was cantering or trotting, go back to walk; if it happened while the horse was walking, bring him to halt for a few seconds, then continue at the walk for a while, and then stop altogether for the day. Should the horse continue to stumble, longer walking exercise will be required – that is, longer distances at the walk over a longer time.

Some horses have very strongly protected joints, while others have weaker joints, but they can all become sufficiently strong to carry out the work required if developed gradually and judiciously.

When work is first started and the horse begins to 'blow his nose' and perhaps give a little cough or two to clear his lungs (this often happens when warming up), it is a sign that the horse is working correctly and understands what is required of him. Warming-up exercises should continue until this activity gives way to quiet work.

Do not confuse high-blowing with lung and nose clearing noises or infectious coughing. When the horse has finished work and feels satisfied with what he has accomplished, he will often repeat the nose blowing; it will sound similar but the practised ear will be able to distinguish it.

At this stage the rider should be satisfied, too, and either return the horse to his freedom (stable or paddock) or change from work to play, if more time in the saddle is required. If this second sign of relaxation does not appear, it usually means that either the horse is not satisfied or there is some antagonism between horse and rider. The rider will only learn to identify these different signs by keeping an alert mind, feeling and listening for the slight changes in the horse's attitude. Many chances to relax should be included throughout the work, whether or not the horse appears to be tired.

The main guide to fitness is the recovery rate of heart and breathing. In the early stages of education it is easy to tell when a horse has recovered from a particularly strenuous period, but later it will be necessary to monitor these signs more thoroughly. This can be done with the help of a stethoscope and by counting the breaths the horse takes. Heart rate can be monitored by taking pulse rates at one of several places, but this is a time-consuming exercise for the amateur as every time the horse moves the count is usually lost.

It is not practical to lay out work programs here for day-to-day work, as each horse is different and much depends on the expertise of the rider. Instead, exercises to be worked in early lessons and those that can be added as the horse develops his ability are outlined here. The rider must make a choice each day and be guided by the temperament of the horse on the day, the success or failure of the previous day's work, and the ability of the horse to carry out the exercises.

Many horses resort to fractious behaviour when being educated and this is caused by the horse's inability to understand what is required. Such behaviour is not corrected by punishment, but by the rider calming the horse and going through the exercise again quietly, step by step, until the horse begins to think calmly and tries to perform the exercise. This is the signal to cease work on that subject for the moment.

Kindergarten work should begin with walking forward on a long rein contact, which should be maintained by the leg aids, tapping the horse up to the bit and using little if any seat or back aids (long-low outline). At this stage, the horse must first learn to answer the legs. One thing at a time is all the horse can cope with.

Many changes of direction are included using direct rein in conjunction with inside leg – do not confuse the horse with outside aids until the inside aids are being obeyed.

Transitions to halt and back to walk should be practised often, the halt coming from the cessation of forward leg aids and the lowering of weight into the saddle, the seat and hands having ceased to follow the movement. Continue until the horse begins to feel uncertain and hesitates a little, then apply pressure on the reins in a feel-give-feel-give movement until the horse stops.

Fairly rapid progress will be made as the horse gains confidence and usually by the end of the first lesson he will be ready to halt as soon as the lowering of the leg and seat are felt. Do not, at this stage, insist that the horse waits for the hand signals; always remember, 'one thing at a time'.

When the horse has halted correctly, maintain contact with the hands, apply the aids to walk forward again and, if left to himself, he will step forward from behind. It is important at this stage to remember that the rider's seat and hands must follow the movement of the horse's back and head. When allowed to bring himself to halt, the horse will almost invariably halt squarely, from the very beginning.

Maintain the halt for 15-20 seconds at first, so that he learns to stand still and wait for the next instruction. Walking around the work area or out in the country for about 20 minutes, with several halts and changes of direction, should be sufficient for the first few lessons.

Over the next few weeks (or months) add the outside leg and rein aids when changing direction, putting the accent on inside hand and leg into the turn and outside hand and leg out of the turn, but never abandoning either completely.

As the horse becomes more proficient, it is here that the rider can introduce the turn-on-the-forehand. Some expert riders will not agree with this, but it has been found to be one of the easiest lessons to teach a horse at this stage when he is not confused with a dozen other impressions. Perhaps turn-on-the-forehand is not the correct term at this stage; it is nevertheless a turn on the forehand.

At this time a semblance of a square halt can be achieved and out of this the occasional turn-on-the-forehand can be requested. This turn should not be repeated often enough for the horse to anticipate it. Once or twice to each direction, once or twice a week in the early sessions is quite sufficient.

Beware that the horse does not get so carried away with his prowess that he tries to turn every time he is halted. In order to prevent this, make at least four or five halts between each turn.

The trot can be introduced at some stage during the early lessons and by the time the horse is ready for primary school he should be working at trot at least as long as at walk – perhaps longer if his balance can be maintained. The trot is the horse's natural gait for travelling long distances; if he has any distance to travel he does it at the trot, occasionally breaking it up with short canter bursts. The horse never gallops unless threatened – or thinks he is threatened – or is playing.

One of the first exercises the horse should perform is work with a long-low outline. This not only improves the horse's reaction to the aids but also develops the back and neck muscles. From this develops the lengthening and shortening of the horse's frame preparatory to the extension and collection movements.

The correct way to produce a long-low outline is to ride the horse forward with a very light contact and to keep him up to the bit with the legs. Always it should be the horse seeking the bit, not the rider seeking the contact. This does not mean that the rider throws the contact away altogether – if the rider does so, the horse will immediately drop on to his forehand.

The exercise should be performed on long straight lines with large half- or quarter-circle corners and long changes of direction (which should be frequent) at walk and rising trot. This is continued until the horse relaxes his frame into the position required and keeps a regular tempo. Developing the horse's ability to move on a long-low outline is so important it may be the only work carried out for many weeks in the early days of education. Many half-halts will be required to obtain this movement, and the horse must remain perfectly straight.

Very little, if any, flexion is required but it is absolutely imperative that the horse is not incorrectly flexed – either on a straight line or when working around corners and changing direction.

A horse with a ewe-neck or higher than necessary head carriage must carry out this

The left diagonal (right hind, left fore) is leaving the ground while the right diagonal (left hind, right fore) is beginning to take the weight. The horse is flexed to the right but is not yet engaging his hocks and is therefore not taking a sufficiently forward stride with the hind legs. The rider is rising on the correct diagonal and using a strong leg to encourage the horse to go forward.

The right hind leg and left foreleg are moving forward to take the next step and the rider has been successful in achieving more engagement of the hocks.

The left diagonal coming to the ground; note the lowering of the horse's hip joint. The improvement in the engagement is quite evident.

The moment of suspension, which is very obvious in the extended trot, is almost non-existent at working and collected trot and is very difficult to catch with a camera. This shot shows the right diagonal leaving the ground and the hip rising. The rider is standing in her stirrups and rising a little high.

A different angle: as the right diagonal prepares to land, the rider is preparing to sit but is incorrectly dropping her shoulder. These photographs were not taken in sequence but were chosen to show the clearest possible picture of the horse's action at the trot. Some include the rider showing what not to do.

The right diagonal is swinging forward and the left side of the horse's back is disappearing from sight, continuing the correct swing of the back. The rider is using her spur to improve the action. *Photographs by Keith Stevens.*

Trot sequence

type of exercise for many months, even after progressing to primary school if necessary.

The basic aims in kindergarten are:
- freely forward, straight and with a long-low outline;
- correctly ridden turns so that the horse does not fall in or drift outwards;
- accurate turns-on-the-forehand with as little forward movement as possible and no backward movement.

Length of working time can be increased to 30-45 minutes, but remember not to bore the horse or he will lose interest in what he is doing and learn nothing. Two 20-minute sessions with a ride-out in between would be better than 45 minutes altogether. However, the whole program depends on the individual horse. Some horses, like some children, enjoy school and others find it deadly boring.

The length of time the horse is in kindergarten cannot be given as a hard-and-fast rule. It depends entirely on the progress made which, in turn, depends on the expertise of the rider and the mental and physical ability of the horse.

However, a rule-of-thumb can be suggested: as soon as the horse is stepping along freely in rhythm and with some semblance of balance, at both the walk and the trot, can come to a halt from the walk correctly balanced and reasonably square, execute a competent turn-on-the-forehand and maintain his balance and rhythm through turns, then he can safely go on to primary school. However, this does not mean that the early work is stopped; it means only that primary school subjects can now be introduced.

PRIMARY SCHOOL

The beginning of work at primary level includes establishing contact between horse and rider through a shorter rein, and if the early work has been successful the horse will be looking for contact with the rider's hands and will relax his jaw to the shorter rein. This contact can be progressively increased by the rider's invitation to the horse – but contact is held by the horse, **not** the rider. If the horse refuses to accept contact there is something wrong with the bit, or with the rider's hands or workmanship.

The trot should now be recognisable as a working trot and should be ridden mostly at rising. It is imperative that the rider changes the diagonal when changing direction so that there is less danger of the horse becoming one-sided, or more one-sided than he already is.

Work at both walk and trot can now be ridden around a carefully planned rectangle, riding each corner as the earlier turns were ridden, but with more precision. Each corner becomes a quarter-circle and the horse must remain upright and not allow his inside shoulder to lean inwards, or his hindquarters to drift outwards. Transitions to walk from halt, to trot from the walk, and back down again should be improved and should still be progressive.

Remember that repetition is the only way a horse can learn, so all the exercises should be repeated several times in each session, aiming for some slight improvement in that lesson.

Work at canter can now be included, even if the canter has been a part of the early work during play time, or even during school time. It should now become part of the curriculum and be improved in the same way as the other exercises.

Time in primary school will be considerably longer than in kindergarten and progress should be made slowly and methodically, working on one new thing at a time, while continuing to practise the earlier lessons. Thus, the sessions will begin to increase in length but should never be more than an hour. Never cease work by the clock, however, only by the results obtained. If a session has been very rewarding, stop early; if problems are encountered in one subject, change to something that the horse can do well, so that the lesson ends on a good note. Then come back to the problem another day.

As the work progresses, it will not be possible to practise everything every day and this is where the diary becomes useful. For instance, the turn-on-the-forehand can now be reduced to one or two to each direction once a week, but if you do not have a diary you will not remember when it was last included.

Some of the trot sessions should now be ridden sitting, and large 20-metre circles and serpentine loops, both at walk and trot, should be included. Work on a long-low outline is continued at the beginning of the session, but now the horse can be asked more persistently for a raised and swinging back by judicious use of forward aids and tactful half-halts.

As the horse warms up, his back will lift even more and his neck will shorten a little as his weight is transferred backwards and he strides further underneath himself. This is **not** collection, nor does it resemble collection as yet, but it is self-carriage with improving rhythm and better balance in preparation for collection.

To improve the horse's ability to carry himself and his rider, gymnastic exercises will now begin.

Easy exercises should be used at first. The lengthening and lowering of the body exercise is a good one to start with. This entails

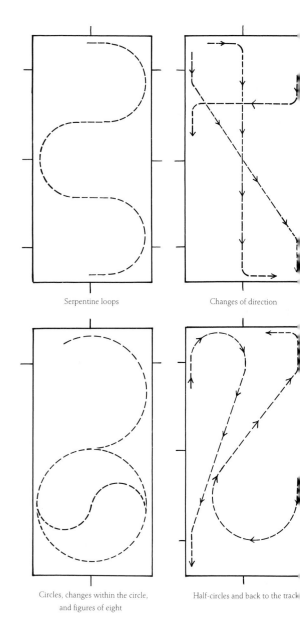

Serpentine loops

Changes of direction

Circles, changes within the circle, and figures of eight

Half-circles and back to the track

CORRECT WORKING FIGURES

lengthening the strides down the long side of the arena and lifting and shortening them before the corner and along the short side of the arena. Continued round the arena for several rounds, changing direction several times, this exercise improves self-carriage tremendously.

At first, the changes of direction can be made by allowing the horse to come to the walk and making the change with a free walk on a long rein. The free walk must be active and forward and not just a meander across the centre. Eventually, the trots will be medium to working and back to medium, but initially just a change in length and height is all that is required. There must be no speeding up or slowing down.

When properly carried out, this is exacting work and should not be maintained for too long at any one time, but it is excellent for developing the back muscles.

The turn-on-the-forehand should now be more accurate and if the horse is carrying it out correctly his turns will be fluent and with a forward desire. The weight should be taken more on the hindquarters, and the inside leg should cross the opposite hind leg with a long stride, while the front legs should mark time quite actively. It is still necessary to make sure that the horse takes one step at a time and does not rush around. Throughout the turn the horse should remain balanced and on the bit and should move fluently forward on completion of the turn.

The next lateral movement which can now be taught is the leg-yield. This exercise has several uses and, despite opposition from some expert riders, its advantages outweigh its disadvantages. Correctly ridden, the muscles on the underside of the shoulder-bone (scapula) come into play and are developed, and the stretch of one hind leg as it crosses in front of the other, while at the same time travelling forward, also helps to develop the driving muscles in the hind legs.

Apart from the benefits received by the leg tissues, the back also must lift and stretch on one side while contracting on the other, thus developing muscles that are not normally used when the horse moves straight ahead.

The exercise is carried out by riding the horse forwards and sideways, while flexed away from the direction of the movement. The horse should remain straight from head to tail. The first attempts will be to teach the horse the movement and correct faults that will creep in. Later, the exercise is invaluable when warming up the horse's muscles ready for work.

As explained in Chapter 9, there are several ways to leg-yield, and the educator should start with the easiest one and progress to the more difficult ones. However, to avoid confusion in the mind of the horse, restrict each work period to one type of leg-yield.

The easiest leg-yield for the horse to understand is that carried out from the inside of the working area to the outside track. At first, only a few strides should be requested and the accent should be on the correct position of the horse rather than the number of strides performed.

The leg-yield on the circle is also reasonably easy but the danger here is that the horse may swing his quarters out rather than step out, or start to leg-yield around every circle. Thus it is necessary to restrict the number of times the leg-yield on the circle is performed, alternating it with correct circle work in exactly the same way that the horse was worked on forehand turns and square halts.

The first attempt at leg-yield may not even move the horse sideways, but if the turn-on-the-forehand has been taught correctly it will not be long before the horse understands what is required. Again, the work must be carried out to both directions and the rider should be satisfied with the slightest sideways movement. The criterion is that the horse has stepped across in front of the outside front and back legs with his inside front and back legs, and not just brought the inside legs up to the outside ones.

For those interested in dressage, the movements required in Preliminary competition are:

- forward on a straight line at all gaits with some impulsion;
- good square halts (on the spot required);
- immobility at the halt;
- rounded corners;
- correct circles.

Work around the arena should be done on the track, as near to the boundary of the arena as is practicable. Rhythm, balance and tempo should be maintained throughout all gaits and transitions. A good free walk is required with sufficient lowering of head and

neck to show that the back is relaxed. Gaits required are medium and free walk, working trot rising and sitting, working canter and halts, all performed in the order in which the test requires them, and on the bit.

Dressage enthusiasts may now start to compete in Preliminary tests, but in practice the test should not be ridden as a complete test. Before competing, one or two practices of the whole test are sufficient – the first time

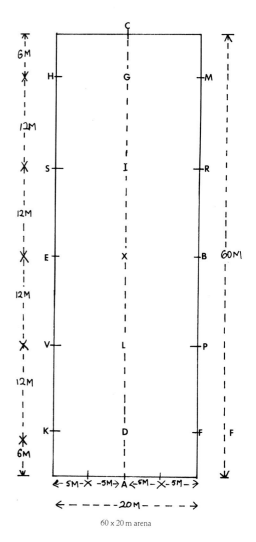

40 x 20 m arena

60 x 20 m arena

to find the weak spots so they can be improved through the educational sessions, and the second time to make sure the rider knows the test. The horse should not know the test and should work only to instruction from the aids.

While competing in one standard, education should proceed in the standard above; that is, while competing in Preliminary, education should be proceeding for Novice and when competing in Novice, education should be continuing for Elementary, and so forth. A great deal of the work is the same, of course, but the new movements help to improve the performance.

To prepare for Novice standard the work should continue as before, improving the rhythm, balance and tempo of all gaits, particularly the canter. If the horse is answering the legs without opposition, the seat, back and weight aids can now be introduced to improve the impulsion.

Transitions may still be performed progressively, but may now be practised missing a gait – trot to halt, halt to trot, canter to walk, etc. However, smooth balanced progressive transitions will mark higher than unbalanced jerky more advanced transitions.

It is necessary to teach the horse that transitions are now to come from trot to halt, without a walk stride in between, but this will come if aids are correctly applied. The rider should be thinking and feeling, and giving the horse time to think and feel, too, so the transition may take several strides to obtain at first. This should be allowed, as no transition can be free and forward moving unless the horse is allowed to make it himself when he is ready. Any attempt by the rider to force transitions will spoil the whole appearance of the movement in the tests, so work at home must be very tactful. Circles and ser-

pentines should be a major part of work by this time.

The horse does not know where the letters in the arena are situated nor does he know their significance, but if he is continually asked for the same movement in the same place he will quickly learn to anticipate that movement and be more concerned in performing it there, than in performing it correctly. Quite often a halt required on the outside track will be excellent, but when the halt is asked for in the middle of the arena the horse finds it difficult to remain straight with no wall or fence to help him. Therefore, it is important to ask for many halts in the centre of the arena, anywhere in the centre, not just at point X.

Medium trot and canter should now be a regular part of the session, and can be used to change direction (trot) or to develop more impulsion around the arena (canter). However, it is imperative that any attempt to move faster, rather than lengthening the stride, should be prevented by the application of subtle half-halts throughout the movement.

Up to now emphasis has been on forward movement, to develop and maintain impulsion; now impulsion should be a little more sophisticated than merely forward. This involves the engagement of the hindquarters and a freeing of the shoulders by transferring a little of the horse's own weight on to his hind legs, which are better equipped to carry the extra weight.

Through all this work, the horse should be predominantly on the bit – **this is not collection** – the horse is not required to be collected until Elementary standard. The position of the head and neck and the movement of the front legs are so tied up with what is happening behind that it is not necessary to concentrate on the forehand. However, as medium trot improves, the eyes of the observer are repeatedly drawn to the shoulder. The forward thrust of these limbs and the position of the head and neck carriage will improve dramatically and this should be felt by the rider.

The requirements of the Novice test are:
- maintenance of a straight line;
- forward movement with improving impulsion and better transitions (still allowed progressively);
- square halts with immobility over a longer period;
- smaller circles without losing impulsion or correctness;
- long periods of trot, including medium trot.

Most of the working trot is performed sitting with the horse's back swinging correctly. The canter movements are increased and include circle work, circles becoming progressively smaller.

While the horse is competing in Preliminary and/or Novice tests, the basic work remains the same as before but there is plenty of variety to keep the horse fresh, especially if the rider creates suitable programs over days and/or weeks, concentrating on continued improvement and variety of work.

New work includes teaching the lateral movements – shoulder-in, travers and renvers – which are excellent exercises (if correctly carried out) to improve flexion and ultimately collection. The application of the aids for these movements is included in Chapter 9, but the rider is reminded that the moment the horse loses his correct outline or his forward movement, the exercise should be abandoned and the horse ridden forward straight.

At first, only a few steps with a slight bend (the natural flexion of the corner is sufficient at this stage) are required. The flexion should increase as the horse's ability to go deeper into his corners improves, but at no time should there be any more bend in the neck than can be obtained throughout the length of the horse's body.

As always, work must be carried out to both directions and should not be continued for very long at any one time. The tempo of the walk and trot must be maintained throughout the exercise and must neither speed up nor slow down. If either error occurs, the horse must be straightened and ridden forward or around a circle with correct flexion and bend for that movement.

TRADE SCHOOL

Work in the early sessions at trade school should include frequent reinforcing of forward straight, introduction of riding deeper into corners, improvement of leg-yields and developing the new lateral movements. The turn on the hindquarters (or half-pirouette) at the walk can be taught and the rein-back and counter canter introduced.

New work includes working towards extended and collected paces in all gaits. The diary is now of great importance, remembering that only one thing at a time should be taught. This does not mean that all the movements cannot be taught over the same period, but it does mean that you should not try to teach the shoulder-in and travers at the same time. Teach each one separately, then combine them when the horse understands them.

By this time the working trot sitting should be the main gait at which most work is carried out, with periods of rest at walk on a long rein, and impulsion improved period-

The inside (left) hind leg initiates the movement by stepping well under the body (engaging the hocks) and transferring more weight to the hindquarters. The inside (right) front leg steps sideways, while the upper body flexes under the rider's seat and develops the bend throughout the body. The rider's left leg on the girth initiates the movement, while the rider's inside seat-bone and outside shoulder maintain the position of the horse's hind and fore quarters respectively. Here, the rider's left arm could be straighter from the elbow, taking the rein slightly away from the neck.

The horse's right hind leg begins to take the weight, while the right foreleg crosses in front of the left foreleg. Note the walk sequence is maintained (left hind, left fore, right hind, right fore). Here, the rider's inside leg is drawn back a little to keep the hindquarters in place.

The horse's left hind leg and left foreleg begin the sequence again. The rider's inside leg is still drawn back; her outside (right) leg, not visible here, is the 'using' leg. The whip in the right hand is ready to assist the right leg if required.

The left foreleg crosses over in front of the right foreleg. Note the rider's right hand maintaining the correct flexion (to the left) by opposing the left hand sufficiently to prevent the horse from over-bending his neck. (The rider's left hand is crossing the withers, which is incorrect.) The whip on the shoulder encourages the horse to move the shoulder to the left.

Continuing the turn, the rider's outside leg is drawn back to prevent the hindquarters from swinging away to the left and to enable the rider's inside (left) leg to return to the girth area.

The final step has been taken and the horse will be pushed forward with the rider's inside (now the right) leg to resume a straight line ahead. *Photographs by Keith Stevens.*

Turn on the hindquarters or half-pirouette (demi-pirouette) ically by medium trot rising. The old problem of faster, rather than forward, should have disappeared and both horse and rider should be looking forward to their educational sessions.

Those educators who are not working towards dressage tests can now include the work for which the horse is intended, such as jumping, novelty events or games, but this must also be introduced a step at a time. For instance, the jumping horse should be taught to jump correctly over small fences, to approach them under the rider's control, to keep the correct bend for the next fence and change leads over the fence when asked. At the same time, educational flat work should continue.

In the earlier tests the whole corner is allowed for the rider to get the horse into canter. Now the horse must be required to canter on request at a given spot and he must be well prepared before that spot is reached to enable him to understand the aid and make the transition smoothly.

Work on all transitions should be stepped up and progressive transitions dispensed with in the educational situation. Work on a circle, half at walk and half at trot, is excellent for improving transitions. It must be a large circle at this stage, at least 20 metres in diameter, and movement should always be to both directions equally. The more sophisticated transitions can commence, also on circles – halt to trot, and walk to canter, each for half the circle in each gait. This is quite strenuous work, but it is far more interesting to the horse, so beware that both horse and rider do not become too enthusiastic and cause fatigue.

Canter circles and half-circles of about 20-metre diameter should be a regular part of the educational work, to improve the horse's flexion and upright position. At no stage should the horse be allowed to lean into the circle or flex away from the circle. This exercise alone requires a good knowledge of the aids and a very sensitive 'feel' from the rider. If this canter work is regularly carried out incorrectly and over a prolonged period, all the good work so far performed can be ruined. Work on a circle is important to the education of the horse, but it must be correct work.

The simple change of lead should be performed in these lessons – the flying change should never be attempted until the horse understands the counter canter.

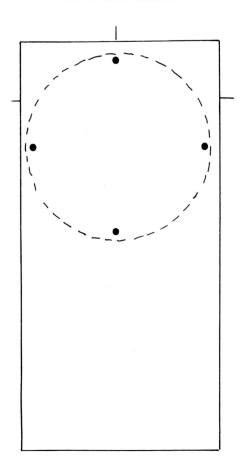

POINTS OF THE CIRCLE

In the show ring the simple change is often performed through the trot, but the correct simple change requires one or two steps at the walk and strike off to canter on the opposite lead. In dressage the simple change is always performed through the walk.

Medium trot can now be maintained for longer periods and should be used quite often to break up two movements, such as between two turns on the forehand or hindquarters, which may result in loss of impulsion. Medium trot is also used to develop the extended trot. The rein-back should be introduced and improved.

The medium trot is now ridden sitting as well as rising and if the rider's ability has kept pace with the horse's education this should pose no problem.

The earlier work of medium to working trot can be duplicated with extended to working trot and, eventually, from extended to collected trot. Smaller circles should be performed in all gaits, but the horse must be in correct form, so care must be taken when reducing the size of the circle and in the length of time devoted to the exercise.

Even though the horse may be fit and well prepared, muscle soreness will still be a problem as new muscles become involved and others are required to work harder. Never lose sight of the possibility that muscle soreness may be the cause of poor performances.

Movements required at Elementary standard are:

- halt to working trot and collected walk;
- rein-back to collected walk and collected canter;
- serpentines at trot and canter (with and without change of lead);
- medium trot (rising and sitting) to collected trot sitting;
- counter canter progressively developed from a few strides in small serpentine loops, to half-circle loops and eventually to full circles;
- working canter to medium canter and back to collected canter;

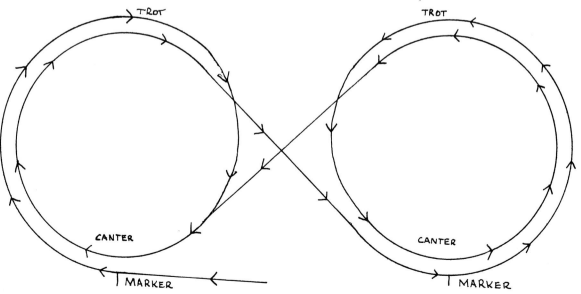

GAITS AND TRANSITIONS
Simple changes in preparation for flying changes – the horse should be taught the counter canter **before** flying changes.

- halts held for longer periods;
- increasing number of rein-back steps;
- shoulder-in and travers combined.

All these movements are perfected by continuing the different exercises and asking for understanding of new movements or improvement of those already understood. In other words, you are increasing the number of 'words' in the 'sentences' and the number of 'sentences' the horse can cope with at any one time.

When the horse is ready to compete at Elementary standard, he should be working at home towards Medium standard, which includes half-passes, flying changes and improvement of all the other movements he has already learned. Transitions will be more demanding and required more often.

The final test in the preparation of the dressage horse is the Advanced test, which has no new movements but requires a higher standard of performance. When the horse has reached the Advanced standard he can be considered a trained horse. The higher tests are recognised as 'High School' or *Haute Ecole* and are the tests that are ridden in international and Olympic Games contests.

Horses trained for other activities will benefit from training to this level. Eventing horses at the top standard are expected to perform Medium tests, and the performance of any novelty or western horse will be enhanced by his ability to perform correct flying changes and keep his balance in tight circles, or to increase the distance he can cover by simply extending his stride rather than by taking shorter, quicker strides.

In my opinion, it will be about two years from the start of education before the horse is ready to compete successfully at Novice standard. This is assuming that the horse is ridden at least five times a week – it will take

A correct halt and salute. Weight evenly distributed over all four legs, lower jaw relaxed to rider's hands, neck bent at the poll and back raised ready to allow the hind legs to step forward underneath the body at whatever length is required. Erica is saluting the judge correctly, sitting squarely to the front with relaxed shoulders and neck, heels lowered without force, legs on the horse ready to apply the necessary aids. Altogether a pleasant picture of alert awareness. (For the purist: yes, Erica's spurs are upside down and low on the heel. She deliberately wears them this way to enable her to use them without displacing her legs.) *Photograph by Russell G. Griffiths.*

much longer if he is ridden only once or twice a week. Worked out by the hour, it will take about 475 hours of work to reach this standard (this is allowing for a break of 5-6 weeks which all horses should be allowed in the year). From this point onwards, the length of time needed to improve the horse's performance and teach him new movements will decrease noticeably, especially if the rider, too, continues to think and feel and learn.

Of course, each horse is an individual and some will come to hand much more quickly than others, but it should be obvious to the rider before the two years are up whether or not the horse will be suitable for the purpose required. It is a waste of valuable time persevering with an animal which is not going to make the necessary grade, but every horse will benefit from this early work regardless of his future activities.

CHAPTER 11

JUMPING

Although jumping is within the ability of every horse it is not an activity in which he normally involves himself unless he has no alternative. Yet a jump is nothing different from his normal everyday movement, as it is purely and simply an extra large canter stride. Therefore, every horse **can** jump if he wishes, but not every horse wants to. Not every horse realises he can jump, but a horse which becomes convinced that he cannot jump has been influenced by traumatic incidents.

Wild horses will jump at anything of reasonable size in their path that they cannot go round. If they consider the obstacle too high, or think that it might have harmful properties on the other side, they may change direction and go left or right, or turn back the way they came. This would be called a refusal in jumping parlance!

It is incorrect to assume, because a horse jumps out of his yard or over a confining fence, that he is automatically a good jumper. In every case the incentive to jump is to escape confinement, either from fear or because of his gregarious nature. Jumping with a rider on his back is something quite different.

A horse does not refuse because he is a coward or dishonest. Horses do not think like people, so their actions and reactions are not prompted by the same stimuli as those which activate people. The horse's reaction to fear and uncertainty is to run away, and he does not think of himself as a coward when he does so. A stop in front of a fence is usually an act of self-preservation rather than cowardice.

A horse often comes to enjoy jumping and become highly skilled at it, but not without training, and he will not continue to enjoy it if ridden by an incompetent rider.

The first considerations when choosing a horse to be trained for jumping are his conformation, temperament and soundness. Of course, all horses can be tried out as jumpers, but schooling of a horse which is unsound, poorly conformed or has an uncertain temperament is a waste of time. Even horses which fit these criteria may never become good jumpers. Like any other athlete, being able to excel in their chosen sport is a bonus not given to all.

However, training is started with the conviction that all horses can jump and a hope that your particular horse will be as good as, or better than, others; but this can only be discovered by jumping the horse.

The horse needs to be sure that the ground on which he is moving is firm and not likely to shift, especially in the early stages, so the initial jumps should be fairly solid so that they will not fall down under his feet. Teaching horses to jump over flimsy little obstacles is asking for trouble, inviting refusals and knock-downs from the very beginning.

The areas of responsibility in jumping should be clearly defined in the minds of both rider and horse. The flat areas between the jumps and the need to present the horse correctly three strides before the jump are the responsibility of the rider; these three strides and the jump itself are the responsibility of the horse.

Although the rider should encourage the horse forward, there should be no interference with the horse's arrangements to negotiate the fence. In other words – the flat areas belong to the rider, the jumps belong to the horse.

When a horse hits a fence with his front legs it is often because he was not properly presented and took off too early, too late or too fast, or the rider has unbalanced him by leaping up the neck. If the horse hits the jump with his hind legs it is usually for the same three reasons, or because the rider sat back prematurely, forcing the horse to drop his hind legs on the fence.

Why three strides? This is because the horse sees the jump for the last time at about that distance from it. If he is properly presented, he need only assess the height and width of the obstacle and prepare himself to jump. If he also has to adjust his stride, say to extend 2½ strides to 3 strides or contract them to 2 strides, his mind is divided between the two problems and he may get one or both wrong.

This is particularly important when the horse is learning to jump. As his expertise improves, he will become adept at arranging things to suit himself and then it will be the rider who makes most of the mistakes, not the horse.

Not only does the horse have to learn to jump, but the rider must also be able to adjust position to suit the situation. The rider's balance must remain over the horse's point of balance and the hands must neither pull back at a crucial time nor suddenly throw the reins away. It is obvious, therefore, that the rider learning to jump should ride an established jumper and the rider who is to train the horse to jump should already be experienced in riding over fences.

Chapter 8 sets out the essentials of the forward, or floating, seat and this should be employed as the jumps become higher.

There are several ways of finding out whether a horse has the ability and temperament to make a jumper. Some trainers put the horse in a 'bullring' – a circular jumping lane where the horse must jump if he wishes to move forward. Sometimes these jumps are set quite high and the trainer chases the horse around from the centre of the ring with a whip. The horse works out the best way to negotiate the obstacles.

There is nothing wrong with this method as long as the horse is allowed to move at his own pace and is not hurried. He should be able to discover for himself that there is nothing to fear and that the activity is really quite exhilarating.

Anxiety and/or fear can be very traumatic for a horse, especially if he cannot exercise his natural instinct to run away. If frightened at this time he will never forget, and may stop at inexplicable moments or make such a drastic mistake that he falls; this in itself will be another traumatic experience.

If the horse is taught to jump over small fences and he has confidence that he can do so, he will understand that a fall is the result of a mistake either on his part or his rider's part, and he will not be so upset. The height and width of jumps should be relative to his experience and can be increased progressively as his expertise improves. This will not then trouble the horse unless the increase has been inordinately large.

Of course, all horses have a limit to their ability, as do humans; some may jump fences of a considerable size while others will reach their limit over medium-sized fences. Only practice will determine your particular horse's ability.

My preferred method of teaching has the added benefit of enlightening the rider about the length of stride of the horse and his jumping style and temperament, before the obstacles become the centre of attention.

It will be assumed that the horse has been educated in flat work to Novice standard. This will have developed the horse's obedience to the aids, and will also have strengthened his muscles sufficiently to enable him to accommodate the extra effort required without too much pain.

The area used can be the same as that for flat work. Materials required include six poles about 3 metres long, 12-15 cm in diameter, either rustic or painted. Six cavalletti are acceptable, but even at their lowest level they cannot be placed on the ground itself and will be raised a few centimetres. This is no problem, but the horse will initially work over poles on the ground better than over cavalletti just above the ground.

Also required are enough wings, cups and poles to erect one or two jumps at a time. Even if it is possible to produce enough material to build a course, this is not necessary at this stage. A cross-country course of small solid jumps is an excellent facility but, if not available, country riding areas with logs and ditches can be just as useful.

The poles (or cavalletti at the lowest level) should be set in line about 90 cm apart, depending on the horse's stride. The horse should be able to step comfortably between each pole.

After some 20-30 minutes work on the flat (dressage exercises), the horse should be walked over the poles, the rider assessing the length of stride and organising the horse on the approach to arrive three clear strides in front of the poles. The horse should step, with one foot only, between each pole and should not leave this exercise until he can do this consistently. If the horse shuffles his stride or steps short or long, he will have to adjust his balance by putting two separate feet within the space, instead of only one.

Work should continue until the horse approaches and walks through the poles with the same length of stride he is using on the flat and moves accurately through the grid. The rider should regularly change the direction after the poles so that the horse is kept mentally alert, and should change direction to come from the other side regularly.

Perfecting the exercise may take several days or the horse may be able to negotiate the poles in the first few attempts. If the problem is difficult for the horse to solve, the time used for this exercise should not exceed 6-8 minutes at any one time. After that it should be abandoned for that day and returned to at another time.

However, it will still be possible to leave the exercise on a good note, as the horse will improve in some small part of the work and this can signal the end for the day.

As soon as the horse can negotiate the poles satisfactorily at the walk, the poles can be reset for the same exercise at the trot. For this, the distance is about 1-2 metres. The problem is again to negotiate the poles in trot with one foot only between each pole.

During this time the rider alters the horse's strides **before** the three strides and makes every effort to arrive in front of the poles exactly three trot strides away. Although the horse will normally be negotiating a jumping course at the canter, this assessment of stride at walk and trot will improve the rider's ability to assess distances by strides.

In later lessons the poles can be placed slightly further apart, or a little closer together, necessitating stretched or shortened strides at walk and trot, but this exercise should not be included until the horse is negotiating the poles correctly over his correct distance with no problems. The horse's demeanour should be alert and lively, but not hesitant or excited.

If the horse is rather lackadaisical, the same exercise can be repeated at the canter with the poles about 3-3.5 metres apart. This is an excellent exercise for the rider learning to ride in a forward position and to assess canter strides, but it is not recommended for the over-keen horse as it will only increase his excitement.

As soon as the exercise is being performed to the rider's satisfaction, the last two caval-letti can be formed into a small jump, or a small jump can be erected after the poles. This jump should be far enough away to allow the horse one good trot stride between the last pole and the jump, or a canter stride if desired.

As the actual effort of jumping resembles a canter stride, the horse should be encouraged to land on a particular front leg — decided by the direction to be taken after the jump. This can be achieved by the rider taking up the position to the direction in which he intends to ride. "Look where you are going and the horse will go where you are

looking." If this is done at this stage, there will be no future problems in getting the horse to take a particular lead over the jump.

If the horse stops jumping and just steps over the jump, the obstacle should be increased slightly in height or width to ensure that the horse does actually jump.

In all early jumping lessons it is imperative that an exercise is stopped as soon as the horse has shown an improvement. This may mean that the second time through the grid the horse has made sufficient progress to stop that part of the lesson for the day.

However, although that particular exercise is finished, another can be started, such as riding out in the bush and jumping over small logs and natural obstacles. At this stage the horse should not be asked to jump anything which he might refuse, but should have as much variety as possible.

This may sound tedious work but, once the rider is able to see his stride and the horse is drawing into his fences, the jumping lessons can include several different kinds of obstacles, not higher or wider, but different. The horse can also be ridden at trot or canter

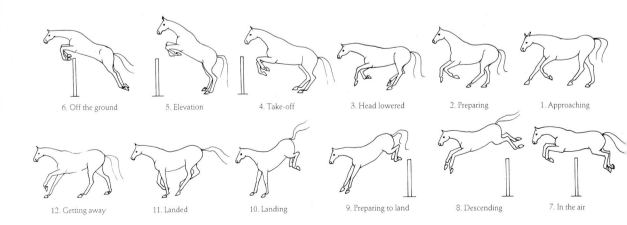

6. Off the ground   5. Elevation   4. Take-off   3. Head lowered   2. Preparing   1. Approaching

12. Getting away   11. Landed   10. Landing   9. Preparing to land   8. Descending   7. In the air

JUMPING POSITIONS

to enable the rider to rearrange the horse's approach and to take a particular lead on the landing side of the fence. In fact there is plenty of variety if the rider's mind and imagination are working.

It should be clearly understood that jumping over the same obstacle time and time again, especially if the jump has been performed correctly, tires the horse and disheartens him, making him believe that he is not doing it right. The rider must allow the horse to understand that he has carried out the exercise satisfactorily.

At this stage the jumps should not be related but, as soon as the horse has developed into an accurate and safe jumper, combination fences can be introduced.

The horse should not be allowed to move faster over the ground than the rider requires and should readily answer the aids to shorten or lengthen his stride. Although a natural increase of impulsion and excited desire to get on with the job should be welcomed, the rider must not allow the horse to race into or away from his fences.

At this time a grid of small jumps can be included, arranged from two or three cavalletti (or wings and poles) one or two strides apart. As the horse's expertise improves, the number can be increased, progressing to no more than six jumping efforts. The rider should allow the horse to make his own way through the grid without interference, except for helping to maintain impulsion. This will improve the horse's dexterity over combinations. The striding distance should be accurate and the jumps small, as the aim is to improve the horse's ability to jump well within his stride.

If the horse is approaching too fast or becomes unbalanced as he comes to the jump, the rider can improve the approach by riding the horse in a circle before the jump. The circle should be arranged in such a way that as soon as the horse has settled he can be ridden through the centre of the circle on to the jump, while still maintaining the three-stride approach.

Should the horse show a tendency to rush away after the jump, he should be brought to a halt after the jump and the halt sustained for 15-20 seconds before moving on again. The halt should be maintained in exactly the same way as for flat work and should be straight, balanced and sustained. Combinations or related fences should not be contemplated until the horse is willing to listen to the rider's aids between the fences.

During these exercises the rider should decide upon, and request, a particular lead for the horse to take after every fence when cantering over them. At this stage, a particular lead may not be important to the horse's balance, as he should have plenty of time to regain his balance before approaching the next fence, but the horse should be learning to listen to the rider's instructions regarding direction and should land appropriately.

Many competitions have been lost because the horse has become unbalanced when approaching a fence on the wrong lead, or in a disunited canter. Care taken in these early stages to establish correct leads and teach changing leads over the fence will pay many a bonus in the future.

The horse should at this stage be learning about the way the rider negotiates a course so that, although the horse himself has not had the benefit of walking the course, he can gain from the rider's knowledge of the course.

As the expertise of both horse and rider improves, the jumps can be arranged in different courses of several jumps — all of reasonable height and width with plenty of room to approach and land correctly. Each fence should be a separate entity until the horse is jumping over everything he is faced with and has perfected his style and competence.

It must be repeated here that the only way a horse can improve his performance is by regular repetition and finding out for himself the best way to negotiate each type of fence. But making him jump the same fence repeatedly will only dishearten him and possibly make him sulky and unco-operative.

He must have sufficient jumping to improve his ability, but not so much that he becomes sick of it. The rider must make this part of the horse's education pleasant and diverting, devising new and interesting changes without over-facing the horse. Height and width can be **gradually** increased as the horse's ability improves.

As soon as the horse is able to approach, jump and leave the fence without getting over-excited or nervous he can be introduced to related fences. His work over the grid should have improved his dexterity and also his acceptance of the fact that another fence is coming up immediately after the one he is jumping.

At first he should be asked to jump two fences which are related by one, two or three exact strides. The distance between these two fences can be continually changed as long as the striding is exact for that horse. Later, the striding can be adjusted so that a long or short stride (or strides) is required, but half – and quarter – stride distances have no place in the early jumping lessons and should be kept for the time when the horse is adept at arranging his bulk over a fence.

All this time the height and width of the fences must remain within the scope of the horse – not so small that he treats them with contempt, nor so large that he is intimidated by them. At this stage he is learning to jump, perfecting his style and stride, and if this work is carried out correctly there should be no refusals to deal with. Later, if and when the horse does refuse, the rider can be sure it is because he believed he could not jump it, and he will certainly not warrant punishment for stopping.

The rider should, nevertheless, always carry a whip. It may be necessary at some time during training or when competing for the rider to use the whip as encouragement, or to chastise disobedience, but it should never be necessary to beat a horse with it. A horse that needs to be beaten to a fence is either not suited to jumping or his education has been hurried. In both cases it is the rider's fault that he has been put in that position.

It is not necessary for the rider to jump around in the saddle to advise the horse of the direction to take after a fence. It needs only a 'look' in that direction with the eyes, shoulders and seat-bones and the horse will do the rest. If it is necessary to change leads, it should be done over the top of the fence, by re-flexing the horse and giving the aids for the new direction, softly, quietly and without force.

CHAPTER 12

SAFETY WITH HORSES

Safety around horses is not given the amount of care and attention it should receive from the average horseman or woman. In theory, if safety rules are followed, no one should get themselves kicked, and broken toes from being trodden on should be unknown. And to allow oneself to be bitten is sheer carelessness. Most of the following suggestions are common sense, but unfortunately 'familiarity breeds contempt' and, unless something happens to teach the handler differently, he/she often thinks "my horse won't kick" or "this horse doesn't bite".

To guard against such painful accidents – or incidents – the handler must know a great deal about the general psychology of the horse: his actions and reactions in certain circumstances and his mental attitude to people in general and to the handler in particular.

The horse's natural means of defence are to kick, bite, rear, strike or run away. Only very frightened or unsuitable horses rear and strike at a person on the ground. Even young horses will not resort to such actions unless very severely frightened, so a horse which regularly acts in this way without cause should be dispensed with as dangerous. However, to sell such a horse to another person without advising them of the problem is tantamount to criminal negligence, so it is better to have him put down.

Many young horses kick, or attempt to kick, when stressed but cease the tendency once they have learnt that no one is likely to hurt them deliberately. However, it is a natural reaction and, if taken by surprise or sufficiently frightened or exuberant, any horse may be guilty of such action.

Therefore, a horse should never be approached from the rear; he should always be able to see the handler and know that someone is coming. The way to approach a horse which is being caught is to speak quietly when within earshot and walk towards his shoulder. If the horse should turn his hindquarters towards the handler he should move so that he is again approaching the shoulder. Many horses which do not wish to be caught will run away, but very few will run over the top of the catcher. Even if they attempt to do so, if the catcher is to one side it is unlikely the horse will knock him down.

Horses which do not want to be caught and regularly present problems must be re-educated or disposed of, as they are time-wasters of the first order.

The well-behaved horse does not go in for biting his handler, but there are occasions when a horse feels justified in biting. Young horses nip for fun – it is their way of showing affection to one another – but this does not mean that a vicious bite is a show of affection, because it is no such thing. If a horse wishes to bite he can inflict a very nasty wound, and even a playful nip can be painful.

When my daughter was a very small child she entered the paddock where her pony mare and a pony gelding were kept. The gelding, which was eventually found to be a rig, lunged at her and picked her up bodily by the shoulder, shaking her like a dog with a rat. She could have been badly hurt but luckily escaped with only a bruised shoulder. Stallions in a rage can be expected to behave in this way, but it is very unusual for a gelding or mare to be so belligerent. Because of such happenings it is important for an older person to be in the vicinity when very young children are around horses.

In contrast, my big 17-hand gelding loved this little girl and would come at the gallop if he heard her cry. She would stand under him and scratch his belly or stroke his legs while he was grazing, because that was all she could reach, and before he moved a leg he would look back to see where she was and carefully move one leg at a time so that he didn't hurt her. Yet this horse had to be put down eventually because he was a complete outlaw when ridden by an adult.

Many women have received painful bites on the breast, and horses that threaten to bite in such a manner should be restrained and chastised. The handler should not stand in front of the horse but keep to one side, so that the horse has first to swing his head and signal his intentions. As the head swings round, a sharp smack on the nose will fore-stall the bite.

Some people say that this makes a horse head-shy, but this is not necessarily so. The horse is well aware of the reason for the smack and will eventually cease his mis-behaviour. Uncalled-for blows to the head cause the horse to be head-shy, but sharp taps with the knuckles when necessary will teach the horse better manners.

Another person who is at risk is the farrier or the person picking up the feet. Usually, it starts as a playful nip to the inviting back-side. However amusing this may be to the onlooker, this action must be prevented from becoming a habit and eventually a vice. Someone should hold the horse or he should be tied up short.

Girthing up is often objected to by the horse and he may swing his head with teeth

bared and will certainly connect if given the chance. The fault lies with the person who saddled the horse, either past or present, and ripped the girth up to its full tightness in one movement. This error can never be undone no matter how careful the subsequent sad-dler is, as the horse never again trusts anyone fastening his girth.

It is significant that a horse will seldom make an attempt to bite a person dealing with a painful wound. He is intelligent enough to know that it is the wound that hurts and is often well aware that the handler is helping him. However, when a tightening girth pinches him he is also well aware that it was the handler that did it.

To make sure the horse does not become antagonistic to being girthed up, the girth should be tightened gradually, one hole at a time. This method takes no more time than tightening in one movement, especially if the horse is moving around threatening to bite or cow-kick.

When a girth is sufficiently tight you should still be able to get a complete finger under it. Very often it is necessary to tighten the girth again just before mounting, or just after mounting, before moving off. This is because the horse breathes in and holds that breath during the tightening process, thus giving the impression that the girth is tight enough. Later, when he lets out his breath, the girth is found to be loose.

Most riders tighten the girth too much and make the horse uncomfortable. This is equi-valent to trying to work with a belt pulled as tightly as possible around the waist. In both cases, the belt and the girth tighten up over long periods and become more and more uncomfortable.

However, leaving the girth too loose is just as bad and could be the cause of a broken neck or other severe injury. Give the horse's girth problems some thought and change the type of girth if the current one is not suitable. There are many different kinds of girth on the market, because it can be such a problem.

When caught, the horse should be led from the side and not pulled along from in front. The handler is in grave danger of being run over by a startled horse if walking directly in front of him and unable to see what is alarming the horse. When walking alongside, the handler picks up the horse's alarm at once and can look behind or to the side to see what is causing the trouble. Remember, the horse can see behind and to the side, as well as in front, at the same time.

All horses should be taught to lead and if one arrives on the property which has not been taught to lead correctly, no time should be lost in teaching him to do so.

When entering a stable, wait until the horse is facing the door before entering. In some cases, the door itself can be used to make the horse change position so that his head rather than his hind legs are towards the door. While in the stable always make sure the horse remains facing up. If necessary, place a headcollar on him and hold him in that position. A headcollar should always be used if the horse is known to kick.

When entering a paddock with several horses at the gate, chase them away a short distance before entering. An accidental kick meant for a horse but finding the handler is just as painful as a deliberate kick.

When passing behind a ridden or tethered horse, make sure the distance is sufficient to be out of range or close enough not to be harmed if the horse should kick. When passing behind the horse, it is a good idea to have a hand on the tail. If the horse is going to kick he must raise his tail as his back lifts in the process of lifting the leg. In this way, the handler can quickly move or discourage the horse by speaking firmly to him.

In a lifetime of handling horses, I have been kicked on only three occasions and all three were my own fault. The first time I came between a mare and her newborn foal, the second time I slipped and grabbed the hock of a sleeping horse, and the third time I was sent flying with one hind leg by a pony passing me as I bent down to remove a stone from the track. Later, I discovered that this pony had been pelted with stones by some larrikins the day before but, not knowing this and being 'sure' the pony would not kick, I was in direct line for a flashing hind leg.

The moral of this story is to be aware of the possibility of danger, be alert to the danger signs and stay out of range.

Horses which have learned to rear when asked to do something they don't want to do become very dangerous and very hard to cure. It is better to prevent them rearing than to have to cure them once they have started.

This vice often begins when the horse is asked to enter a stable or float or pass through a gateway to leave his friends. In the case of the stable and the float, it may be the dark interior that frightens him or the memory of a bad experience in them.

Forcing a young horse forward against his desires will almost certainly initiate evasive action. His most useful defence in such a situation is to rear and/or move backwards away from the supposed danger. Taking the precaution of fitting a rearing bit before the first attempt is made will give the handler a chance to prevent the horse from rearing. A breeching rope behind will discourage the animal from running backwards.

Remembering that the horse's power-house is in the rear, it is folly to try to pull the horse forward. It is also folly to get behind him to chase him forward as his hind legs are lightning fast.

Standing to one side and encouraging him forward may be sufficient or, if not, two people with hands linked behind him may do the trick. Otherwise, the breeching rope can be used.

If a horse is taught to lead as soon as he is first handled, before he encounters any great traumas and before he realises his own strength, he will always remember this lesson and however reluctant he may be he will eventually give in. However, if he discovers he is stronger than the handler, every subsequent handler will suffer.

Every horse's natural reaction to fear, pain or potential danger is to run away, so if he is allowed to run away from his rider's actions he will quickly become a bolter – dangerous and difficult to cure. Only a very good rider should pick a fight in open country and she must be very sure she can win before doing so.

Subjecting the horse progressively to situations which he might consider dangerous during his initial schooling is the most sensible way of making sure the horse does not continue to think these situations are dangerous. The most frequent cause of bolting is allowing inexperienced riders to ride inexperienced horses in open country. The rider does something that feels different to the horse, he begins to panic, the rider begins to panic, and very quickly we have a no-win situation from which the horse tries to escape by bolting.

Re-education is the only solution and that does not always work.

Almost any situation will be acceptable to the horse if he is in company with another horse which is unconcerned about the sup-posed danger. A calm self-assured rider is imperative in such situations.

The most dangerous idea prevalent among people who are not familiar with horses is to believe that the young horse and the young child can grow up together. If only people realised they were preparing for a potentially lethal situation they would certainly not consider such a course. A young child or inexperienced adult should be exposed to the quietest, oldest pony or horse that can be found and, until they have learned how to handle horses generally, they should not be allowed to deal with young animals.

Having a foot trodden on by a horse is very painful; having a hand trodden on is not only painful, but completely irresponsible as well. The horse cannot tread on anything which is not on the ground, so it is only sensible and very easy to keep the hands off the ground when near the horse. If something is dropped under the horse, move him away before attempting to pick it up. Easy, sensible, but not always practised by the inexperienced.

The feet, of course, are different because they are always on the ground or near the ground. However, when working around a horse, make it a practice to lift the foot nearest the horse when the horse lifts his foot. It takes quite a while to perfect this habit, but once achieved it is infallible.

In all my years of involvement with horses, I have only once been trodden on sufficiently hard to cause injury. Occasionally, I have been pinned to the ground with a hoof on the edge of the boot. It goes without saying that no horse handler should be near a horse without shoes or boots – bare feet or sneakers are unacceptable to the experienced horseman. It is also bad practice to crouch or kneel around any horse. The body should be bent from the waist with the weight always on the legs to allow fast movement away from danger.

It should be understood that horses prefer not to stand on anything which is not solid ground, so a fallen rider is often safe if he/she curls up and keeps still. The rider's own horse and others following will hurdle the body if they can see it and have the chance to do so. This is not because of love for the rider but for self-preservation. Shifting ground is anathema to the horse.

Despite this fact, the occasional horse has learned that he can inconvenience his handlers by stepping on their feet and will take every opportunity to do so – this is a particularly bad habit with ponies which are around small children. Probably the child yelped every time he was accidentally trodden on and the pony has learned this bad habit, in the way he always learns, by repetition. Therefore, if the horse treads on you, it is better to suffer in silence lest the horse learns to do it regularly.

Horses have a very definite pecking order but unfortunately it does not run down the scale in order. The horse which appears to be at the top of the order may be underdog to a horse well down the line and, although the top horse can intimidate all the others, he cannot intimidate the underdog. Thus, at feeding time there is considerable chasing about before they all settle down to their own portion.

The person feeding horses is in considerable danger unless he is aware of the pecking order and keeps a close eye on developments. It is not the intention of the horse to hurt the feeder, but accidental damage is just as painful and potentially as disastrous as intentional damage. Occasionally, a horse will become belligerent at feeding time and in this case it is necessary to carry a whip or stick.

The best way to deal with this situation is to have feed bins or piles of hay sufficiently far apart to allow both horses and feeder to keep clear of the belligerent ones. There should be more than three horse lengths in all directions between each bin or pile so that no horse can hog two of them or reach another horse with a kick.

When turning horses loose in a paddock they should never be allowed to go free while facing into the paddock. Each animal should be taken into the paddock, turned to face the gate (which should be closed, of course), then let free. Should the horse be exuberant and leave in a hurry with flying heels, he must first turn away from the leader. At the same time the leader can step back out of range. If allowed to rush forward past the leader, a backward kick can cause severe damage to the leader.

This method should be practised at all times, no matter how quiet the horse appears to be, as it is the unexpected that catches the handler unawares.

When catching a horse in the paddock, get the lead rope around the neck at the first opportunity, then put on the headcollar or halter. While fiddling around to find the right way for the noseband, the other horses, or even the horse being caught, may take it into their heads to gallop away. The least of the resulting problems will be losing the horse, as it will have to be caught again and this will be more difficult with everything careering around madly. At worst the catcher can be knocked over and injured.

It seems ridiculous to say that no one should stand in front of a herd of horses, expecting them to stop, yet people are often seen doing just that. The horses may stop but the handler may also be flattened in the attempt.

Recently, a woman was knocked onto her back by a group of horses; they were not horses on the move but jealous mares who objected to interest being taken in a lesser member of their group. Although a considerable distance from the group, the woman was standing towards the front of the mare she was talking to, and not to one side, as recommended. As the other mares lunged at them, the woman stepped sideways but she was unable to move too far because the other horses were coming up on each side of her.

The mare hesitated as she did not wish to knock the woman over, but then jumped forward and a little sideways, hitting the woman with her large belly as she passed. The woman fell flat on her back almost in front of the other mares racing up alongside. A very dangerous situation developed from nothing more than an interest in a particular mare though, in this case, the woman was only winded.

Much has been written about methods of teaching a horse to float, or retraining it to be transported pleasantly. All the methods outlined are excellent, provided they work. A method may work with some horses and not with others, but if the horse is properly prepared and carefully floated retraining will not be necessary.

Firstly, the youngster should be trained to walk into and out of a float as he would walk into and out of a stable. The best time to do this is when he is weaned, but it is certainly preferable to have it done by the time the youngster is broken in. A short journey without hassles at this point will set the stage for the animal's subsequent attitude to the float and, if at any time he becomes disenchanted

with the idea, it will not be too difficult to get his confidence back.

Occasionally, one comes across a horse which is float-shy for no known reason. Travel trauma in humans may be caused by travel sickness or claustrophobia, and the horse is just as likely to suffer from both these ailments. We don't know for sure because the horse cannot speak, but there is evidence to suggest that these situations do occur.

A person in the same situation might take relaxant medicine, but horses travelling to competitions, either racing or sports, may not be given any kind of drug. It is illegal for both horse and rider to compete under the influence of drugs. The horse cannot vomit, although he can feel nauseated and may retch, probably suffering acute anxiety on this account alone.

If he shows any sign of anxiety, the horse should be prepared for travelling immediately before his trip. Getting him ready and leaving him standing around for a long time can only increase his uneasiness. It may not be the float journey itself which causes the horse to be nervous. He may associate the float with something that is going to happen when he arrives at the journey's end. Many horses which are difficult to load when leaving home enter the float with alacrity for the return journey.

Before loading the horse, make sure that everything is in readiness to travel as soon as the horse has been successfully loaded, and have the vehicles in a position which will facilitate the loading. When the horse has entered the float the breeching fastening should be closed, whatever type it is, and the ramp closed **before** the horse is tied up.

Before the ramp is let down the horse must first be untied, then the back let down and the breeching unfastened. This is particularly important if the horse is inclined to rush out. Any attempt to hold him forcibly in the float will only increase his anxiety and fear.

There are other ways of discouraging the horse from rushing out, such as a breeching rope – the same as the one used to help get the horse into the float. A person with a whip held against the quarters or gently tapping them may discourage the horse from running out. Whatever method is used, the horse should not be forcibly detained. It is better to try to calm him verbally from in front and from the side of the float (not from directly behind) than to let him think he is being restrained by force.

Most floats have a bar or chain which is fastened behind the horse before the back is put up (referred to here as breeching fastenings). When letting the back down, these fastenings will usually hold the horse and allow a handler to calm him a little before it is undone. However, if there is no fastening – for any reason – the person who lets down the back must stand to one side and not directly in front of the opening door.

He should also be ready to drop the door if the horse starts to rush out, as very severe injuries can be sustained by the person lowering the ramp if he is in the way when the horse is leaving the float in a panic. This also applies when fastening up the ramp after the horse/s are in the float ready to travel.

It is potentially dangerous to ride in the float with horses which are fractious, although a human presence can be calming. Horses have been known to try to leave the float by the access door or the front window and for someone in the front of the float there would be no escape route. Passengers are not allowed to ride in caravans, but as yet this does not apply to horse floats.

The driver of the vehicle pulling the float or the transport should do his best to give the horse a trouble-free ride and this usually means driving at a reasonable speed and slowing down well before corners and intersections.

Many drivers appear to have no consideration for the animals behind them, flying round corners and breaking fiercely at intersections, throwing the horse about with reckless abandon. The driver should always have his mind fixed on the equine passengers and approach every hazard, corner or intersection at reduced speed. Brakes suddenly applied at speed can throw the animals off their feet and thus cause future troubles even if they are not physically hurt. When driving with a float behind, I will take the chance of hitting the hazard (be it man or machine) rather than throw the horses down.

The best way to learn to transport horses is to ride in the float with someone else driving. Stand where the horse stands and remember that the horse has no arms to hold on with. Get the driver to drive at different speeds and determine which will be the easiest one for the horse to keep his balance.

As in every other activity with the horse, he must first be taught to trust his handler and enter the float, then he must travel quietly without kicking, pawing or scrambling, and finally he must remain good-mannered and get off soberly. Once established, bad behaviour in any of these areas is hard to cure.

Some people have used hobbles for horses which paw, but the horse must first be made familiar with hobbles in the stable or yard, and they must be put on after the horse is in the float and removed before the horse is taken off. For the horse which kicks, it is the noise of the kick which gives him satisfaction and induces him to continue. If this noise can be eradicated, the horse gets no pleasure from continuing the practice. A well-padded ramp will not only frustrate the horse's actions but will prevent injury to hind legs.

Horses that scramble should have the centre partition removed as they cannot scramble if there is nothing to lean on. A woman who travels horses throughout the United States once told me that she always removed the centre partition when travelling two horses together over long distances, and never had any trouble. Yet before she started this practice she often reached her destination with injured horses. She does not make a practice of heavily bandaging her horses to travel, but applies bandages and/or boots only to the inside legs of each horse.

Horses that are difficult for the farrier are usually made so by human hands, by lack of thought on the part of either the handler or farrier. The horse's first visit to the farrier should be carefully policed. If the youngster has his feet cut back at the same time as his mother, then regularly throughout his life, there will be few hassles. This is not always possible but, whatever the circumstances, the horse's first visit to the farrier must be hassle-free even if it takes a long time to achieve anything or if the farrier has to come back more than once to complete the job. This also applies to clipping, grooming and veterinary visits. The first approach is the most important.

Search diligently for talented, good-tempered farriers and veterinary surgeons and guard them jealously – they are worth their weight in gold.

Patient, firm handling can re-educate a badly behaved horse. There is no point in beating such a horse as he seldom understands the reasons for the beating but, conversely, sickly sentimental handling can do as much damage as brutality.

A good position for the showjumping rider: nice straight back, balanced over her seat, head up and looking ahead to the next jump, elbows bent with hands ready to follow the horse's head and neck down as he lands. The rider's toes are turned out, a position being taught by modern instructors, but this position turns the back of the calf on to the horse's side and does not allow the rider to be consistent with aids taught on the flat in the early lessons. Photograph by Russel G. Griffiths.

CHAPTER 13

LUNGEING

Lungeing is an art which will improve a horse if carried out expertly or develop more problems if executed incorrectly. It is an area of expertise that needs to be learned and practised by the operator under instruction, before attempting to improve a horse's gaits, balance or activity.

A horse which is correctly lunged will improve his rhythm, his understanding of his rider's requirements, his balance and his muscular system. The horse which is incorrectly or inexpertly lunged will learn to evade, to run rather than move correctly, to lean in or out and to flex incorrectly. He may also learn how much further up the 'pecking order' he is than the operator, a disaster in itself!

The area required to work correctly is about 20 metres in diameter – not much larger and never smaller. It should be identified by some form, preferably a fence, but single barrels around the perimeter will serve. If barrels are not available, poles or tyres on the ground may suffice, but only for well-educated and correctly trained horses.

I have witnessed a horse being successfully lunged in a jumping area using the jumps themselves as the perimeter of the circle. This is only possible if they are set out to allow such space between them. Without some form of perimeter the horse tends to pull away from the operator, particularly when being taught.

It is important for discipline that the horse is saddled with riding equipment, i.e. saddle, bridle and lungeing cavesson or headcollar, or lungeing roller with bridle and carefully fitted side-reins. If the horse is being lunged purely for exercise, it is better to turn it loose into a round yard and keep it moving freely forward than to try to lunge it without the symbols of authority.

The length of time the horse should be lunged should not exceed 45 minutes, and this should be developed from 10-minute sessions over a period of time, increasing as the horse's muscles develop and are able to maintain the effort for longer.

The operator requires one (or two) lunge reins of standard length (about 30 metres), a lungeing whip and gloves. The lunge rein should be of a reasonably soft canvas. Hard materials such as rope will burn the operator's hands if the horse should pull away. This is, of course, the reason for the gloves.

The whip should be long enough to reach the horse on a 20-metre circle; it should be light enough to enable the operator to wield it without difficulty, yet firm enough to apply a touch to the horse that is as light or heavy as required. The lunge whip is an aid which takes the place of the rider's legs, so cracking or hitting are, or should be, rarely used.

The aims of lungeing are:
- to improve tracking (gaits), bending (flexibility), and balance and rhythm;
- to strengthen the horse's musculature and improve his impulsion;
- to provide exercise and improve obedience.

The faults that can occur and, if continued, will get progressively worse and more difficult to correct are:
- incorrect flexion (bending away from the direction of the movement), leaning in with the inside shoulder and/or hip;

- two-tracking (hindquarters spinning outward), moving too fast, too slowly or unevenly;
- refusing to stay out on the circle and intimidating the operator by cutting across the circle and forcing him to retreat;
- kicking at the operator or attempting to turn away and pull him along.

The first principle of lungeing is to ensure the horse will answer the voice aids, so the words used must be the same for every similar exercise. The operator should make sure the words are spoken with the same inflection and loudly enough for the horse to hear. A raised or angry voice is a reproving voice so do not raise the voice unnecessarily or use an angry voice when the horse has merely misunderstood. Keep both for obvious disobediences. Raise the voice only if the horse deserves it and lower it again as soon as he has settled to correct behaviour.

The words 'walk' and 'whoa' sound so much alike it is better to use the word 'halt' for stopping, then there is no chance of a misunderstanding. The word 'halt' is also much easier to command than 'whoa'.

The words to be used should be walk (not walk-on), trot (spoken 'tr. .ot') and canter (spoken 'can. .ter'), halt, steady (to reduce speed or length of stride) and up-forward (to increase length of stride). The speed of the gaits should never be increased – only the height and length of the stride.

When teaching a horse to lunge, the operator can enlist the help of another person or handle the whole thing himself. If the horse has already been taught to lead correctly from both sides, it is a simple matter for the operator to start the horse by leading him on a small circle then gradually to move away until the horse is maintaining the circle without the operator, who is now pivoting in the centre opposite the horse's shoulder. The operator must not get in front of or behind the horse at this stage.

If the horse has not been taught to lead correctly, it is well worth the extra time taken to do this before starting to lunge.

Should the horse stop or move inwards once started, the operator returns to the leading position and starts the horse again. Lungeing should be taught when the horse is in a tranquil mood and not when he feels like 'setting the world on fire'.

I have found that it seldom takes more than 5-10 minutes to get the horse to walk out on the lunge in a 12-15 metre circle, but it will take longer to sustain that position for any length of time; in fact, it may take several sessions. Most horsemen and women do not give themselves sufficient time to get the horse working. Only time and patience will produce results and it is a fact that the horse will give up before the person, if the person is persistent enough.

Teaching the horse to lunge involves teaching him to stop on command as well as to start the movement, so once the horse is moving he should be taught to halt on his line of progression and should **not** be allowed to turn in towards the operator. Repetition of words and the patience to allow the horse to think and react will be rewarded, and it will be unusual if the horse is not walking and halting when requested to do so in the first lesson.

If the horse does not start again after halting, walk in and quietly start him forward again, repeating the act of moving away until he is continuing on his own again. Carry the whip, but do not use it at this stage.

Should the horse turn in when halted, walk over and put him back on the line of progression; then move away a little, leaving him standing there. Repeat until he stays where he is required to stay. The whip can be used to point towards the horse's shoulder and touch him there if necessary.

Do not ask for another step forward until there has been a semblance of obedience to the correct position at the halt. Should time be running short, ask the horse to walk as you move away, giving him no chance to turn in again. Then halt and walk towards him to finish.

These exercises are carried out to both directions and it may be found that one side is easier than the other. Do not concentrate only on the bad side, but continue to work to both directions until they are basically correct. Do not move forward to trot until the horse will stay out on the 20-metre circle and walk and halt, while remaining on the line of progression and keeping the lunge rein stretched.

This may be tedious work for both horse and operator but if it is not perfected before moving on the operator will be unable to perfect it later.

If side-reins are used they should not be fastened until the horse has completed some warm-up work; during this time they should be clipped together across the neck or to the dee-rings on the saddle. The bridle reins are removed or looped and fastened through the throat-latch. They must not be left to flap and entangle in the horse's legs.

The stirrup irons should be removed or run up the leathers and secured with the stirrup leather. If they are allowed to remain down to accustom the horse to them flapping against his sides, they should be shortened. Heavy stirrup irons should be used in this case so that they do not bounce too much. The only time when it is advantageous to leave the stirrups down is in the early stages of a horse's education. Allowing them to dangle at any other stage can be quite dangerous, as they may get caught up on something and the horse will undoubtedly panic.

The side-reins, when attached, should never be tight. At first they should be quite loose, a hole or two at a time being tightened until the horse can maintain a light contact on the bit while working forward. Side-reins are not designed to force the horse to accept the bit, nor should they be used in this way. The horse is more likely to go forward into his bit if it is light and pleasantly firm, without pulling.

The basis of all education is to get the horse to move forward from his hindquarters up to his bit, and tight side-reins or tight reins prevent the horse from achieving this. Contact is one thing, but pulling or holding tightly is quite another.

Horses being lunged should have leg protection, especially when being taught or if over-excited. Boots and/or bandages should be correctly applied over the vital tissues of the legs, below the knee and down over the fetlock joint. If the operator is inexpert in the application of bandages, boots should be used instead, as bandages incorrectly applied can cause more damage than they prevent.

When lungeing, the operator should loop the lunge rein backwards and forwards through the hands – it must never be wrapped around the hand. When using one rein, the end attached to the headcollar or cavesson should be held in the hand on the side of the direction to which the horse is moving, with the fingers inside the rein (held as when riding) and the loops held in the other hand with the whip, paying out the rein to the 'leading' hand as required, and taking up again when necessary.

The whip should be held in the non-leading hand with lash and handle held behind the operator's back when not in use and turned in the hand to face the horse when in use. The horse should be working between the operator's leading hand and the whip, with the operator facing the horse's inside shoulder.

When teaching a young horse to lunge, he should first be introduced to the whip, which is rubbed all over him until he accepts it without flinching – it is not an instrument of punishment but a tool for teaching. Even horses which are used to being lunged can have a session of whip-rubbing if they show any fear of it.

The whip can now come into play, the operator dropping the lash behind the horse as the commands are given. This is repeated without touching the horse until he moves forward at the required gait.

Once the horse is moving forward at the walk on a 20-metre circle, keeping the lunge rein taut, halting when requested and staying out on the line of progression, he can be asked to move forward at the trot. If he rushes, he should be quietly and repeatedly asked to 'steady' until he either does go more steadily or drops back to walk. In either case, do not react, just keep him moving forward. If he dropped back to walk, repeat the instruction to 'tr. .ot' until he does so.

To change direction, ask the horse to halt, walk out to him and make much of him; then move to his other side and start him again in that direction.

As the horse's understanding improves, the whip can be dropped behind him in a rhythmical movement, keeping him moving forward with a good stride, but not forcing him to move faster. The operator can occa-sionally touch the inside hock with the lash to improve his forward stride or point it towards the shoulder to keep the horse out.

I am very loath to lunge a horse at canter, but if the operator wishes to canter the horse on the lunge, it should not be started until the horse is working in balance and rhythm at both the walk and the trot. The same procedure applies as for trot and the horse given time to understand and obey. Cantering on the lunge is very demanding and it should be kept to a minimum until the horse is able to carry out the movement correctly flexed and with his hindquarters properly engaged.

Assuming the horse has already been taught to lunge, any faults or omissions in his training should be corrected before trying to improve gaits, posture or obedience. Many horses are taught to face the operator or even come in to the centre; if this has been taught it will be difficult to correct.

A horse should be able to halt correctly (straight and square) which he will do of his own volition if the exercise is repeated often enough and the horse understands what is required. He should be able to walk, trot and canter to voice command, and to lengthen and shorten his stride as requested. While working he must remain upright (not leaning in or out) and be correctly flexed (bent towards the inside of the circle along his whole length to the arc of the circle).

He should readily understand voice aids and not be afraid of the whip, but respect it. He should have complete confidence in the operator, without being contemptuous of him, and must obey every command.

Two reins can be used for lungeing, the second rein coming from behind the horse's quarters and attached to the cavesson or headcollar on the offside.

GLOSSARY

This section gives the meaning of words used in this book or among horsemen and women in 'horsey' conversation.

Treatment of diseases is not included as it is expected the horse handler would consult a veterinary surgeon whenever treatment is required. Some ailments are covered in the book *Care of the Australian Horse and Pony* (published by Rigby in 1966).

above the bit: an evasion of the bit when the horse holds his head upwards, sometimes to the extent of being ewe-necked; also referred to as stargazing, when the bit is not in contact with the bars of the mouth. Results from the horse not using correct hindquarters and/or back muscles and from the lack of response to, or use of, the rider's legs.

action: way of going, the way in which the horse moves his legs and propels himself forward, as in 'good' or 'bad action'.

aids: the means by which the rider communicates with the horse. They are head, leg, seat, weight and hands. Artificial aids are whip and spur.

amateur: a person who does not make his living working with horses; e.g. a mounted policeman is not a professional as he makes his living as a peace officer and only rides the horse in the performance of his duty. A stablehand is a professional but the rider of a jumping horse is not, unless he actually gets paid for riding the horse; the horse wins the prizes, not the rider.

azoturia: a disease affecting the muscular and nervous system of the hindquarters, usually caused by not reducing the energy content of the horse's fodder when he is given a day off. Usually affects horses which are in work and is associated with too much energy and insufficient exercise. A very painful condition which requires immediate cessation of work and veterinary treatment. Any attempt to keep the horse moving, such as riding it or walking it back to the stables, could be fatal.

He should either be floated home or left where he broke down. Prevention is better than cure, as once having suffered from this malady it is always a possibility in the future.

balance: a horse is said to be balanced when he moves along in complete control of his own weight and, when ridden, also balances his rider. The distribution of weight will vary according to the work performed – more on the forehand for fast work and more on the hindquarters for slower work. In other words, a horse with self-carriage.

behind the bit: often referred to as overbent, a position where the horse is holding his nose in towards his chest and flexing his neck sharply, in an attempt to escape the bit. Should not be allowed to continue for any length of time, but it is quite a useful exercise in developing back and neck muscles when asked for by the rider.

belly: the correct reference to the outside area of the horse's stomach. The stomach is inside the horse.

below the bit: an evasion by the horse where the head is lowered towards the ground and the horse is leaning on the bit. It should never be allowed to continue and must be corrected by leg and seat aids, not by hand aids.

bit: the instrument placed in the horse's mouth to enable the rider to communicate with the horse through the hands. Also describes the curb bit as used in a double bridle, i.e. bit and bradoon for curb and snaffle bit.

bog spavin: soft swelling on the inside front of the hock joint resulting from inflammation of the bursa and an increase in synovial fluid. Unsightly but seldom causes lameness. Can be treated by draining and therapy but unless the cause is removed, the spavin will return. Often due to faulty conformation (straight hocks) or overwork (fast halts before animal is ready, as in western riding) or nutritional deficiency when young.

bolt: a mindless gallop in which the horse has no

thought but to put distance between himself and the situation that caused him to panic. Running away with a rider (in which the horse quite often indulges if the rider is incompetent or makes unreasonable requests) is not necessarily a bolt. It is impossible to stop a bolter until his mind starts to work again and he may cause severe injury to himself and rider before stopping. A runaway may be stopped at any time and the horse will seldom knowingly indulge in activities which will cause himself pain.

bone spavin: bony enlargement at the front of the hock joint, resulting in limited use of the joint and lameness. Causes are faulty conformation, excessive concussion, nutritional deficiency or hereditary disposition. Can be treated with success leaving only a blemish but can also result in permanent lameness. Spavin can also occur inside the hock joint itself, with no visible swelling, and this is often chronic with little hope of recovery.

bowed tendons: inflammation and enlargement of the flexor tendons at the back of the cannons (front legs). Can be severe enough to rupture the tendon or mild enough to show a slight stretching. Caused by severe strain, as in racing, or faulty conformation; incorrect shoeing can also predispose the animal to this injury.

break: apart from the usual meaning of broken bones it also refers to the act of changing from one gait to another without the rider's permission, as in canter to trot when the rider has intended to remain in canter.

breakdown: when a horse sustains a serious injury and cannot continue with his work. Most often applied to racehorses but can refer to any injury sustained by a horse which prevents his continued use, either temporarily or permanently.

broken knees: a term which is a legacy of the horse and buggy days, meaning injury to the knee of the horse which causes scar tissue to form. A horse with broken knees was rigidly avoided as it suggested the horse could stumble or fall at any time, causing injury to the rider or driver and putting the horse out of action. The injury which caused the broken knees may have injured the small bones of the knee or the tendons which run over the knee. There is no flesh in this area and, once the skin is broken, injury to the mechanics of the knee is almost certain. Today, injuries such as chipped bone fragments in the knee or damaged bursa, giving the horse a permanent big knee, are considered to be more serious than broken knees. Chipped bones need veterinary attention, as the chips moving around within the knee joint can cause further injury. Big knees need attention until they calcify and then may not cause any further trouble, although remaining unsightly.

broken-winded: pulmonary emphysema or heaves are other names given to this malady. It is a serious condition of the lungs often confused with a less serious ailment referred to as 'roaring'. Requires veterinary advice. Can be caused by over-extending an unfit horse or by the dusty condition of fodder.

brushing: a faulty action in which the front and/ or back feet brush against each other. The injury can be low down, between the coronet and fetlock joint, or higher up the leg, depending on the gait and speed of the horse at the time of injury. Caused by poor conformation, incorrect shoeing or predisposition by other injuries. Requires attention for the actual injury and prevention by the use of boots or bandages.

bulldog jaw: see **undershot.**

bursitis: inflammation of the bursa, i.e. the fluid-filled sacs which protect all tendons, ligaments and joints. Appears as a soft swelling wherever undue stress has been applied and the bursa injured. Requires initial inspection by a veterinary surgeon but may remain as a calcified swelling.

cadence: a combination of correct balance and regular rhythm and tempo, resulting in elegance of movement.

canine teeth: also known as tushes, these teeth usually appear in male animals around the age of four years. Occasionally, they also erupt in

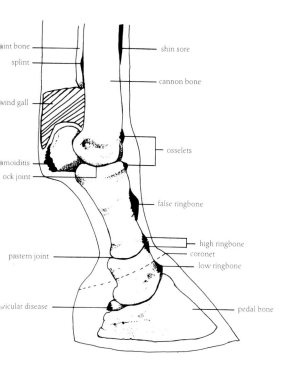

splint bone — — shin sore
splint
— cannon bone
wind gall
— osselets
sesamoiditis
fetlock joint
— false ringbone
— high ringbone
pastern joint — — coronet
— low ringbone
navicular disease
— pedal bone

INJURY SITES IN THE INNER STRUCTURES OF THE FOOT
AND LOWER LEG

females. Sometimes referred to as bridle teeth, they appear in the space between the incisors and molars. Seldom cause trouble once they are established.

capped elbow: soft swelling on the point of the elbow which will respond to treatment if caught early enough and prevented from recurring by the use of a 'shoe boil'. Caused by contact with hard surfaces when the horse lies down or rolls, and aggravated by the end of the front shoe. Can cause lameness. Prevention is better than cure – use deep bedding in stables and deep sand in rolls and yards. Seldom occurs in the paddock.

capped hock: soft swelling on the point of the hock which, if not successfully treated, becomes a fibrous lump and remains as a blemish. Unsightly but not serious and does not often cause lameness. Caused by continual contact with hard ground, kicks or blows, and aggravated by hard surfaces. Can be drained by a veterinary

surgeon but this means the draining must continue periodically. Hock boots, or padded ramps for horses which kick while travelling will help to prevent such an injury.

caps: the young horse's deciduous or milk teeth are referred to as caps when the next set of teeth erupt before the first teeth have been shed. Can be removed with a flick of the thumb in most cases.

cast: refers to a horse which has got down and cannot get up again, such as when trying to roll in a small place, or against a fence, and becoming caught up. Often happens to stabled horses which lie down too close to the wall or with the head underneath the feed bin. If cast for any length of time, internal damage can result. It is often dangerous for the person trying to release the horse, from his flailing hoofs and struggling body.

change diagonal: carried out by the rider at rising trot. Refers to the change of position from one diagonal to the other at the trot by remaining in the saddle for one extra beat, then rising on the new diagonal. Necessary to the correct development of the horse's back muscles by ensuring that both sides receive equal work.

change lead: carried out by the horse. Refers to the moment when the horse changes his leading leg in canter. A simple change is through the trot or walk, and a flying change is within the canter gait without either walking or trotting.

chestnut: colour of the horse's coat; also refers to the calcified formations just above the knees on the inside of the front legs. Occasionally found on the hind legs below the hocks. Believed to be residual toes of the prehistoric horse. Layers can be peeled away with the fingers as they grow.

clench: refers to the downward bend of the horseshoe nails which have secured the shoe to the foot. When the horse needs re-shoeing these clenches become loose and/or risen. Risen clenches can cause injury to the opposite leg tissues by gouging through the skin and flesh.

coarse: refers to the apparent lack of breeding, sometimes due to indiscriminate crossing of breeds. Although the presence of heavy horse blood in animals is sometimes referred to as 'coarse', this is not the original meaning, which inferred out-of-proportion bones, head, etc.

coat: the hair on the horse's hide – not the manufactured protection which is correctly referred to as a 'rug'. A good coat, shiny and lying flat, is an indication of good condition.

cob: English name for a heavily built, middle height horse, capable of carrying weight over a distance without distress. Used also as a description of middle sized saddlery, such as cob size bit and bridle.

cold backed: horses sometimes appear uncomfortable when a saddle is placed on their backs, objecting by humping the back, bucking and/or cow-kicking. Usually the horse settles down without incident if walked around for a few minutes before mounting and after tightening the girth.

cold blood: heavy work horses are said to be cold-blooded as opposed to Thoroughbreds and Arabs which are known as warm bloods. Scientists claim that there is a slight difference in the temperatures of both types but the terms are generally recognised as metaphorical.

combined training: any combination of dressage, showjumping and endurance test, i.e. dressage and showjumping, dressage and endurance, or showjumping and endurance.

condition: the physical appearance of the horse; he is said to be in good or bad condition depending on the appearance of the coat and the fleshing of the frame. Good condition in a racehorse will be different in amount of fleshing from good condition of the hack, but the appearance of the coat would be identical, i.e. bright, shining and lying flat, with a silky texture. Mane and tail hair is also a barometer of condition: it should be bright and shining, not dull and lifeless.

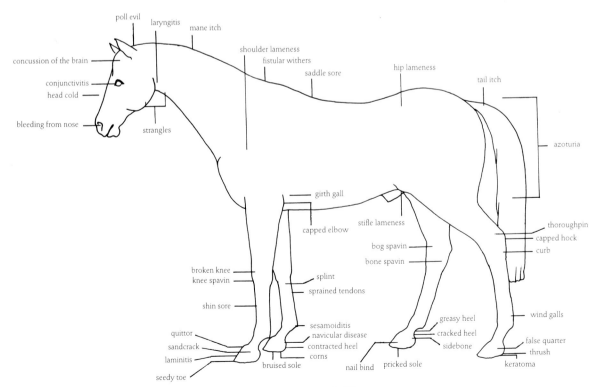

SITES OF AILMENTS

conformation: the physical build of the horse – often spelt incorrectly with an 'i' as confirmation.

conjunctivitis: inflammation of the membrane on the inside of the eyelids, the third eyelid and the cornea. Eyes become bloodshot and a watery discharge is noticed; can become acute, when discharge is thicker and stickier. Contagious in some cases. This is a symptom of several diseases, but can also be caused by dust, pollen, etc. Requires treatment as soon as discovered. Often alleviated by bathing in solutions suitable to the human eye. Veterinary surgeon will supply soothing eye ointments.

contracted heel: often the result of poor conformation (upright pasterns) but can also be caused by incorrect shoeing. If the result of poor shoeing, it is easily corrected by going to a more knowledgeable farrier who will remove the shoes, allow the toes to grow a little and cut back the heels to widen the foot again. If congenital, the farrier can still help but cannot be expected to alter drastically the conformation of the foot.

corns: caused by poor workmanship by the farrier, or neglectful owner. If shoes are not removed as the foot grows, every 6-8 weeks and sometimes more often, the shoe is carried forward by the growth of the toes. This causes the heel of the shoe to press on the sole itself and form a bruise. A stone bruise has the same effect and both require attention to alleviate the pressure. If necessary, apply healing dressings.

counter canter: a horse is said to be counter cantering when he is moving to the right but is on the left lead, and vice versa. When the rider has asked for this lead it is correct, but if the horse moves himself on to the counter (or contra) lead he must be stopped and restarted. When requested, it is a suppling exercise, when not requested it is disobedience on the part of the horse. Not to be confused with disunited.

curb: a hard enlargement of the ligament, the tendon sheath, or the skin below the hock. Begins as an inflammation but thickens into scar tissue. Caused by kicks, blows or conformational defects such as cow hocks or sickle hocks.

May cause temporary or permanent lameness, depending on tissues involved.

diaphragm: the chest cavity, defined by the ribs, the breast-bone (sternum) and the chest. Must be spacious to allow for lung expansion and heart room.

dishing: throwing one or both front feet out to the side instead of moving them straight ahead. Sometimes seen at all three gaits but often obvious only in the more active gaits or when the horse is unbalanced. Can be improved or corrected by a talented farrier.

disunited: the act of cantering on one lead with the forelegs and the opposite lead with the hind legs. Always incorrect and should not be confused with the counter canter. A horse will often become disunited while trying to carry out an exercise or movement when off balance. Good riders should be able to recognise this action by feel and correct it immediately.

dominant: all body tissues are developed from hereditary genes. These are grouped into 'dominant' and 'recessive' genes. Dominant genes show up in the first generation progeny or not at all.

dressage: (pronounced 'dress-arge'); specialised training of the horse. "Educating the horse to understand the international method of communication between rider and horse to a state where the horse is keen and obedient." (FEI definition). Requires obedience, balance, suppleness and rhythm in all movements under a rider.

education: teaching the horse what is required of him as opposed to merely demanding blind obedience.

EFA : Equestrian Federation of Australia. The governing body for all Australian and international competitions in dressage, showjumping and eventing. Also co-ordinating body for many other equestrian activities such as instructor training, listing judges, and registering competitive horses. Each State and Territory has a branch which is responsible to the Federal body.

engaged: a term referring to the activity of the hind legs of the horse. Involving the hip, stifle and hock joints, it allows the hindquarters to accept more weight from the forehand and increase the forward impulsion.

eventing: refers to a combination of activities in one competition, including dressage, endurance and showjumping; known as one-day and three-day events.

ewe neck: a neck which appears to have been put on upside down; a conformation defect or acquired by incorrect use of back muscles.

exercise: the act of working a horse to get him fit and keep him fit and well, a necessary daily chore in any preparation for sport or competition. Also necessary if a horse is stabled, even if not being prepared for anything in particular.

farrier: person who shoes the horse. May be a qualified blacksmith or involved only in putting shoes on the horse. A farrier becomes expert only after many years of training and practical shoeing.

favour: a horse which is slightly lame in one leg is said to favour that leg, i.e. keep weight off it as much as possible, and is therefore lame.

FEI: Federation Equestre Internationale. The body responsible for devising the rules and applying them to all international and official national competitions in dressage, showjumping and endurance tests. It is also involved in other international equestrian activities such as horse driving.

fettle: an old-fashioned word meaning condition of the horse. It is inferred that the horse is in poor condition if it is not in good fettle.

fistula: a suppurating, inflammatory condition which often occurs at the poll or withers. Poll evil is usually caused by a blow to the head, and fistulous withers by pressure on the backbone by the head of the saddle or from an ill-fitting rug. Both conditions require immediate treatment by a veterinary surgeon.

fodder: the food which the horse consumes.

forehand: from the girth area forward of the horse.

forging: hitting the sole of the front feet with the toe of the hind feet. When the horse is shod this produces a continual clicking sound. Horses ridden forward beyond their capacity, or when unbalanced, will forge and can injure themselves if they accidentally hit the flesh of the leg instead of the foot. This injury is commonly known as an over-reach.

founder: see **laminitis.**

Galloway: once the name of a breed of British pony. Has now become a reference to size and type in Australia. Galloway classes range from 14-15 hands.

girth galls: sores or lacerations caused by friction of the girth. Often the result of unclean horse or girth, girth too tight or too loose, or particularly sensitive skin. Some horses which are thin-skinned are prone to galling when they first start to work, or when they come back into work after a rest, but will harden up over a period of time. Applying methylated spirits to the area in moderation (not when the skin is broken) will help to harden the skin.

greasy heel: a skin irritation which begins in the heel area but which can travel up the leg and eventually invade the whole body if neglected. Infection enters the tissues in unclean or cold damp conditions. Immediate cleansing of the affected areas and application of soothing antiseptic ointment will arrest the infection but the horse must be removed to clean, dry quarters. Hosing mud off a hot animal with cold water forces the bacteria from the mud into the open pores, then the pores contract with the cold water and an infection is inevitable. Allow mud to dry, then brush off.

hack: the dictionary definition, 'a horse kept for hire; a worn out horse' is very wide of the meaning of the present-day hack. A show hack is a well-conformed, well-educated, beautiful animal of 15 hands and over. A Galloway hack is between 14 and 15 hands and a pony hack is usually under 14 hands, although it can be up to 14.2 in some pony breed classes.

hands: a horse's height is quoted in hands which, in imperial units, was 4 inches, the average width of a man's hand. This was the way a horse was usually measured before measuring sticks were universally available. Size is still stated in hands but a hand is now 10.2 cm and each point is 25.5 mm, i.e. 14.2 hands is 193.8 cm. Measurement taken at highest point of withers.

hard feed: the feed provided by man as opposed to that obtained by the natural act of grazing. Includes chaff, bran, oats, barley, etc.

Haute Ecole: High School training, the art of riding in its highest form. Divided into two parts: 'airs above the ground' and 'airs on the ground'. The most famous establishment of the exponent of the art is the Spanish Riding School of Vienna.

herring-gutted: poor conformation where the belly of the horse narrows dramatically and runs up towards the hind legs, resulting in lack of room for many vital organs. Sometimes a horse in very poor condition may appear herring-gutted, as his stomach has shrunk inside, but proves not to be so when his condition improves.

high blowing: a rhythmic snorting sound produced by some horses when exhaling during work. It is considered by many old grooms that high blowing suggests a really good horse. Distinguishable from broken-winded or roaring by the horse's relaxed demeanour.

hindquarters: the back end of the horse from the point of the hip backwards, but often indicates the whole of the body behind the saddle.

hors concours: non-competitive. Increasingly used in equestrian competition where it acknowledges that the partnership involved is taking part in the competition for experience only, and will not be considered for a prize regardless of the result.

impulsion: the horse's natural desire to go forward, often discouraged by the early work in breaking and training and must be regained as education proceeds. Without rhythm and balance the horse cannot produce sufficient impulsion to be able to carry out the requests of the rider. Impulsion is obtained by riding the horse **forward,** but fast is not forward.

in hand: a horse led from the ground.

jog and jig: when a horse insists on attempting to trot instead of walking as required he is said to be jogging. A horse that jigs is usually uneducated or has an inexpert rider. When jigging, the horse may combine the walk, trot and canter, taking a few steps of each, throwing his head around at the same time. A horse may be allowed to jog for some distance on a lengthy journey, but it should never be allowed to jig. Both are tiring to the rider.

joint capsule: the membrane that encloses, protects and feeds the tissue within the joint.

laminitis: a fever of the feet usually caused by trauma – over-eating (by breaking into the feed store), spring grass eaten too greedily (especially by small ponies) or galloping on hard surfaces. Other causes of laminitis include trauma during foaling, etc. but these are problems which arise without warning. The first three can be prevented by good management and should be dealt with immediately they occur. In lush spring grass conditions, small ponies and any other grossly fat equine should be locked away for hours or days at a time, with only small amounts of hay and plenty of water. Always requires the attention of a veterinary surgeon once developed.

leading leg: the front leg that appears to be taking the lead in canter is referred to as the leading leg, although in fact it is the last leg to move in the canter stride. The horse should always be asked to lead correctly unless a counter canter is requested in a particular exercise. A disunited canter should never be allowed.

navicular disease: injury or disease of the navicular bone deep within the foot. Horse gradually becomes chronically lame. Needs the services of a veterinary surgeon to diagnose and treat.

nearside: the left-hand side of the horse, traditionally the side from which most handling is done, although the horse should also be handled from the offside from time to time so that he is not afraid of anything that may happen on that side. The horse is invariably afraid of the unfamiliar.

novelty events: games such as musical chairs, flag and barrel, barrel racing, etc. carried out on horseback. Some horses become champions at this type of event and win continually.

offside: the right-hand side of the horse.

on the bit: when the horse is maintaining contact with the rider's hands and his whole frame is supple and ready to carry out the bidding of the rider. The hindquarters must be engaged, neck flexed at the poll and nose held just beyond the vertical with a soft lower jaw. To be on the bit requires a noticeable state of readiness to move on when requested.

osselets: bony outgrowths resulting from inflammation of the periosteum on the surface of the fetlock joints. Unless new bone formation restricts the joint it is unsightly but not serious. Lameness appears when they are forming and may continue if joints are affected. Often caused by too-straight pasterns or other conformational defects which place more strain on the areas than is warranted.

over at the knee: congenital, or acquired as a foal when legs must be bent to enable the foal to reach the grass. If congenital, the fault will remain, but if acquired, will improve as the foal gains strength and size.

over-reach: the act of striking the heel of the front hoof with the toe of the hind hoof. This often causes a deep painful gash. Can be caused by incorrect shoeing or incorrectly applied protective boots. See also **forging.**

overshot: also referred to as parrot mouth. Congenital conformation, or a defect of the jaw in which the incisor teeth of the upper jaw overshoot those of the lower jaw. Many degrees of parrot mouth are found, although some need close inspection to find them. In its chronic form it prevents the horse from grazing and, if not hand fed, the horse would probably die or live in a less than satisfactory condition. Horses with any form of this affliction should not be used for breeding as it is recessively inheritable.

over the bit: or overbending, where the horse brings his nose into his chest and leans down on the bit and travels along in that position. Develops from behind the bit if allowed to continue in that form and often caused by too strong hands.

paces: the gaits of the horse, often used to dif-ferentiate between the length of stride within the gait; as, collected, working, medium and extended paces within the walk, trot and canter gaits.

parrot mouth: see **overshot.**

passage (pronounced 'pass-arge'): "This is a measured, very collected, very elevated and very cadenced trot" (FEI definition). Impossible to perform correctly unless the horse is fully collected, with self-carriage and maximum impulsion. Often seen being performed in the paddock by young horses who are showing off to each other.

pharyngitis: inflammation of the pharynx, or sore throat. Needs veterinary attention and the horse must stop work until healthy again.

piaffe: "A highly measured, collected, elevated and cadenced trot on the spot" (FEI definition). As in the passage, the horse must be fully collected, with self-carriage and maximum impulsion.

pirouette: "A circle executed on two tracks, with a radius equal to the length of the horse, the forehand moving round the haunches" (FEI definition). Opposite to the turn-on-the-forehand, it can also be described as a turn on the hindquarters. A half-pirouette is a half-circle also executed on two tracks. Usually performed at a walk or the canter, but can also be performed at piaffe.

plaiting: has two meanings. First, the braiding of the mane and tail; secondly, the crossing of the front legs in front of each other while supposedly moving on a straight line. Usually caused by poor conformation such as pigeon toes or incorrect shoeing. Both causes can be corrected by a good farrier. Also referred to as 'paddling'.

pointing: the act of resting a front leg in front of the body, often the first indication of soreness. The horse often rests a hind leg, but seldom rests a front one unless there is some kind of soreness or injury.

points: the collective name given to all outward parts of the horse. They are identified on a chart and should be learned off by heart by all horsemen and women.

presence: the indefinable quality or class of the potential champion, a combination of correct conformation, rhythm, balance and cadence in movement.

professional: in the equestrian sense, a very complex term which usually refers to one whose principal means of livelihood is obtained by working with horses, or who receives a substantial sum of money for his association with horses. E.g. racehorse trainers, jockeys and riding instructors are professionals. A person who rides a horse for another person without payment and wins substantial prize money (except in rider class) is not considered a professional on that score alone, as the horse is the prizewinner. If, however, this money is the rider's sole means of support, he might still be considered a professional. The FEI and EFA are the authorities which rule on this classification.

quarters: the horse has two kinds of quarters, the forequarters and the hindquarters of his body, and the left and right quarters of his hoofs.

quittor: a sore or wound which arises at the coronet. Very painful and almost always causes lameness, the coronet being equivalent to the 'quick' of the fingers and toes of the human. Occasionally, is the result of a deep-seated injury which breaks out at the coronet. In this case the original injury must be found and cured. Unless completely cured it can become the seat of a fistula.

recessive: as opposed to dominant genes. Recessive genes may miss several generations and appear at any time in the future.

refuse: when a horse stops in front of an obstacle he was supposed to jump, he is said to have refused.

respiration: the art of breathing, intake and expelling of the breath into and out of the lungs. When counting the respirations, inhalation and expiration are counted as one.

rhythm: the regularity of the gait, in which each leg takes the same amount of time to cover the same distance, raising each leg exactly the same height.

rig: or cryptorchid – horse with only one descended testicle or one which has had one testicle removed, leaving the other intact but possibly retained within the scrotum. A responsible veterinary surgeon will refuse to geld a horse with a retained testicle unless he is allowed to perform an operation to remove the internal testicle. It is illegal to sell a rig without informing the purchaser of the problem and, if it is later found that the horse is a rig, the original owner must take the horse back and refund the purchase price if requested to do so.

ringbone: ossification of the pastern bones, due to stress or injury. Poor conformation and/or hereditary genes may predispose the horse to ringbone. High ringbone is found on the upper pastern bone and low ringbone on the lower pastern bone. Low ringbone is usually the most traumatic as it involves the very vulnerable coronet. Both need veterinary consultation.

roaring: a noise made by the horse when asked to work hard or fast. It is caused by partial paralysis of the vocal cords in the larynx. Often incorrectly referred to as broken-winded. Can be alleviated by an operation known as a 'hobday', or by other more modern methods.

Salvation Jane (Paterson's Curse): a noxious weed which has recently been found to cause permanent damage to the liver of some animals, including horses. It has a blue flower and broad leaves; very difficult to eradicate because it is propagated by both seeds and roots. If not kept in check it takes over whole areas and prevents the growth of all grasses.

sandcrack: a crack which begins at the coronet and extends downwards towards the ground. Often results from a quittor or other injury to the coronet. Must be treated professionally by both a veterinary surgeon and a farrier. Without treatment, this crack tends to continue to extend down the hoof with the movement of the horse. Often painful and causes lameness.

schooling: a term often used by racehorse trainers to indicate teaching hurdle-jumping and steeple-chase horses. Also refers to teaching the horse the aids.

seedy toe: separation of the hoof from the ground upwards, often caused by working unshod horses over rocky ground or by stone-bruise injuries. Needs farrier's attention and possibly that of the veterinary surgeon.

self-carriage: the ability of the horse to carry his own and the rider's weight distributed over all four legs. A horse which is said to be 'on the forehand' does not have self-carriage nor does the horse which moves with a ewe neck, or in a star-gazing position.

sesamoiditis: inflammation of the sesamoid bones caused by stress through working young or unfit horses too hard, or by injury. Causes lameness but easily repaired by a short rest unless the sesamoid bone/s are cracked or broken, in which case healing will take longer. Excessive lungeing of young unformed bones can spread the sesamoids, in which case they will not return to their original position.

sidebone: ossification of the lateral cartilage of the foot, resulting in impaired flexibility. There is often a genetic predisposition to this affliction particularly in heavy horses.

slab-sided: where the ribs do not swell outwards sufficiently, giving the horse the appearance of completely flat sides. Leaves insufficient room for heart and lungs, therefore is not desirable conformation.

slipped stifle: the stifle is equivalent to the human knee, so a slipped stifle corresponds to a displaced cartilage in the knee. Once having slipped, the horse is predisposed to this injury unless given a long rest in restricted quarters. Even then the injury may recur at any time. Unlike the human knee the stifle cannot be strapped.

sound: a horse with no obvious defects in wind or limb and able to carry out the tasks required of him is said to be sound. However, a horse which is sound for work is not necessarily sound for breeding, and vice versa. It is now the practice to declare the horse 'suitable for the purpose' rather than sound.

spavin: see **bog spavin** and **bone spavin**.

speedy cutting: hitting the hind leg on the pastern or fetlock with the toe of the forefoot. Caused by a lack of co-ordination in movement, the hind leg moving more quickly than the front leg can move out of the way.

splints: calcification or bony growth on the inside of the leg usually involving the cannon and the splint bones. Mostly confined to the front leg but occasionally seen on a hind leg as a result of injury. Usually caused by trauma, but can be the result of injury such as when kicked, slipping or jumping. Often painful when forming but once formed causes few problems unless it is fouling a joint. The splint is thrown up to strengthen the leg and as such is not the dreaded happening that many horsemen believe; should be recognised as a blemish rather than unsoundness.

stargazing: a horse above the bit; when the nose is poked out and held too high. Means that the neck and back muscles are being used incorrectly. It is often the fault of the rider's too strong hands, or asking too much from the back muscles before they are strong enough to support the neck muscles correctly.

stone bruise: a bruise of the inner, sensitive tissues of the feet due to the horse standing on a sharp obstacle with all his weight. Flat-footed horses are more prone to this condition than horses with good foot formation.

string halt: an involuntary sharp lifting of a particular hind leg which is then set down with extra force. Believed to be a nervous disease and difficult, if not impossible, to cure.

substance: the build of the horse. A horse which is expected to carry heavy weights must show more substance than one which is expected to carry only light weight.

supple: as opposed to being stiff. Suppleness is necessary for most activities particularly dressage, jumping and sporting events.

swan-necked: a horse which is flexed in the centre of the neck rather than at the poll. It is an indication that the back muscles are not being used correctly.

sway-backed: a conformational defect where

the back in front of the loins dips down and rises again to the withers, instead of remaining level then rising a little at the withers. Sometimes congenital but can be caused by working the young horse too hard, or with a heavy rider, before the bones are mature (also referred to as 'swampy').

synovial fluid: the fluid which protects the joints and is contained in the joint capsule.

tack: items of saddlery used in working with horses.

temperature: the temperature of the horse's body should be 100°F or 38°C. All horsemen and women should have a thermometer on hand, as temperature is a very reliable guide to health or sickness in the horse. It is taken in the anus.

tempo: when all four legs take the same length of stride and the same time to move, the horse is said to move in even tempo.

thoroughpin: a soft fluid-filled enlargement in the hollow above the hock. The swelling can be pushed backwards and forwards through this hollow with the fingers. Caused by strain on the flexor tendon which allows synovial fluid to escape into the hollow. Rarely causes lameness but will leave a blemish.

thrush: a disease of the frog resulting from dirty stables or continual standing in wet, muddy conditions. Easily prevented by good husbandry and not serious unless neglected, when the frog will rot away.

tied up: a lesser form of azoturia where the horse appears stiff and disinclined to stretch out. Exercise and feeding must be adjusted and the horse should be given light work until this has been corrected.

transitions: changes of gait and changes within the gaits. In fact, any change up or down in the movements of the horse.

tushes: sometimes called bridle teeth or canines. See **canine teeth.**

undershot: or bulldog jaw, the opposite defect to overshot or parrot mouth. A condition which is congenital and recessively inheritable and has all the same problems as the overshot mouth.

unsound: the opposite to sound – when a horse is not suitable by lameness, illness or conformation for the tasks required of him.

volte: a small circle of 6-metre diameter. If larger, the description is 'circle', stating the size.

wall eye: an eye which shows only the cornea in colour and in some cases this has an opaque appearance. The sclera round the eye is completely white. Not to be confused with showing the white of the eye.

white of the eye: where the normal eye colour is shown but a white circle can be seen around it. A horse often shows the white of the eye when frightened or angry, but the term is used to describe a horse which habitually shows the white of the eye.

wind galls: soft swellings of the bursa sac located at the fetlock joints. Results from excessive speed, working on hard ground or jumping horses when unfit. Usually painless and seldom causes lameness. Considered to be a blemish rather than an unsoundness.

wolf teeth: small residual teeth which erupt in front of the molars. Usually a source of trouble and should be removed as soon as possible.

Riding a corner correctly. The horse is slightly behind the bit but otherwise the movement is being performed correctly. Photograph by S. Sobey.

INDEX

Italic numerals refer to an illustration

above the bit 74, *75, 80*
Achilles heel 45
Advanced test 142
aids 96-100, 126, 128, 137, 140; *see also* body
    language
    for canter 112-3
        change of lead, flying 114-5
        change of lead, simple 114
        circles 117-8
        collection 109-10
        contact 104-5
        corners 116-7
        counter canter 113-4
        downward transitions 105
        figures-of-eight 118-9
        flexion 105-6
        forward movements 110
        gallop 115
        half-halt 103
        half-pass 125
        halt from canter or gallop 104
        halt from trot 104
        halt from walk 103-4
        impulsion 106, 109
        lateral movements 119
        leg-yields 120-2
        on the bit 109
        rein-back 115-6
        renvers 124-5
        serpentines 118-9
        shoulder-in 122-3
        travers 124
        trot 111-2
        turn-on-the-forehand 119-20
        turn on the hindquarters 123-4
        turns and tracks 117
        volte 119
        walk 110-1
        walk on long rein 111
aids, how to apply them 100-3
    back and seat 101
    hands 101-2
    legs 100-1
    reins 102
    weight 101
alimentary canal 27, 30, 32
anabolic steroids 21
anticipation 100, 129, 131, 137
anxiety 127, 144, 154, 155
Appaloosa 46
approaching a horse 149
Arab 10, 11, 20, 46, 49, 50
area, suitable for education 127
arena, dressage 127, 134, *136, 137*
artificial aids 97
atlas, *see* poll
attention span 56, 127, 128
autonomic nervous system *25, 26*
azoturia 129

back 48, 50, 73, 75
    muscles, development of 25, 69, 70, 73, 75,
        131, 135

backbone 19, 21-2, 26, 47, 73
bad manners 56
balance 69, *79,* 80, 81, 93
    horse's point of 69, 80, 144
    of horse 66, 68, 70, 73, 80, 126
        helped by rider 69, 79
        loss of 74, 91
    of rider 69, 79, 82, 83, 91, 144
    when jumping 94-5, 144, 147
ball and socket joint 19, *20*
bandages 156, 159
bars of the mouth 29
base narrow 40, *43,* 44
base wide 40, *43,* 44
behind the bit 74-5, *75*
below the bit 74, *75*
bench knees (off-set cannons) 40, *40*
binocular vision 57
bit 29, 30, 46, 75
    correct fitting 59, 159
biting 10, 149, 150
bleeding 34
body conformation 22, 37-50, 143
body language (aids) 96-7
    hands 97-8, 99
    head 97
    legs 97, *97,* 99
    seat and back 97, 99
    spurs 97, *97,* 98
    voice 98
    weight 97, 99
    whip 97, 98, *98*
    see also aids
bolting 152
bone marrow 15
bones, functions of 15, *15,* 24
bone structure 14-23, *23,* 24, 38-9
boots (for horses) 156, 159
bowed hocks *43, 43*
breaking in 86, 126
breeching rope 151, 152, 155
bridle, fitting correctly 59
broken-mouth snaffle 59
bronchitis 33
brushing (injury to legs) 48
bucked shins, *see* shin soreness
bulldog jaw (undershot) 45
bullring 144

caecum *27,* 31-2
calf knee 40, *40*
canine (bridle) teeth 29-30
cannon bone *14, 16, 19,* 38, 39, 40, 41
    off-set, *see* bench knees
canter 37, 62, 64, *64,* 133, 140
    aids for 112-3
    collected 66, *67, 89*
    extended 66, *67*
    medium 66, *67, 77*
    rider's position *83,* 91
    sequence of footfalls *63*
    three-time beat 101
    working 66, *67*

cantle 80, 81
capped elbow 16
capped hock 16
cat-hammed, *see* cut-up behind
cavalletti 127, 145, 146, 147
cavesson 157, 159, 160
change of lead
    flying 114-5, 140, 141, 142
    simple 114, 140, 141, *141*
changing leads over fence 147, 148
changing muscle reaction 84-5
character traits, of horse 51
children, young 149-50, 152, 153
circle 73, 74, 75, 102, 137, 140
    aids for 117-8
    correct working figure *134*
    definition 103
    in horse's natural state 70, 79-80
    points of *140*
    to left *84*
    to right *84*
circular movements, aids for 116-9
circulation 26, 32, 34, 38, 128
circulatory system 24, *33,* 34
    function of plantar cushion 38
claustrophobia 154
clipping 156
colic 31-2
collection 61, 74, 75-6, *99, 134,* 137
    aids for 109-10
    lowering of hindquarters *69*
combination fence 147
concentration 128, 129
concussion 22, 34
conformation, good and bad
    forelegs from front *40*
    forelegs from side *40*
    hindquarters from behind *43*
    hindquarters from side *44*
conformation, *see* body conformation
contact 104-5, 131, 133, 159
corners 75, 101, 131, 133, 138
    aids for 116-7
coronet *14, 19,* 37, 38
coughing 129
counter canter 102, 138, 140
    aids for 113-4
cow hocks *43, 43*
crib-biting 33
croup *14,* 49, 50, 69
curves, negotiating *53,* 74, 101, *134*
cut-up behind 44, 49

demi-pirouette, *see* turn on the hindquarters
dental caps 29
desire to please 52, 56, 96, 100, 129
diagonal, changing of 88, 91, 133
diary, teaching 128, 134, 138
diet, change in 32, 129
digestion 27, 28, 30, 128
digestive system 24, *27,* 27-32
direction, changes of 135, 147
    correct working figure *134*

direct rein aids 102, 126
discipline 56, 126, 157
dislocation 19
drenching 30-1
dressage 26, 87, 91, 99-100, 141
    definition 7-8
    paces within the gaits 66
dressage tests 90, 98
    Preliminary 136
    Novice 138
    Elementary 141-2
    Medium 142
    Advanced 142
drugs 21, 154

ears 45, 58
education 126-142
    stages of 126
    aims of early stage 133
elbow joint 14, 19
Elementary test 137, 142
    requirements 141-2
energy cycle 128, 129
epiphysis 19, 20-2, 23
Equus przewalskii 10, 13, 71
ergot 14, 39
eventing 142
evolution, of horse 9, 9-11, 10
ewe neck 47, 50, 131
exercise 128
    gymnastic 134
    warming up 128, 129, 134, 135
eyes 46, 56-7

faeces 32
fair play, sense of 52
fall by rider, horse's reaction to 52, 55, 153
falls, by horse 93, 144
farrier 36, 37, 150, 156
fear of the unknown 51, 52
feeding, how to arrange safely 153
feet, stepping on 152-3
fetlock 14, 19, 38-9, 41, 159
figures-of-eight 118-9
fistula 16
flexion 74, 75, 131, 138
    aids for 105-6
    extent of foreleg 42
    extent of hind leg 49
    left 76, 78
    right 76, 78
float 151, 155
    driving 155
    riding in 155
    training 154-6
floating (filing) the teeth 29
floating seat, see forward seat
foal 20, 40, 48
foot 37, 39
    evolution of 9, 10
foreleg flexion, extent of 42
foreleg, lower, structure of 39
forward (floating) seat 94-5, 144

forward movement 97, 102
    aids for 110
frame (outline), of horse 101, 131
    extending 62, 74
    shortening 70, 74
frog 34, 37, 37-8

gaits 60-7, 69, 136, 137
    different forms of 87
    paces 66
    timing 60
gallop 53, 62, 64, 66, 131
    aids for 115
    rider's position 92
gas build-up 32
gaskin 14, 44
ginglymoid joint 19, 20, 21, 44
girthing up 150-1
gliding joint 19, 21, 22, 23
goose rump 49, 50
grass seeds, in mouth 30
grid of jumps 147, 148
grip 93, 100
grooming 156
growth, of horse 20-3

half-circle 118, 119, 140
    correct working figure 134
half-halt 76, 86, 102, 131, 137
    aids for 103
half-pass 125, 142
half-pirouette, see turn on the hindquarters
halt 65, 73, 86, 130-1, 137, 142
    from canter or gallop 104
    from trot 57, 65, 104
    from walk 66, 103-4
hands, as riding aid 97-8, 99
Haute Ecole 142
head 45-7
    carriage of 78, 131
head and neck, structure of 46-7, 47
headcollar 151, 153, 157, 159, 160
head-shy 150
hearing 57-8
heart (cardiac muscle) 24, 34
heart recovery rate 72, 130
high-blowing 129
hind leg flexion, extent of 49
hindquarters 49-50
    engagement of 137, 160
    lowering of, in collection 69
    muscles, development of 69, 70
hinge joint 19, 19, 20, 44
hipbone (point of hip) 14
    damage to 44, 45
hip joint 19, 44, 74
hitting a fence 144
hobbles 155
hocks 14, 16, 19, 21, 43-4, 45, 74
    bowed 43, 43
    cow 43, 43
    engagement of 43
    sickle 43

hoof 37, 38
    structure of (fore) 38
horse
    as athlete 55-6, 60, 143
    as farm worker 11, 11, 12
    as transport 11-2
horse behaviour, understanding it 51-9
horse, in straight position 68
hosing out the mouth 30

impulsion 95, 97, 137, 138, 147
    aids for 106, 109
incisor teeth 29
independence of rider's muscles 85, 100
inexpert rider 80, 80, 96, 108
intelligence 52, 55
intestines 27, 27-8, 31, 32

jealousy 154
joints 16-9, 19, 129
    giving way 129
jumping 37, 43, 44, 45, 49, 143-8; see also
        showjumping
    horse initiative needed 100
    lessons 126, 140, 145-8
    materials needed 145
    positions 146
    rider's position 94-5

kicking 10, 149, 151, 155
knee 22, 23, 39-40, 41, 45
    back at the knee (calf knee) 40, 40
    bench knees 40, 40
    knock knees 40
    over at the knee 40, 40
    problems 39, 41
    tied in below the knee 40

lactic acid 128-9
lameness 61
lampas (inflammation of palate) 30
lateral flexion 42, 75
lateral movement 97, 119, 138
leading a horse 151, 152, 158
learning ability 56, 126
learning rate 55
leg aids 97, 97, 99, 100-1, 126
leg bones 22-3
    lower 19
    upper 20
leg protection 156, 159
legs 37-45
    as aid 83
    muscles, development of 70
leg tissue 15, 40, 135, 159
leg-yields 120-2, 135-6
lengthening the stride 25
lesson plans 128
lessons
    length of 129, 133, 134, 138, 145, 146
    variety in 138, 146-7, 148
ligaments 19, 41
    damage to 24

load carrying 68, 127
loins 48-9, 80
long-low outline 69, *69, 77,* 130, 131, 134
　　incorrect *70*
lop ears 45
lumbar vertebra *22*
lungeing 22, 74, 85, 157-60
　　aims of 157
　　area required 157
　　cavesson 157, 159
　　faults 157-8
　　roller 157
　　whip 157, 158, 159, 160
lunge rein 157, 159, 160
lungs 33, *33*
　　efficiency of 33
luxation 19, 44

Mairinger, Franz 126
mandible (jaw) *14, 16,* 19
materials, for jumping 145
maturation 20-3
Medium test 142
memory 26, 55, 126, 144
monocular vision 57
mouth, injuries to 27, 30-1
movements, of horse 60
moving with the horse 79, 80, 87
　　when jumping 94
mullen-mouth snaffle 59
muscles 24-6, 50, 128
　　damage to 45
　　of propulsion ('pulley belts') 76, *76,* 78, 86,
　　　　87, *87*
　　soreness of 141
muscular system 24-6, 50

navicular bone *16, 19,* 22, 38
navicular disease 38
neck 46, 47, 75
　　muscles, development of 70, 131
nervous disorders 26
nervous rider 128
nervous state, of horse 127
　　assessed by ear movements 58
nervous system *25,* 26
nose blowing 129
not tracking up *94*
Novice test 137, 145
　　requirements 138
nutrition 27, 28, 42

oesophagus 27
one-sidedness 84, 133
on the bit 59, 74, 75, *75, 76,* 78, *99*
　　aids for 109
on the forehand 69, *73,* 80
osseous system 14-23
ossification 38
overbent, *see* behind the bit

pace (special trot) 66
paces (within gaits) 66
paddling, *see* plaiting
paddock
　　catching horse in 153
　　how to enter 151
　　turning horses into 153
pain, low tolerance to 26
panniculus muscle 25, 59, 86
parrot mouth (overshot) 46
passage 103
pastern bones *14, 16, 19,* 38-9
pecking order *6,* 56, *56,* 153, 157
pedal bone *16, 19,* 38
pelvis *20,* 44
periosteum *19,* 22-3, 40
peritonitis 32
piaffe 103
pigeon toes *41*
　　to correct *35, 36*
pirouette 123-4
plaiting (of feet) 48
plantar cushion 37, 38
pleurisy 33
points of the horse *14*
poll *14,* 47, 69, 76
　　evil 16
polo 26, 73, 96, 126
pommel 81, *81, 95*
positive thinking 85
Preliminary test 137, 138
　　requirements 136
problems, of riders
　　collapsed hip 92, *94*
　　collapsed rounded waist 92
　　head tilted to one side 92
　　looking down 92
　　rounded or collapsed shoulders 92, *94*
　　stiff back 92
propulsion 68, 76, *76,* 78
Przewalski horses 10, *13, 71*
psychology, of horse 24, 51-9, 149

quarter-circles, *see* corners

rearing 10, 149, 151
rearing bit 151
refusal (to jump) 51, 143, 146, 148
rein aids 102
rein-back *64,* 64-5, *73,* 102, 126, 138, 141
　　aids for 115-6
　　incorrect *85*
rein of opposition 102
reins 86, 101-2
related fence 147, 148
relaxation 130, 138, 142
renvers 124-5, 126, 138
respiratory rate 34, *72,* 130
respiratory system 24, 32-4, *33*
retching 154
rewarding the horse 58
ribs 15, *16,* 26, 73, 75
rider, good, characteristics of 51

rider's position 79, 80, 81-2, 83, *86, 87, 107*
　　ankle 93
　　arms 85-6, 93
　　hands 85, 86, 93-4
　　head 92
　　heels and toes 83, 93
　　knee 93
　　legs 81-2, 85, 86
　　seat 80, 83
　　shoulders 81, 86, 87, 92
　　at canter *83*
　　body in three sections 92-3, *93*
　　faults 83, *83,* 85, 86, 92, 93, *94, 95*
　　on jumping horse 94-5
ringbone 38, 39
rising trot 83, *83, 85,* 87, 88, 133
roach back 48, 49

sacrum *16,* 19, *21,* 49
saddle 11, 48, 80-1, *82,* 93
　　good flat-work shape *82*
　　problems *81*
saddling 48, 150
safety 149-56
salivary glands 27, *27*
scapula 135
scrambling 156
seat and back aids 97, 99, 101, 126
seat, of rider 80, 81, 83, 87, 92
　　incorrect *91*
　　when jumping 95
seed spikes, embedded in mouth 30
self-carriage 129, 134
self-defence 12, 144, 149, 151
　　natural instinct of horse to flee 10, 51, 79,
　　　　143, 152
serpentine loops 102, 134, 137
　　aids for 118-9
　　correct working figure *134*
sesamoid bones *19,* 22
shin soreness 23, 40
shoulder 19, 41-2
　　injury to 45
　　point of *14,* 41-2
shoulder-in 122-3, 126, 138
showjumping 26, 73, 96
sickle hocks 43
sidebone 38, 39
side-reins 157, 159
sitting trot 87-8, 134, 138
skeleton
　　equine *16*
　　horse with rider *82*
　　human and equine compared *25*
　　of head, equine *27*
　　organs protected by, (mare) *31*
slab-sided 48
smell, sense of 58
splint bones *16, 19,* 39
splint formation 39
spurs 97, *97,* 98, *142*
stabled horses 29, 128, 129
stable, entering, with horse 151

stargazing, *see* above the bit
stifle *14,* 19, 43, 44, 74
    slipping 44
stirrups 82-3, 93
    bar, correct position of 82
    for jumping 94-5
    for lungeing 159
stomach 27, *27,* 31
stops, sudden 70, 73
straight ahead position *84, 88*
stumbling 129
superficial muscles *25*
suppleness 80, 81, 85, 87, 88, 92, 93
suture joint 19, *21*
swan neck 47, 75
sway back 48
synovial membrane 16, *19,* 41

tactile hairs 59
tail 151
    set-on of 50
taste buds 58
taste, recognition of 58
teaching methods 126, 128, 130, 133, 134,
    138
teeth 29-30
    canine 29-30
    floating (filing) 29
    incisor, indicate age 29
    uneven wear 46
    with sharp edges *28,* 29
    wolf 30
tempo 70, 73, 131, 136, 137, 138
tendon 38, 39, 40, 41

    damage to 24
    sheath 41
thoracic vertebra *22*
Thoroughbred 10, 20, 21, 43
timidity 51-2, *55*
titbits 58
tongue 58
    accommodating abnormal size of 59
trainer's status, horse's opinion of 56
transitions 65-6, 102, 103, 126, 133, 137
    downward 105
travel sickness 154
travers 124, 126, 138
trot 49, 61-2, 66, 87, 101, 131
    aids for 111-2
    collected 66, *67, 70, 90*
    extended 66, *67,* 141
    long-low outline at *69*
    medium 66, *67, 70,* 141
    rider's position 87-8
    rising (posting) 83, *83, 85,* 87, 88, 133
    sequence *132*
    sequence of footfalls *63*
    sitting 87-8, 134, 138
    tempo 88
    working 66, *67, 70,* 133, 138
trust, in people 51
turn-on-the-forehand 119-20, *121,* 131, 134,
    135
turn on the hindquarters 123-4, 138, *139*
turns 70, 73, 74, 75, 79, 101
    aids for 117
tying up (disease) 129

urogenital system 24

vertebrae 15, *16,* 22
veterinary visits 29, 30, 156
vices 33, 51, 150, 151
vision 57
    binocular 57
    limited straight ahead 57
    monocular 57
    wide field of 56
voice aids 98, 158, 160
volte 103, 119

walk 60-1, *62,* 66, 87, 101, 130
    aids for 110-1
    collected 66, *67*
    extended 66, *67*
    free 66, *67, 84,* 135, 136
    medium 66, *67*
    sequence of footfalls *61*
wall eye 46, *46*
warm-up exercises 128, 129, 134, 135, 159
water, entering 59
weight, of rider 82
    as aid 86, 97, 99, 101, 126
weight adjustment, by horse 68-9, 70, 74,
    127, 129
whip 97, 98, *98,* 144, 148, 153, 155
whip-rubbing 160
white of the eye 46
wind-sucking 33
withers *14,* 24, 47, 48, 50
wolf teeth 30
worms 21, 32